IMAGES
of America

MOUNT VERNON

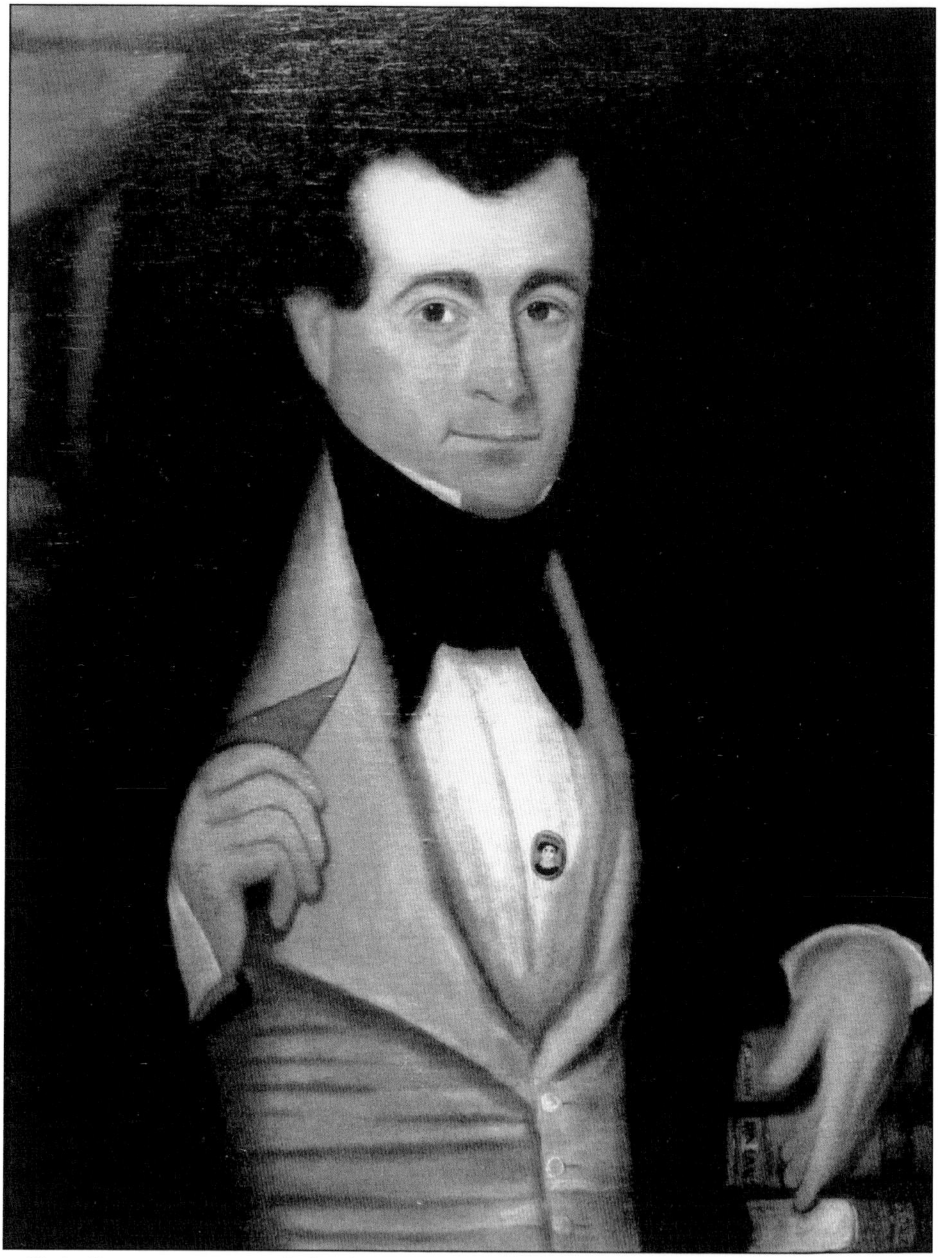

New York City was overcrowded, when in 1850, John Stevens's Industrial Home Association No. 1 reached 1,000 members. As their agent, he purchased five Eastchester farms and divided them into quarter-acre parcels. The borders of the village of Mount Vernon covered what is now Union Avenue on the east to Fifteenth Avenue on the west, and from Valentine Street on the north to Sandford Boulevard and a small portion of Kingsbridge Road on the south. The portrait above of John Stevens was made around 1837. (Courtesy of the John Stevens estate.)

On the cover: Please see page 43. (Photograph by Henry Sihler, courtesy of the Mount Vernon Public Library Virginia McClellan Moskowitz Local History Room.)

IMAGES
of America

MOUNT VERNON

Larry H. Spruill, Ph.D.
Foreword by Mayor Clinton I. Young Jr.

ARCADIA
PUBLISHING

ISBN 978-0-7385-6265-0

Published by Arcadia Publishing
Charleston, South Carolina

Printed in the United States of America

Library of Congress Control Number: 2008932699

For all general information contact Arcadia Publishing at:
Telephone 843-853-2070
Fax 843-853-0044
E-mail sales@arcadiapublishing.com
For customer service and orders:
Toll-Free 1-888-313-2665

Visit us on the Internet at www.arcadiapublishing.com

To the late Cecil H. Parker, Mount Vernon educator, who inspired me to become a historian, and Virginia McClellan Moskowitz for modeling the practice, passion, and legacy of a municipal historian

Contents

ACKNOWLEDGMENTS

Mount Vernon could not have been possible without the collaboration of Opal Lindsay, director of the Mount Vernon Public Library, and Shirley Garrett, supervisor of the Virginia McClellan Moskowitz Local History Room. Their access and guidance to the archives and photographs was most helpful. I would like to thank Jeffrey Williams, planning commissioner, and Traci Thompson and Daniella Jackson from the mayor's office for believing in the project. Also many thanks to Donna May-Jackson for use of images from her collection of Mount Vernon memorabilia; William (Billy) Thomas for his pictures from the Mount Vernon Boys and Girls Clubs; Leslie Alpert for her picture research, editing, and marketing support; Dorothy Brown and Ted Jenkins for their photographic expertise; Hanns Marshalleck and Marjorie Lipan for their digital and technical assistance; William Sullivan for the use of the art gallery and availability of the images in the permanent collection of the Association of Community-Based Artists of Westchester (AC-BAW) Center for the Arts; and Rebekah Collinsworth, Arcadia project editor, for her persistent professionalism. A special thanks to Dr. Giles Conwill, chairperson of Morehouse College's history department, for his encouragement and support. Finally, I am grateful for my family's patience and consideration of my passion for all things Mount Vernon. Thanks Doris, Michael, Hassan, Miriam, and Mikeshia for sharing me. Unless otherwise noted, all images appear courtesy of the Mount Vernon Public Library Virginia McClellan Moskowitz Local History Room.

FOREWORD

As mayor, I am honored to have the opening words to this important publication. There comes a time in the life of every city when it must reflect on its journey to the present. Now is such a moment. As I move Mount Vernon in vastly new directions, it is important to take time to look back and better understand the vision, goals, and accomplishments of those who came before us. Local history is an important tool in assessing the present, as well as charting an innovative and progressive future.

Although the faces of our neighborhoods have changed, some things have not. Mount Vernon's strategic location and easy access by all types of transportation to the cultural and financial centers of the metropolitan area remain enviable. *Mount Vernon* is a timely visual review of the vitality of rail transportation, the old downtown district, the suburban splendor of neighborhoods, the earliest medical, postal, educational, and religious institutions, and other essential city services.

The images in *Mount Vernon* indicate that these advantages were not accidental but achieved by planning and talented and courageous leadership. The challenges facing my administration are no different than those of my predecessors. Dr. Spruill has presented us with inspirational pictures from our past that confirm that there is very little new in the life of cities. Our citizens are equally as gifted and able to shape a new, exciting, and sustainable Mount Vernon.

I have spent nearly my entire life living on these four square miles. These pictures stir memories of the city that nurtured and led me into public service. Like the founding settlers, I now understand why I needed to serve my community as it created opportunities for new generations to live the American dream. These fascinating photographs helped me to remember the things that made Mount Vernon one of the greatest small cities in New York. They confirmed what really makes our city great—its deep reservoir of talented people and unique location.

Great cities have two things in common: confidence and a sense of continuity. Both are gained by a rich sense of their past. *Mount Vernon* introduces us to Adelina Patti, the extraordinary 19th-century opera singer, and scientist Emile Bachelet and his 1912 Third Street laboratory where the magnetic levitation train was invented. In the 20th century, Mount Vernon was home to Art Carney, Dick Clark, Humphrey Bogart, Arthur Krimmer, Art Buchwald, Denzel Washington, Hazel Scott, Adam Clayton Powell III, Bella Abzug, Dr. Betty Shabazz, Bessie and Sadie Delany, Sidney Poitier, Nina Simone, Debbie Allen, Felicia Rashad, Stephanie Mills, the six daughters of the late Malcolm X and Dr. Betty Shabazz, Sean "P. Diddy" Combs, Doug E. Fresh, Heavy D, Linda Fairstein, Jay Hoggard, Michael Philips, the late treasury secretary Ronald Brown, and many more. We launch into this new century with new generations of extraordinary residents.

Our city and county are changing daily. We have often been misunderstood but never unnoticed. My administration has created a new vision, a balance between our suburban past and the best elements of urban living. Many have moved away and are often nostalgic about our city. Longtime and new residents, as well as our neighbors in Westchester and Bronx Counties, should read *Mount Vernon*. They will better understand the journey to reclaiming our legacy as the "City of Happy Homes." It is a new day; our heritage of success continues.

—Mayor Clinton I. Young Jr.

INTRODUCTION

Everything in a city has a beginning, a place of departure. Local history is the record of a people's relationship to other people, places, and events. It provides continuity from its earliest settlers to its newest residents. Citizens who know their history find that tapping into local historical treasures gives special meaning to their collective pilgrimage. From time to time, a community must come together to weave yesterday into today. This ritual bonds people in the past and present. We get a chance to see people and neighborhoods locked in another time, often beyond our everyday reach.

Mount Vernon initiates a period of self-reflection. These images and narrative are missing pages in our public memory. When it appears that we are losing touch with traditional civic pride and values, reflections on the olden days are important. Yearning for the old Mount Vernon is in fact a plea for continuity. We often hear people talk about what Mount Vernon used to be like. Some have lived long enough to remember who and what we were. Most residents do not know the city's heritage. They take for granted and think that schools, a hospital, a city hall, houses of worship, police and fire stations, a library, parks, and long-established neighborhoods and commercial district have always been where and what they are. This is why Mount Vernon demands a special time to preserve and share our heritage.

Reenvisioning and rethinking about our city's then and now while simultaneously planning for future generations can be complicated. Today is an excellent time for a look at how far we have come. *Mount Vernon* gives us a tool to do just that, measure the distance and direction we must yet travel.

Mount Vernon has a rich Colonial and early American heritage. It is impossible to understand it without knowing its relationship to the town of Eastchester. From 1626 to 1664, this area was under Dutch rule and called New Netherlands. From 1665 to 1776, it was part of the English colony called New York. The present city limits were the center of Eastchester. In 1850, five large farms were sold to John Stevens and a group of New Yorkers and Mount Vernon was born.

From 1853 to 1891, the small frontier village grew into a stable suburban community. Houses, businesses, schools, roads, neighborhoods, and public services and institutions were established to the point that the village had outgrown Eastchester. By 1892, Mount Vernon had over 15,000 people and was ready to shed its village swaddling cloth.

In 1892, Mount Vernon became a city under the laws of New York State. At the dawn of the past century, Stevens's dream of a prosperous and progressive gateway city to New York City was a reality. From the Gay Nineties to the years following World War II, Mount Vernon was called the "City of Happy Homes." Its tree-lined streets, spacious homes, and fine schools attracted home buyers looking for a suburban paradise close to New York City. It became the bedroom of prominent leaders and quickly became attractive to people from all walks struggling to find their way in American life. The city was able to sustain its original suburban goals until the Great Depression and the end of World War II. The nation and city began to change.

From 1954 to 2000, there was a dramatic population shift. Its ethnic composition went from predominately white to largely African American and Hispanic American. Many of its classic south side suburban neighborhoods fell victim to urban elements, while most of its north side communities maintained their traditional characteristics. This nearly five-decade transition was polarizing and altered the city's outlook and image.

By the new millennium, Mount Vernon's future was often presented in extreme terms. The two most asked questions were, first, will the city become a cultural and environmental appendage of Bronx County? Second, will it once again become more like its wealthier neighbors in Westchester? We are well into the new century with its difficult challenges. Mount Vernon remains resilient. It is always innovative and pacesetting. It will find its future in the best elements of its heritage, while pursuing the advantages of its rich human resources and geographical location.

Mount Vernon is a book of photographs highlighting the role ambitious people and transportation technology played in the city. Mount Vernon is an optimistic city. The diversity of its people and their faith in the American creed of life, liberty, and a chance to pursue the things that make them happy made it attractive. Mount Vernon inspired and gave hope to so many and continues to do so.

Let's take a look at familiar and unfamiliar people, places, and things from the past century and a half. It is only a glimpse, though a panoramic one of hundreds of names and faces of doctors, teachers, businessmen, activist women, athletes, artists, clergy, families, politicians, and ordinary people connected to these four square miles. Get acquainted and enjoy the experience of *Mount Vernon*.

—Larry H. Spruill, Ph.D., city historian

One

THE TOWN OF EASTCHESTER 1664–1852

Mount Vernon's affiliation with Eastchester makes it a young city in an old locality. In the 17th century, land east of the Hudson River to the northern shore of Long Island Sound now including Westchester County and southwestern coastal Connecticut was inhabited by Siwanoy Indians. During the summers, they lived by the clam and oyster beds along Eastchester Creek. The Siwanoys' concept of individual land ownership was different than the settlers. In the ensuing quarrels, both settlers and natives were massacred. The Siwanoys were gradually driven north and westward.

Modern Mount Vernon is bounded on the west by the Bronx River and Parkway and on the south by Bronx County. The Hutchinson River and Parkway are the eastern boundary. It was named for Anne Hutchinson, a religious rebel banned from Boston in 1639. She settled about a mile south of the current city line. In 1643, during hostilities with the Dutch, Native Americans killed Hutchinson and her family. In 1654, Thomas Pell, a Connecticut Englishman, obtained a Native American land grant, which contained part of what became Eastchester. In 1664, he gave a land deed to 10 families who settled Eastchester.

St. Paul's Church and Cemetery (1693), now on South Columbus Avenue, faced the village green and the settlement grew around it. By the American Revolution (1776), Eastchester consisted of scattered farm families, a mill, and several taverns. The 1790 census shows Eastchester with 740 people. Farm products commanded good prices and were inexpensively delivered to New York by water and market wagons. The town prospered as a rural community.

In 1844, the New York and Harlem Railroad reached White Plains while skirting the western edge of Eastchester on the way. In 1849, the New York-New Haven Railroad passed directly through the town's farms and forests. Eastchester was doomed to fall victim to the nation's first urban "affordable housing movement." New York was slowly becoming the Empire State and Manhattan its metropolis. City living costs were high, particularly housing and rent. The extension of railroad tracks subjected large tracts of Eastchester farmland to purchase. With two commuter railroad lines in town, rural Eastchester was endangered and would never be the same. In 1850, Mount Vernon was conceived, and the founding villagers were within a short commute of New York.

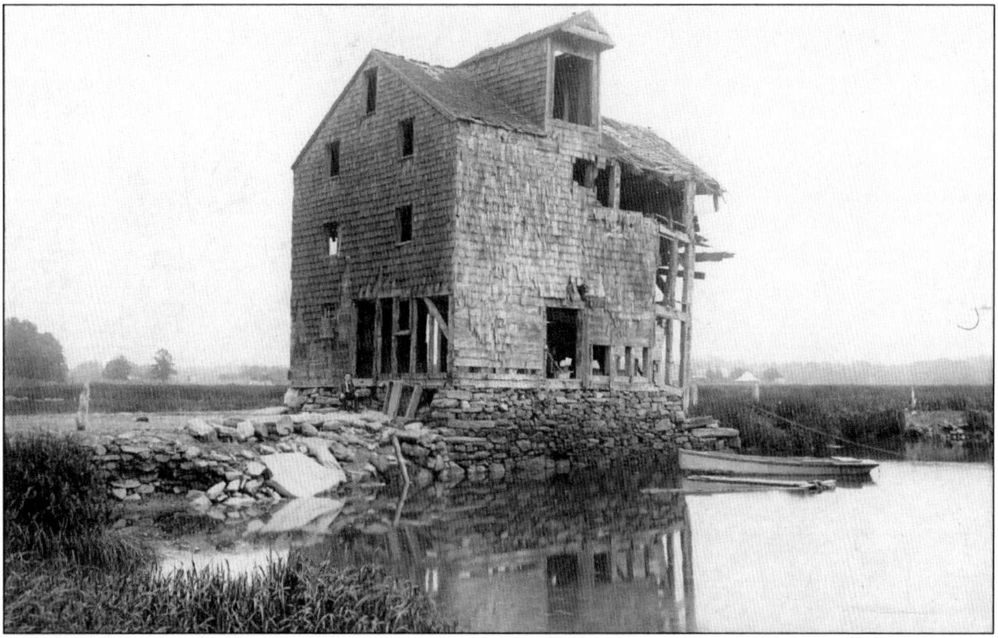

Pictured above are the 1897 remains of Reid's Mill, built in the early 18th century. During the Colonial settlement of Eastchester, the mill grinder was an important person. All the local farmers brought their grain to the mill to be ground into flour. Reid's Mill was located on Eastchester Bay not far from Co-Op City in the Bronx. The remaining frame came down many years ago.

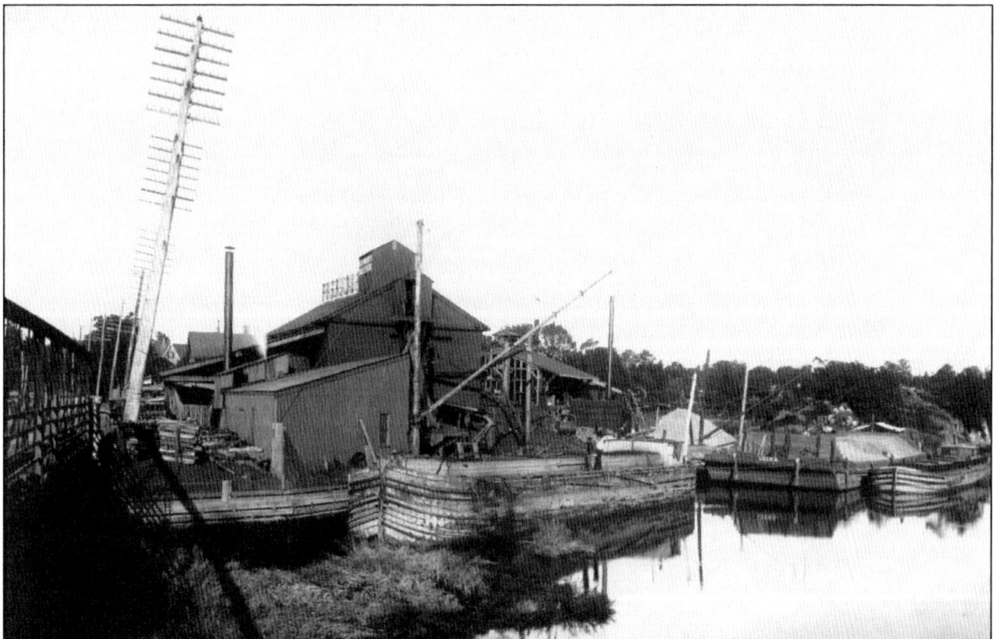

This is a view of the town dock around 1900. Mount Vernon became a fast-growing suburban-urban community. Today residents do not associate the community with a port and harbor. Yet, it remains so.

St. Paul's Church and Cemetery is the site of the 1664 founding of Eastchester and the village green. It is one of the oldest church buildings in New York State. It is currently a national historic site operated by the National Parks Service located on South Columbus Avenue between Fulton and Third Avenues. (Courtesy of the St. Paul's Church National Historic Site.)

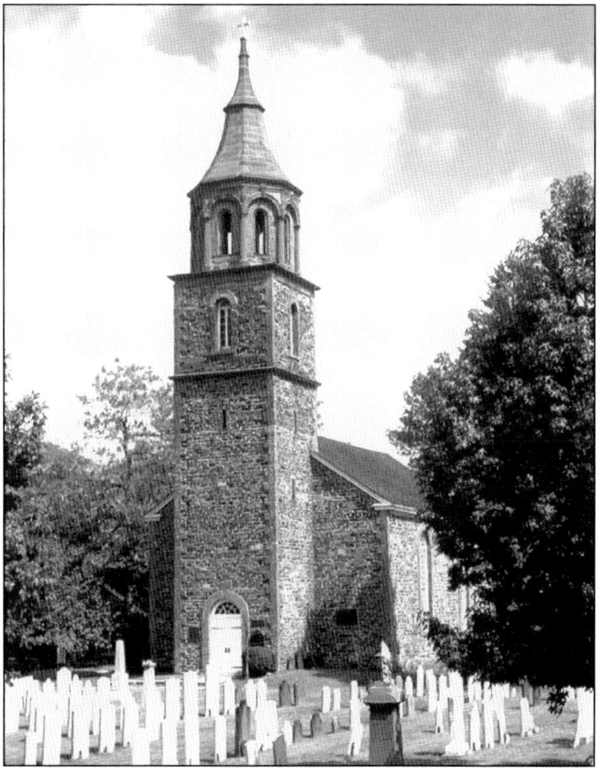

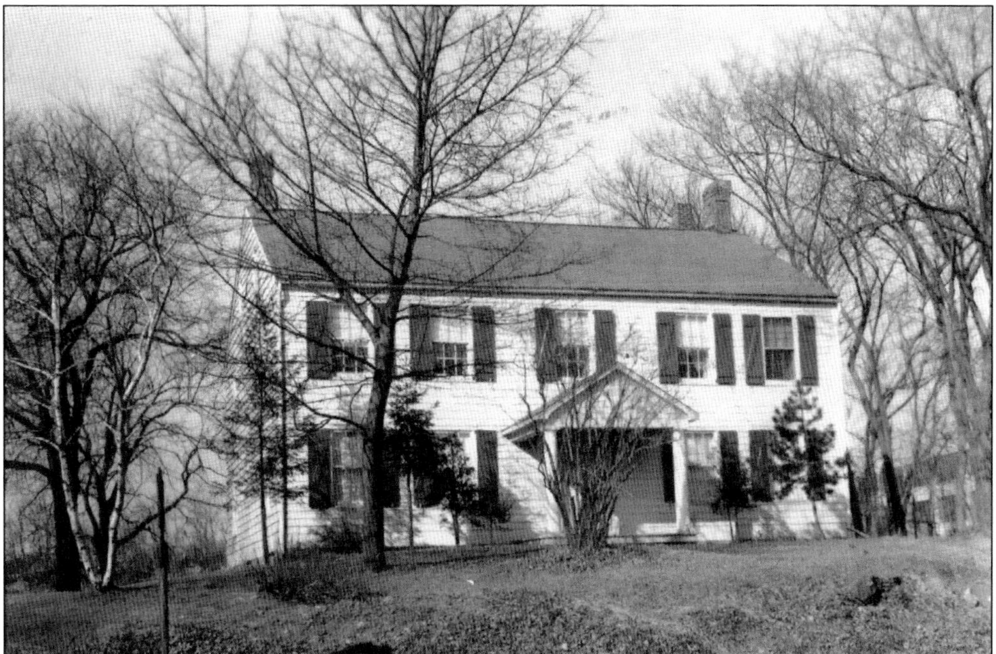

Crawford's Tavern, built in 1732 and also known as the Fay-Griggs homestead, was opposite St. Paul's Church. William Crawford operated it during the American Revolution. In 1966, it was torn down to make room for industrial development.

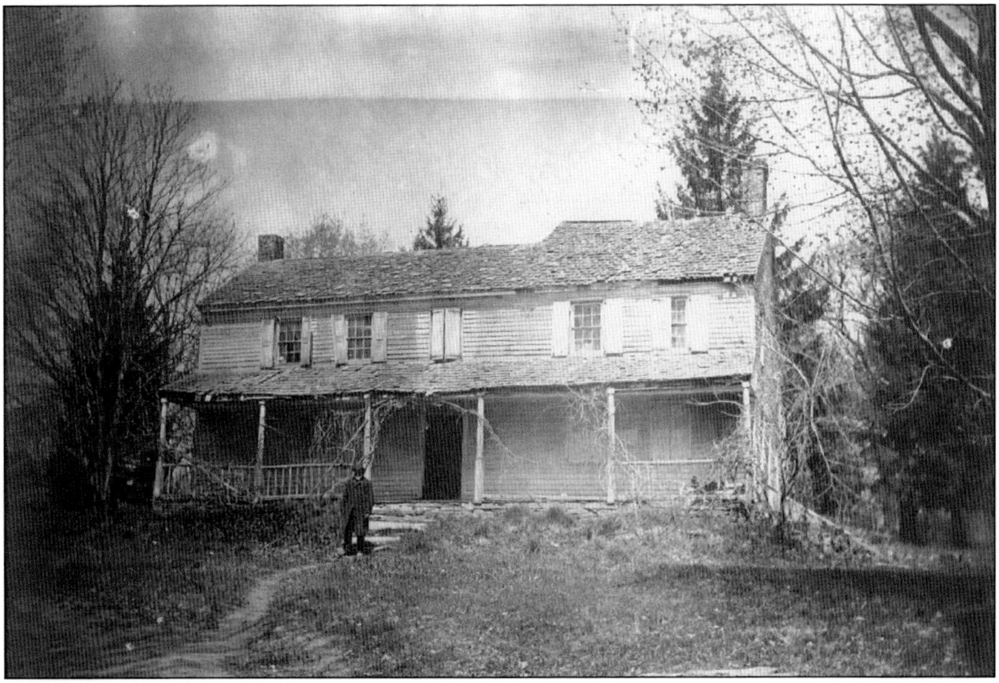

This is a picture of Philemon Fowler's Tavern, built in 1733 and once located at South Columbus Avenue at the western corner of Third Avenue. It was here Loyalists gathered during the American Revolution. It was rebuilt in 1799 and torn down in 1911.

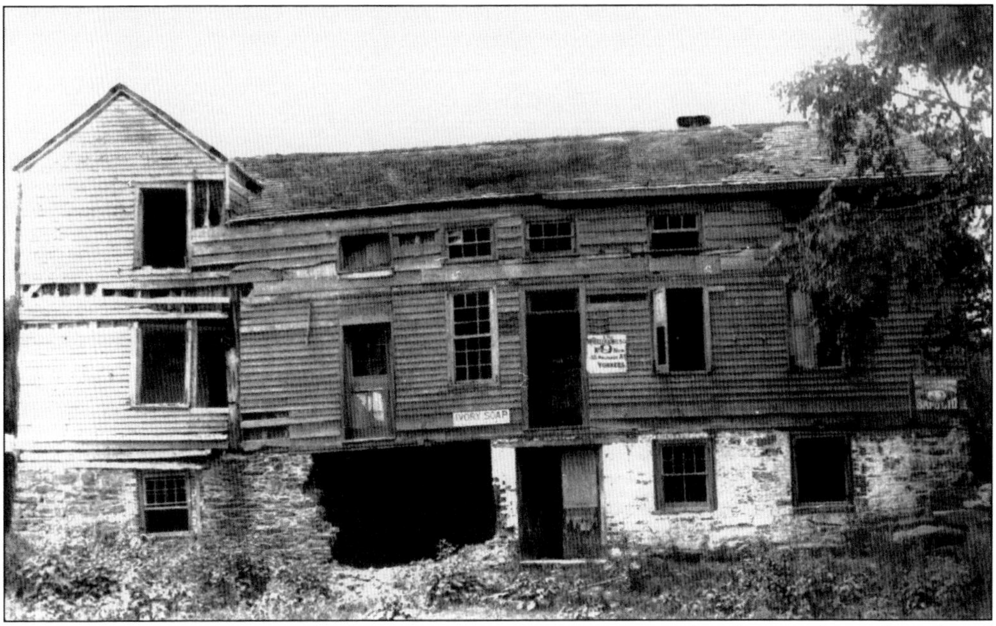

The 1907 picture above is Charles Guion's Tavern. It was popular during the Colonial and Revolutionary era. During the war, it hosted Gen. George Washington. It was on the west side of what is now Route 22 just before Kingsbridge Road. The 18th-century village of Eastchester used it as a post office. Rebecca Turner, a former slave, was a famous tavern cook. It burned down in 1909. While pulling down the masonry walls, a large amount of gold coins were found.

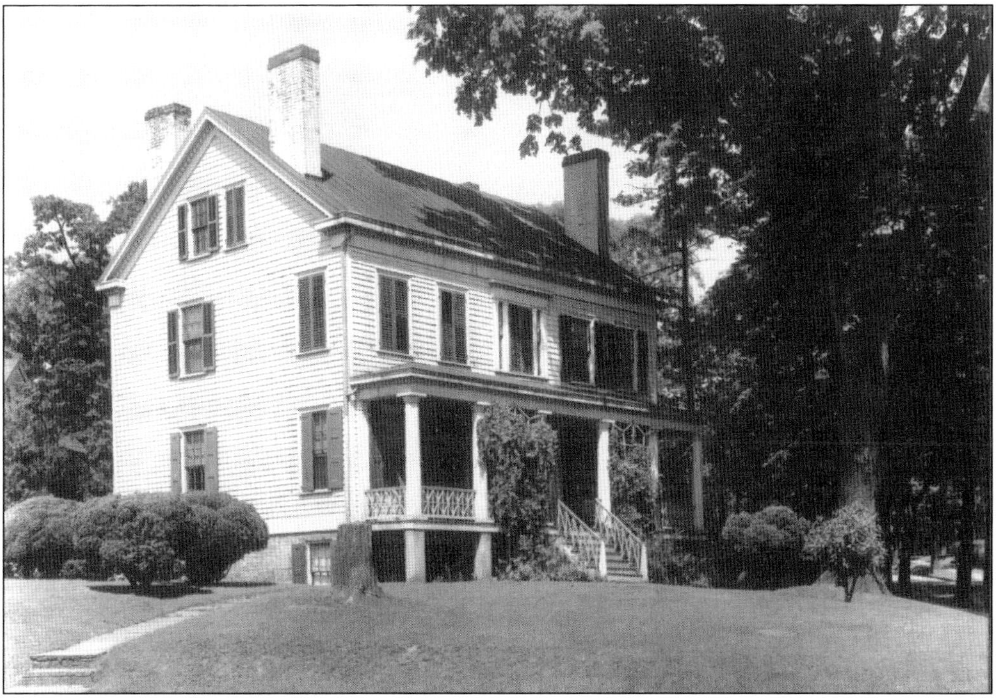

On July 2, 1851, Mount Vernon's founder John Stevens moved his family into the house above, built by Sylvanus Purdy in 1849. He purchased it at the time his association took possession of the five Eastchester farms. It became known as the Stevens House. It was built as a farmhouse along the old Mile Square Road from St. Paul's Church to Yonkers. Located at 29 West Fourth Street, the property, bordered on the west by Sixth Avenue, was in the center of a charming rural setting nearly overshadowed by a magnificent ancient elm tree (below), an attraction in its own right. Some called it the "[City] Charter Elm." Due to disease, it was cut down in 1953.

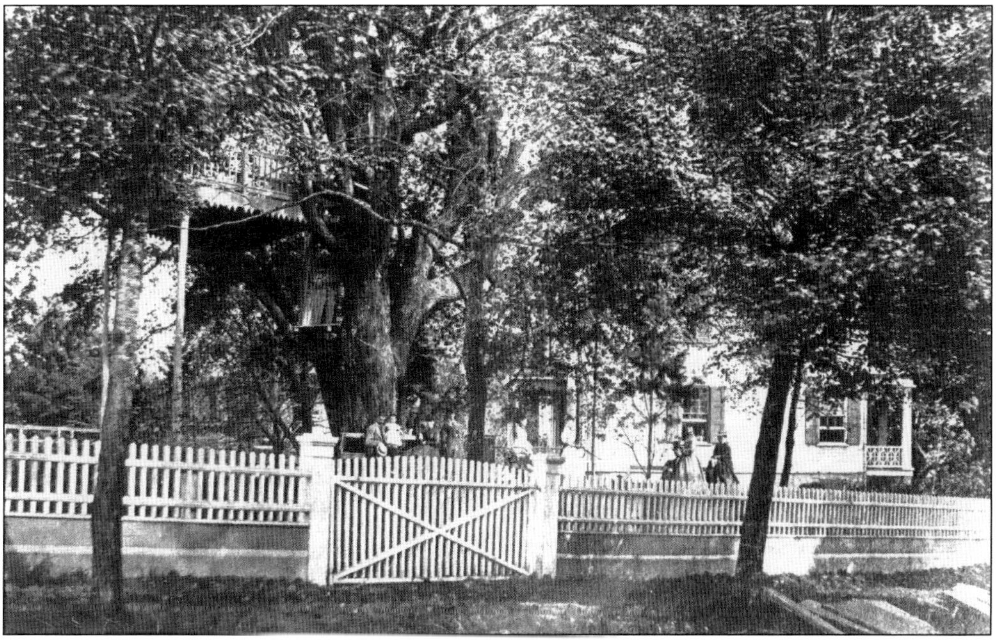

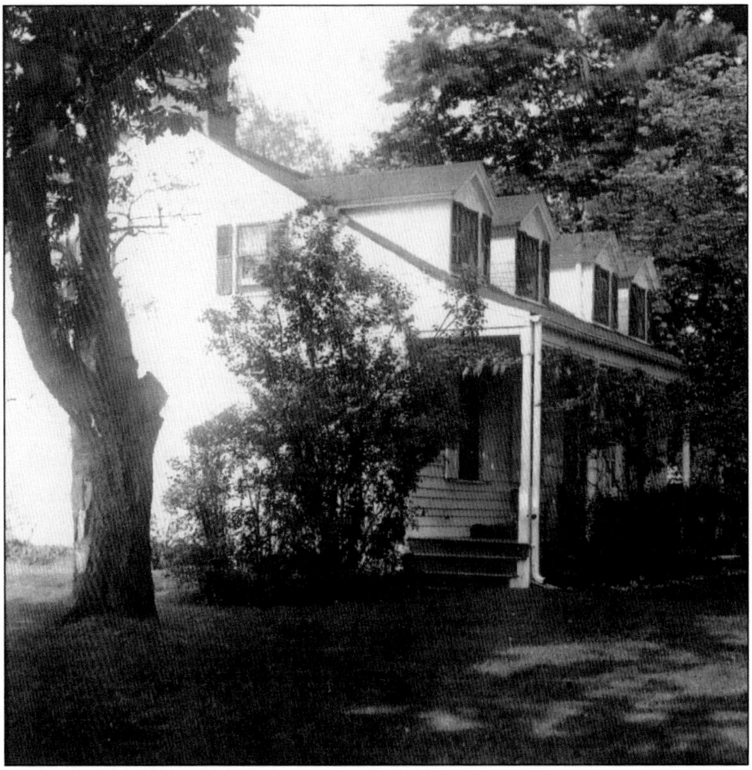

On the left is the Hunt house at 396 North Columbus Avenue. It dates back to a purchase by Israel Hunt from Thomas Lawrence. The house had been remodeled several times. Five generations of the Hunt family occupied the premises before it was torn down in the 1960s to widen the Cross County Parkway. (Courtesy of the Westchester County Historical Society.)

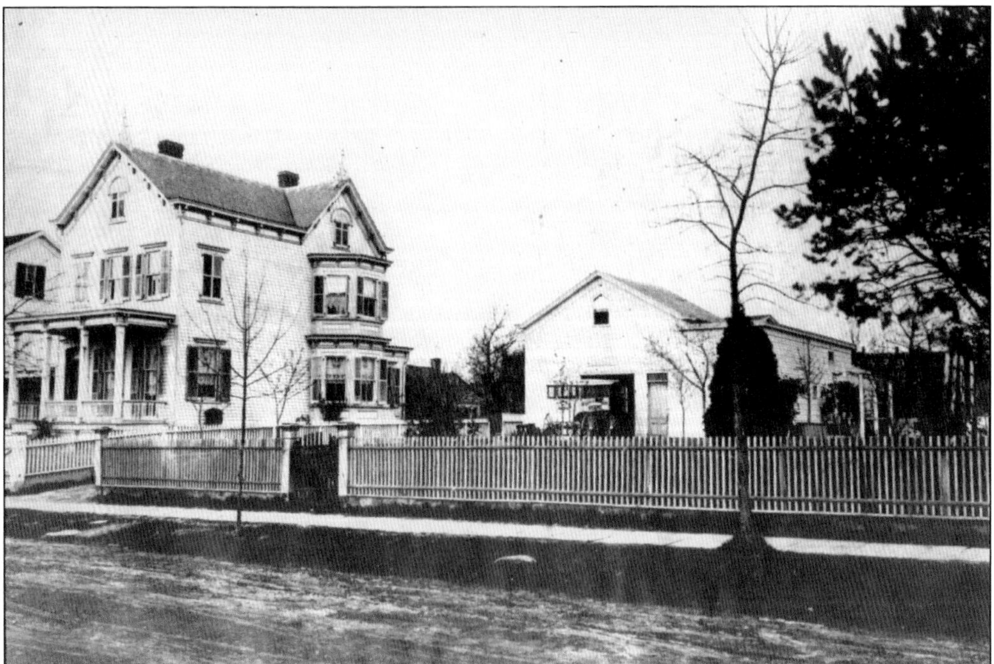

The 1892 photograph above is of the Valentine farmhouse at 27 South Sixth Avenue. The family ran the stagecoach from Mount Vernon to Yonkers. There is a glimpse of the coach in the barn. (Photograph by Walter A. Miles.)

On the right is Rev. William S. Coffey of St. Paul's Church. He served as rector for 59 years, from 1850 to 1909. His scholarly work and historical recollections of early Mount Vernon are often quoted in modern publications. He also served as a controversial pastor during the inaugural years of Trinity Episcopal Church on Fourth Avenue between Fourth and Fifth Streets.

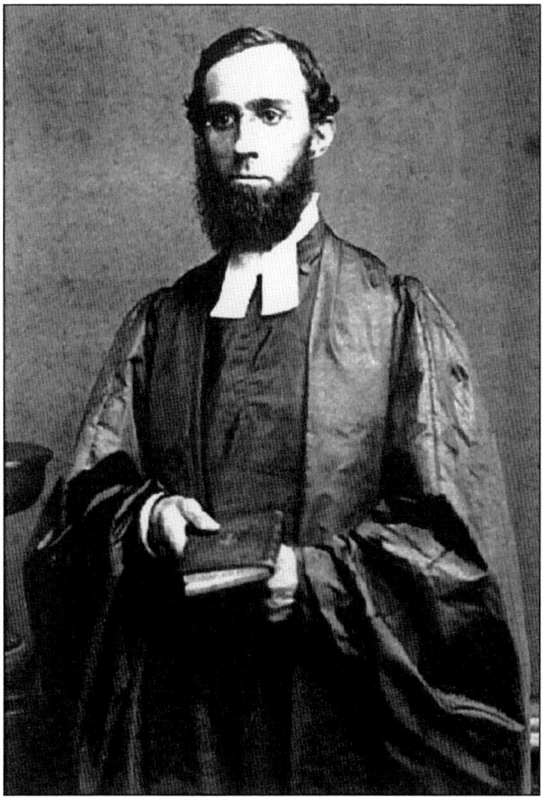

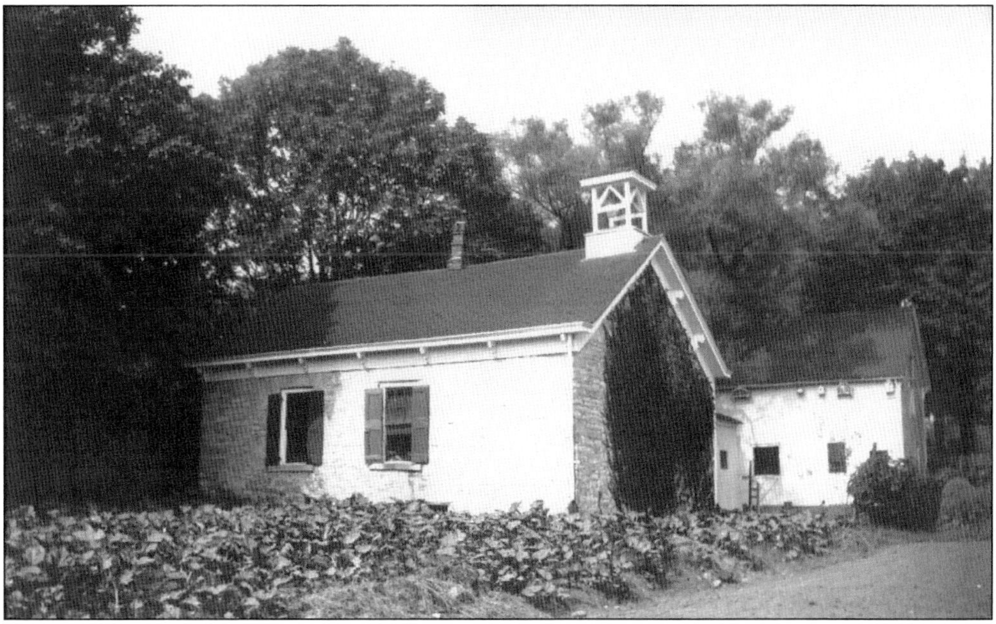

This picture is of the building called the Marble School House, erected in 1835. It is one of the oldest schools affiliated with Mount Vernon. It was built with stone from the Tuckahoe marble quarries. It was later moved from Mount Vernon to the intersection near California and New Rochelle Roads. It is still standing and houses the Eastchester Historical Society.

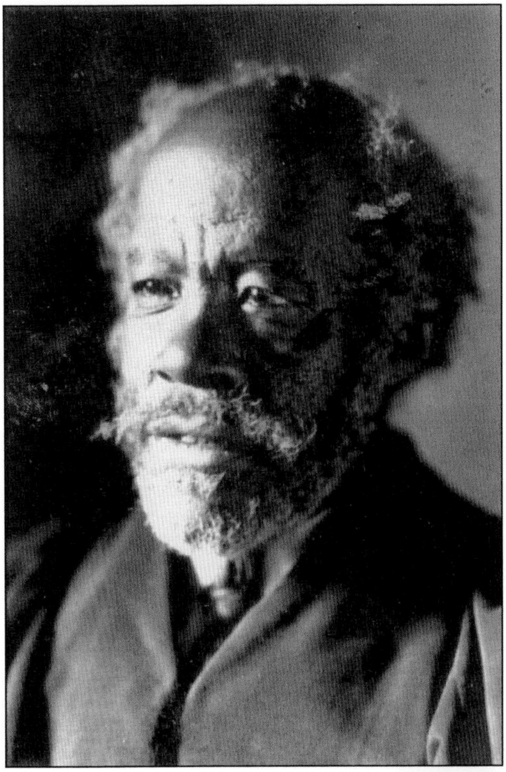

Pictured are Andrew and Anna Casten Johnson. Andrew was born on a village farm in 1872. Anna was also born in Eastchester. It is believed that Andrew is a descendant of Nat and Hannah Franklin, former slaves of Glorianna Franklin, a descendant of Thomas Pell, lord of Pelham Manor (around the 1650s). Nat Franklin was a Revolutionary War veteran. There were significant numbers of African Americans born in Colonial Eastchester. These two photographs are to date the oldest of people of African descent born in the city. (Courtesy of the Tuckahoe Public Library.)

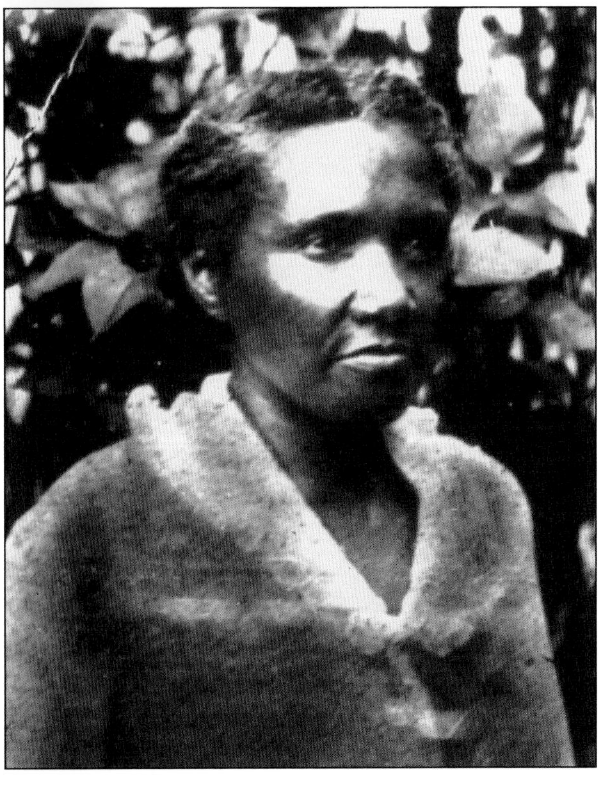

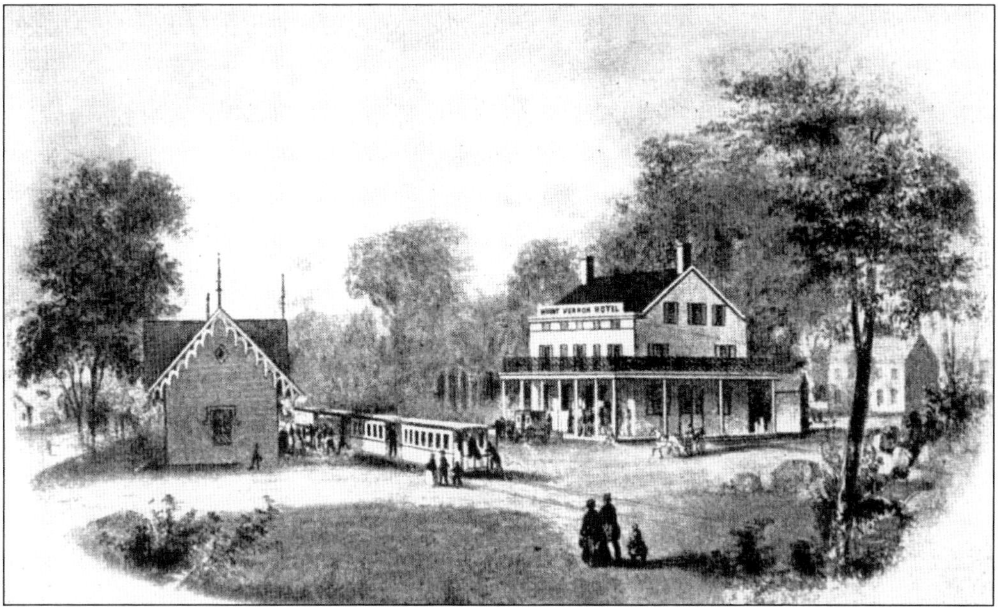

The illustration above is the earliest view of Mount Vernon. There were only a handful of houses. At the heart of the settlement were a small train depot, a single-direction rail track, and a hotel aptly named the Mount Vernon Hotel (Gould's Hotel). In 1851, the hotel was at the southwest corner of what is today Gramatan Avenue and Fiske Place. The hotel property included land now occupied by a bank, Mount Vernon City Hall, and the Proctor and Lucas buildings.

This is the November 1, 1852, New York-New Haven Railroad timetable on which the Mount Vernon station first appears. The stations were Canal Street, Thirty-second Street, Harlem, Williamsbridge, Mount Vernon, and so on up the line. At that time, horses drew the railroad coaches between Canal Street and Thirty-second Street. A train, starting from Canal Street at 7:00 a.m., arrived at Mount Vernon at 8:06 a.m. There were only four trains daily each way. Getting the train company to make an official stop and place a listing on the timetable was a major victory for the villagers.

Commutation	Port C. Special	STATIONS.	Accom'dation	Bost. Express.
9.00 A.M.	7.00 A.M.	Ar. 75.98 N. Y., Canal St. --- De.	7.00 A.M.	8.00 A.M.
8.30 "	6.35 "	2.50 De. 73.48 .... 32d St. .... 2.50 "	7.25 "	8.30 "
8.18 "	6.22 "	5.00 " 68.48 .... *Harlem* .... 7.50 "	7.41 "	8.42 "
7.58 "	6.07 "	6.00 " 62.48 *Will'ms' Bridge* 13.50 "	**7.58** "	8.55 "
7.50 "	6.00 "	3.09 " 59.39 Mount Vernon 16.59 "	8.06 "	9.00 "
7.42 "	5.52 "	3.09 " 56.30 New Rochelle 19.68 "	8.13 "	9.05 "
7.34 "	5.43 "	3.64 " 52.66 .. Mamaroneck .. 23.32 "	8.21 "	9.12 "
7.24 "	5.34 "	3.65 " 49.01 ..... Rye ..... 26.97 "	8.29 "	9.17 "
7.20 "	5.30 A.M.	1.64 " 47.37 . Port Chester . 28.61 "	8.34 "	9.20 "
7.13 "		2.57 " 44.80 .. Greenwich .. 31.18 "	**8.42** "	* 9.25 "
7.09 "		1.56 " 43.24 Cos Cob Bridge 32.74 "	8.46 "	9.28 "
7.00 "		3.64 " 39.60 ... Stamford ... 36.38 "	8.56 "	9.42 "
6.46 "		4.63 " 34.97 .... Darien ... 41.01 "	9.05 "	9.50 "
6.38 "		3.40 " 31.57 ... Norwalk ... 44.41 "	9.13 "	9.55 "
6.28 "	Bridgeport	2.93 " 28.64 ... Westport ... 47.34 "	9.21 "	10.00 "
6.20 "	Special.	4.76 " 23.88 .. Southport .. 52.10 "	9.31 "	10.07 "
6.17 "		1.58 " 22.30 ... Fairfield ... 53.68 "	9.35 "	10.10 "
6.07 "	11.00 A.M.	4.80 " 17.50 .. Bridgeport .. 58.48 "	9.50 "	10.25 "
5.57 "	10.51 "	3.47 " 14.03 ... Stratford ... 61.95 "	9.57 "	10.31 "
5.54 "	10.47 "	1.50 " 12.50 Housatonic Riv. 63.45 "	10.01 "	10.34 "
5.48 "	10.39 "	3.01 " 9.52 ... Milford .... 66.46 "	10.09 "	10.39 "
5.35 "	10.21 "	7.02 " 2.50 .. West Haven .. 73.48 "	10.25 "	10.51 "
5.30 A.M.	10.15 A.M.	2.50 De. ----- .. New Haven .. 75.98 Ar.	10.30 "	10.55 "

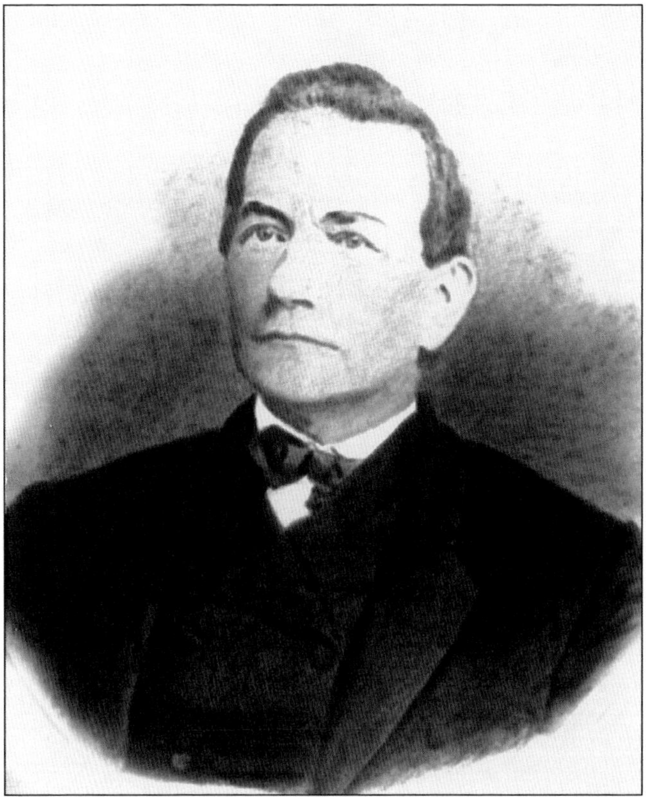

In 1851, John and Emeline Megie Stevens and their three children left New York City looking for a new life. Stevens dreamed of building a new community within a half hour of downtown New York. He was a nature lover. Mount Vernon was his opportunity to return to country living. He was able to convince 1,000 other families to embrace the Industrial Home Association No. 1. Stevens's integrity, perseverance, and force of personality brought out the best in others. He had a distaste for strife and conflict and was a staunch advocate for hard work and simplicity. Their years of patience and persistence brought them success and made them worthy to be called the "Founding Family of Mount Vernon, the City of Happy Homes."

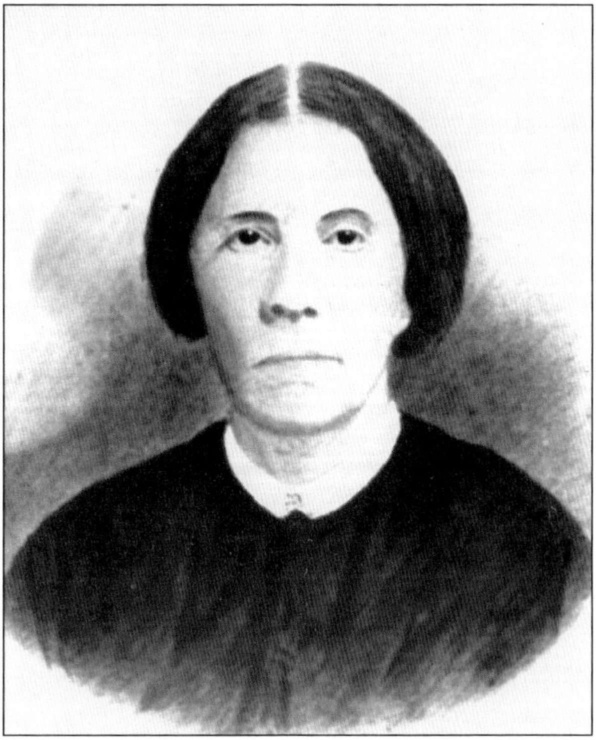

Two

BUILDING A NEW VILLAGE 1853–1891

In 1850, a group of New Yorkers led by John Stevens organized the Industrial Home Association No. 1. Stevens was dedicated to building a new city, making home ownership possible for people of modest means. He believed ordinary people should be able to own homes without abandoning connections to the city. This new community of well-constructed houses along tree-lined streets, parks, excellent schools, and reliable transportation to New York would happen and flourish by their collective support.

In 1851, the association's 1,000 members purchased, at a cost of $205 per acre, five Eastchester farms along the New York-New Haven Railroad. The land was mapped and divided into quarter-acre parcels. The members met in a large barn behind the Stevens house. Each subscriber drew a number and was allowed 10 minutes to choose a lot. Building began promptly, and the name Mount Vernon was chosen. Stevens's dream city within 30 minutes by train from New York became a reality. By August 1852, 300 houses were finished or under construction. In December 1853, there were 1,370 residents, and it was incorporated.

Shortly after the settling of Mount Vernon, three other adjoining communities, West Mount Vernon, East Mount Vernon, and Central Mount Vernon, were laid out. The largest was West Mount Vernon, settled mostly by German immigrants, and was located northwest of Mount Vernon between the two railroads. Its inhabitants traveled on the Harlem Railroad, and their depot was Hunt's Bridge, later called Mount Vernon West. In 1853, Central Mount Vernon, Fleetwood, Washingtonville, and Jeffersonville were developed. In 1869, the Chester Hill section along East Lincoln Avenue was started. East Mount Vernon joined the original village in 1874. West Mount Vernon and Central Mount Vernon incorporated as West Mount Vernon in 1869. It was annexed to the John Stevens settlement in 1878.

Mount Vernon's success as an attractive home for middle-class families and later southern migrants and impoverished immigrants planting new roots spread throughout the region was established by 1892. That year, its 15,513 residents voted on a proposition of annexation to New York City or become independent. On March 12, they voted in favor of becoming the City of Mount Vernon. It was free to chart its own course in the 20th century.

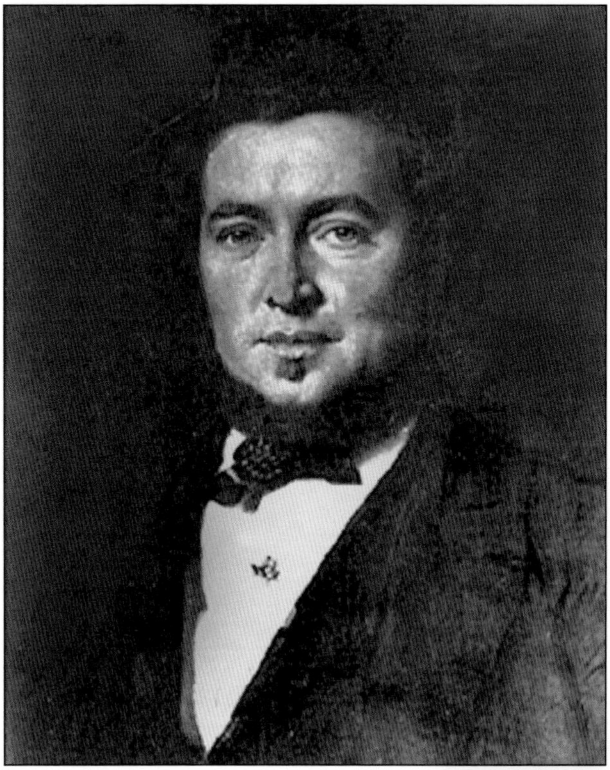

George Gould (left), proprietor of the Mount Vernon Hotel, fully embraced John Stevens's vision to build a community within a half hour of New York City by railway. His hotel was the cradle of Mount Vernon's earliest civic and social life. Gould's son Theodore (below) was the first child born in the village and was presented with a lot at the corner of Eighth Avenue and First Street. Modern politicians have sought the secret to Gould's success with hotel services centered around the train station. There are current plans for a hotel near the railroad depot.

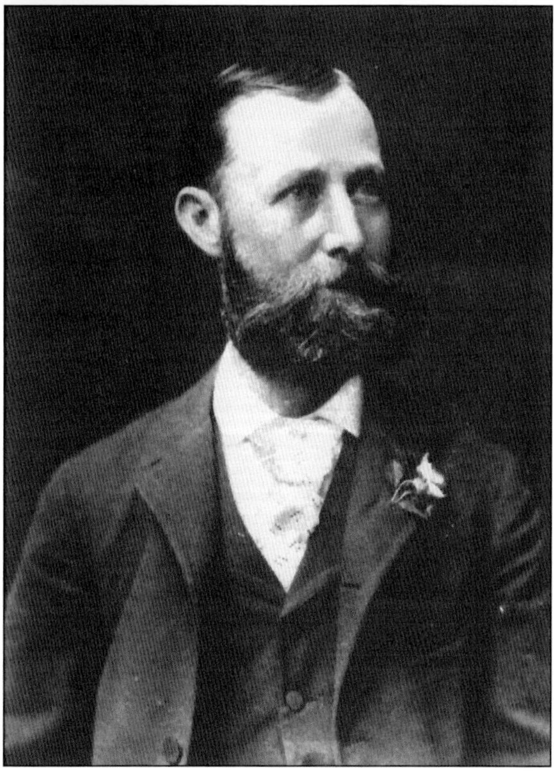

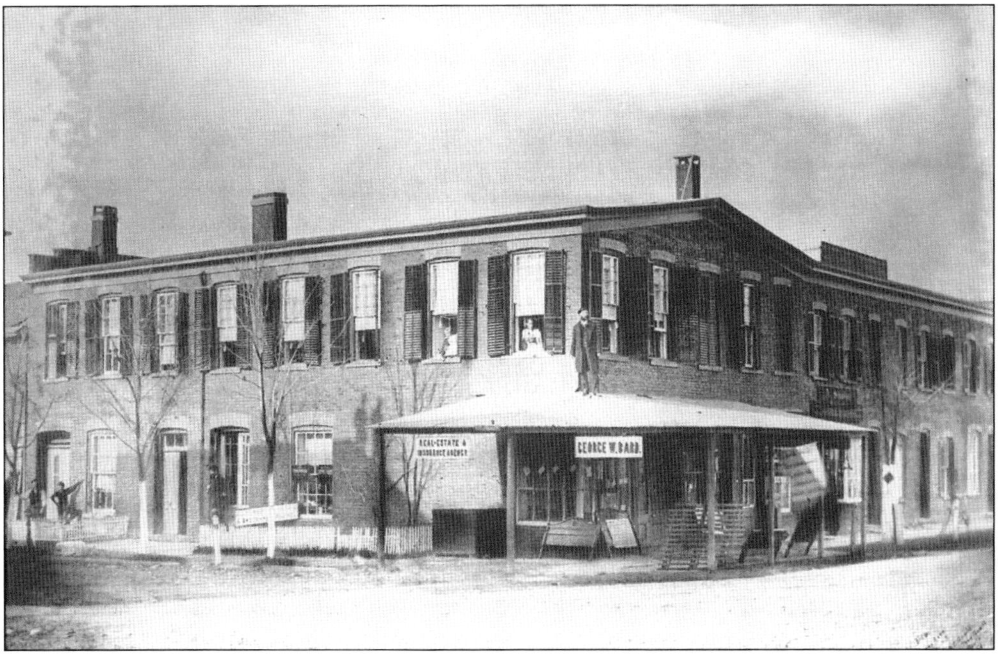

The Gould's Hotel (also known as the Mount Vernon Hotel) was the early center of civic life. It was the meeting place for politicians, and the ballroom was the scene of many prominent social affairs. The upper floor of the hotel was used as a gymnasium. Horace Greeley, Cyrus Field, and Frank Leslie patronized it. As a child, Adelina Patti performed in the ballroom in connection with a benefit for Sacred Heart Catholic Church. Her singing attracted broad attention. She became the most renowned opera singer of the 19th century.

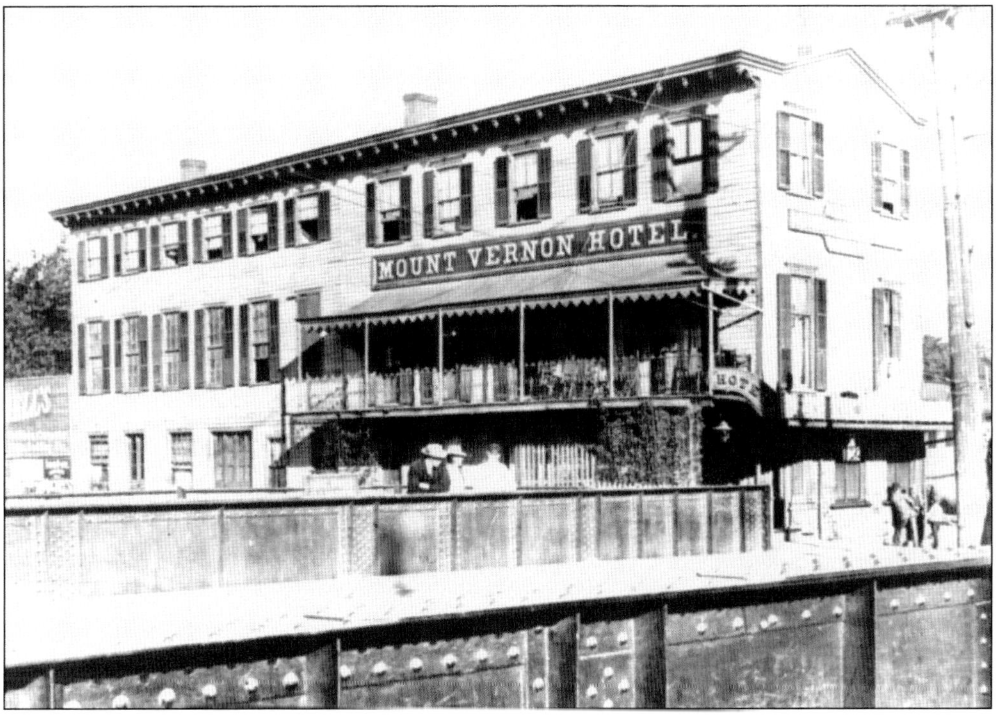

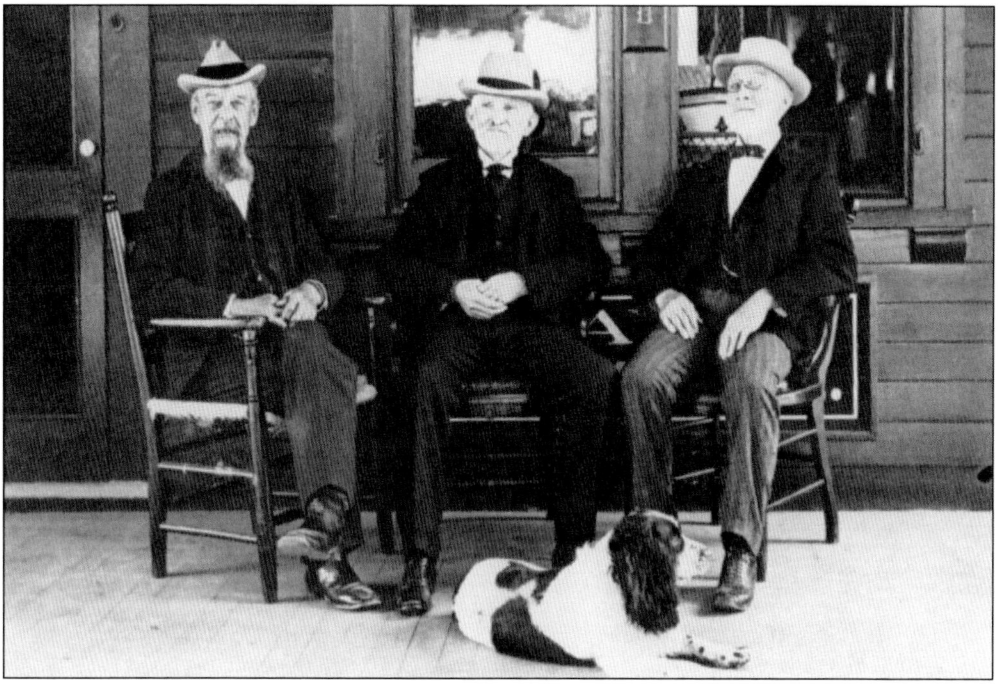

The photograph above is a flashback to the olden days when folks gathered in front of Burr Davis and Son's Funeral Parlor (started in 1863) to gossip and thresh out municipal affairs. Seated are, from left to right, John Stoothoff, Burr Davis, and Nathaniel B. Hayt. They were lifelong friends. Davis presided at both of their funeral services. This picture was taken in 1900. The 1903 photograph below is the Burr Davis building and employees at 15 South Fourth Avenue.

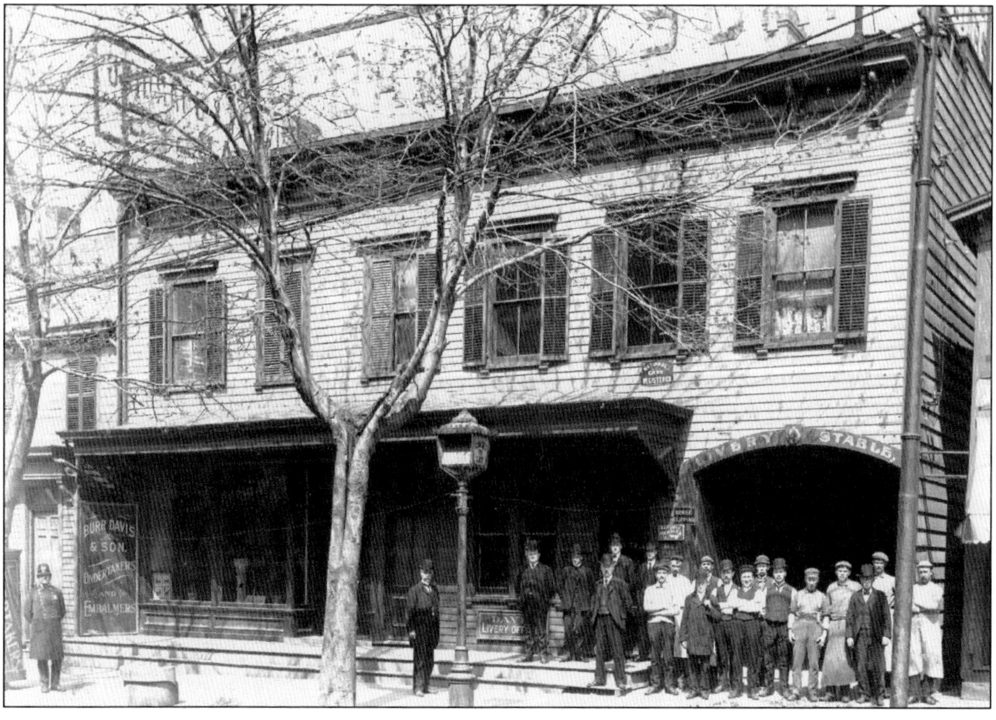

In 1854, a talented Italian family lived near South Street and West First Street. The neighbors soon heard extraordinary music flowing from the two-family house. It was the voice of Adelina Patti, a child prodigy with a remarkable destiny. Patti often sang for her classmates at school No. 3 (Grimes). At 16, Patti made her operatic debut at New York's Academy of Music. In 1862, she sang "Home Sweet Home" at the White House for Abraham and Mary Lincoln, mourning their son Willie, who died of typhoid. They were moved to tears and requested an encore. She was the most requested singer by Queen Victoria at Buckingham Palace. The program below is only one from numerous performances. Patti was the embodiment of the prima donna and the most extravagant singer of the day. Patti demanded $5,000 a night, in gold, before the performance. (Courtesy of Alif Archives.)

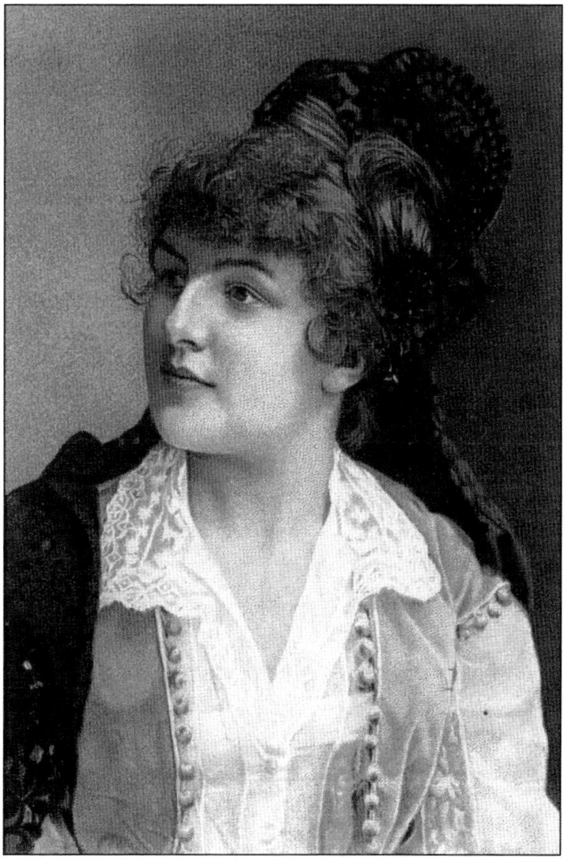

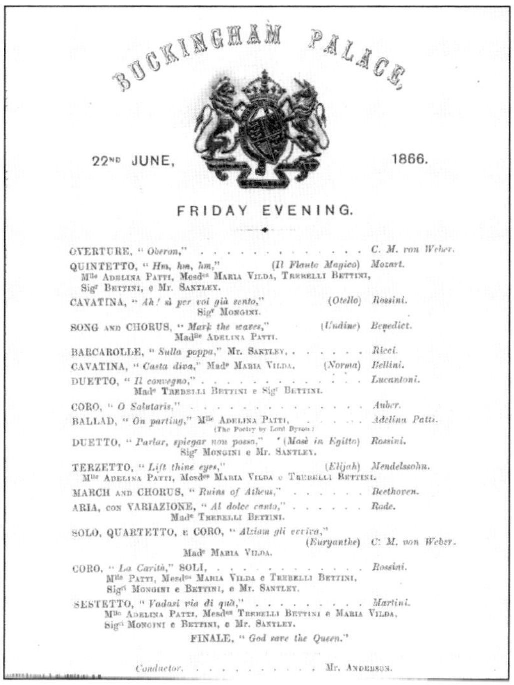

BUCKINGHAM PALACE,

22ND JUNE, 1866.

FRIDAY EVENING.

OVERTURE, "*Oberon*," . . . . *C. M. von Weber.*

QUINTETTO, "*Hm, hm, hm*," (*Il Flauto Magico*) *Mozart.*
Mlle Adelina Patti, Mesdes Maria Vilda, Trebelli Bettini, Sigr Bettini, e Mr. Santley.

CAVATINA, "*Ah! sì per voi già sento*," (*Otello*) *Rossini.*
Sigr Mongini.

SONG and CHORUS, "*Mark the waves*," (*Undine*) *Benedict.*
Madlle Adelina Patti.

BARCAROLLE, "*Sulla poppa*," Mr. Santley, ... *Ricci.*

CAVATINA, "*Casta diva*," Made Maria Vilda. (*Norma*) *Bellini.*

DUETTO, "*Il convegno*," . . . . *Lucantoni.*
Made Trebelli Bettini e Sigr Bettini.

CORO, "*O Salutaris*," . . . . *Auber.*

BALLAD, "*On parting*," Mlle Adelina Patti, ... *Adelina Patti.*
(The Poetry by Lord Byron.)

DUETTO, "*Parlar, spiegar non posso*," (*Mosè in Egitto*) *Rossini.*
Sigr Mongini e Mr. Santley.

TERZETTO, "*Lift thine eyes*," (*Elijah*) *Mendelssohn.*
Mlle Adelina Patti, Mesdes Maria Vilda e Trebelli Bettini.

MARCH and CHORUS, "*Ruins of Athens*," . . . . *Beethoven.*

ARIA, con VARIAZIONE, "*Al dolce canto*," . . . . *Rode.*
Made Trebelli Bettini.

SOLO, QUARTETTO, e CORO, "*Alziam gli evviva*," (*Euryanthe*) *C. M. von Weber.*
Made Maria Vilda.

CORO, "*La Carità*," SOLI, ... *Rossini.*
Mlle Patti, Mesdes Maria Vilda e Trebelli Bettini, Sigri Mongini e Bettini, e Mr. Santley.

SESTETTO, "*Vadasi via di quà*," . . . . *Martini.*
Mlle Adelina Patti, Mesdes Trebelli Bettini e Maria Vilda, Sigri Mongini e Bettini, e Mr. Santley.

FINALE, "*God save the Queen*."

Conductor, ... Mr. Anderson.

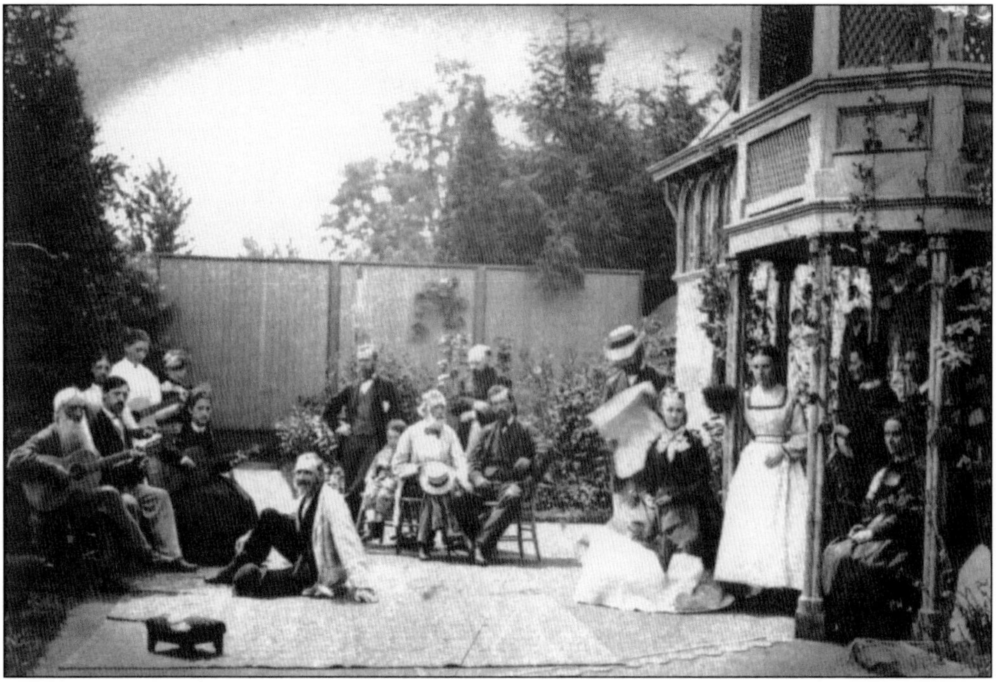

The pioneers of Mount Vernon were concerned with the quality of cultural life in their fledgling village. This is a photograph of a group of musicians gathering on Fourth Avenue between Second and Third Streets. It was located on the west side of the street near the current location of AC-BAW Center for the Arts. This photograph is from the 1860s.

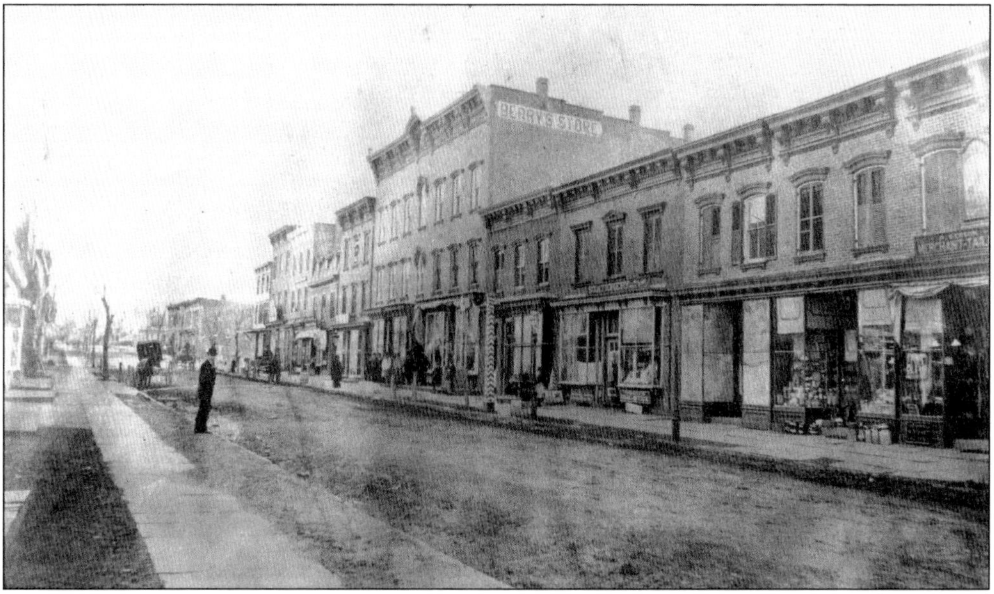

Both culture and commerce were alive and well in the early village. Above is an 1881 view looking southward down Fourth Avenue from First Street. On the west side of the street is Berry's General Store. It grew to become the city's first department store. Its customers were from around the county. It stood where the more modern Genung's store replaced it in the 20th century.

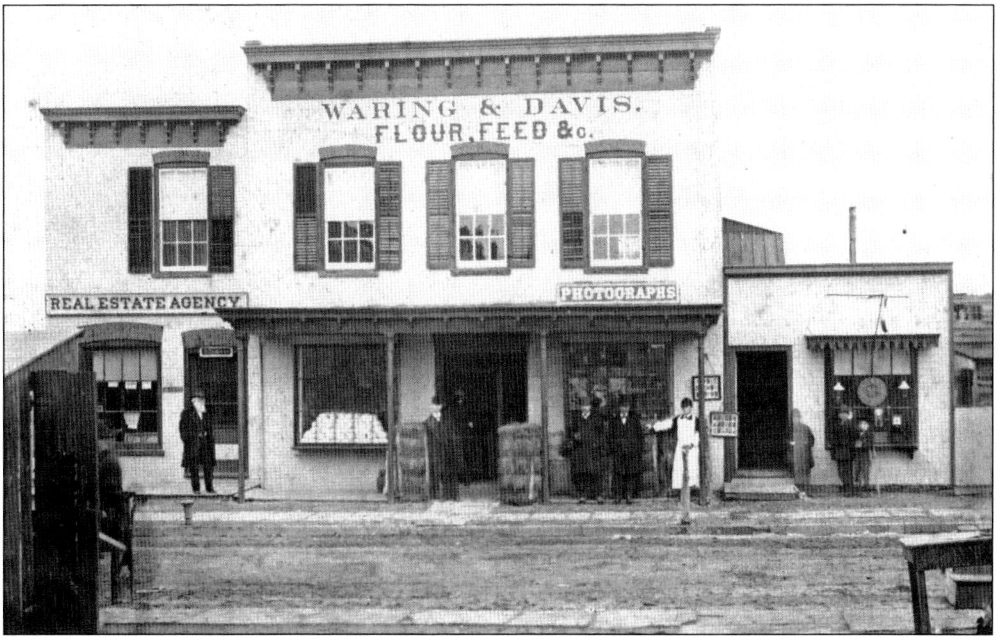

This 1863 photograph of 8 South Fourth Avenue, near First Street, shows the frontier nature of the commercial district. The street was a dirt path. The gentlemen standing in front of the business represent their ownership. Through the 1970s and 1990s, there was a camera store and studio in the same address as this Civil War–era photography studio.

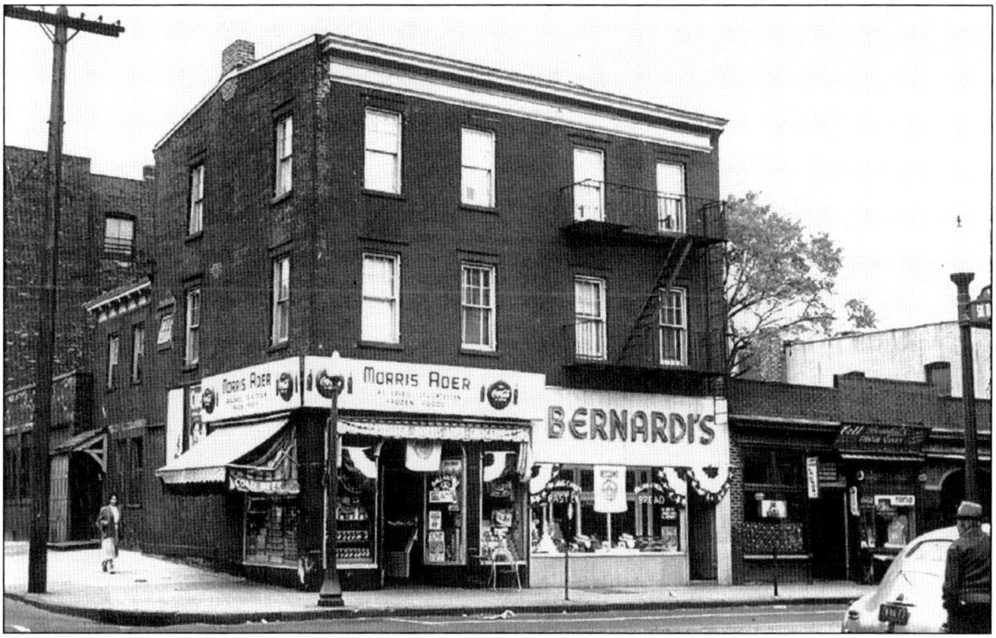

This brick building at the southwest corner of Third Street and Third Avenue is the oldest of its type in the city. Built in 1852, it was a cigar store owned by William McCaffe. It became the site of a heated debate on the issue of incorporating the village. On December 3, 1853, in McCaffe's store, voters favorably decided the question by a vote of 82 to 52. The building has been remodeled several times. This image was taken in 1947.

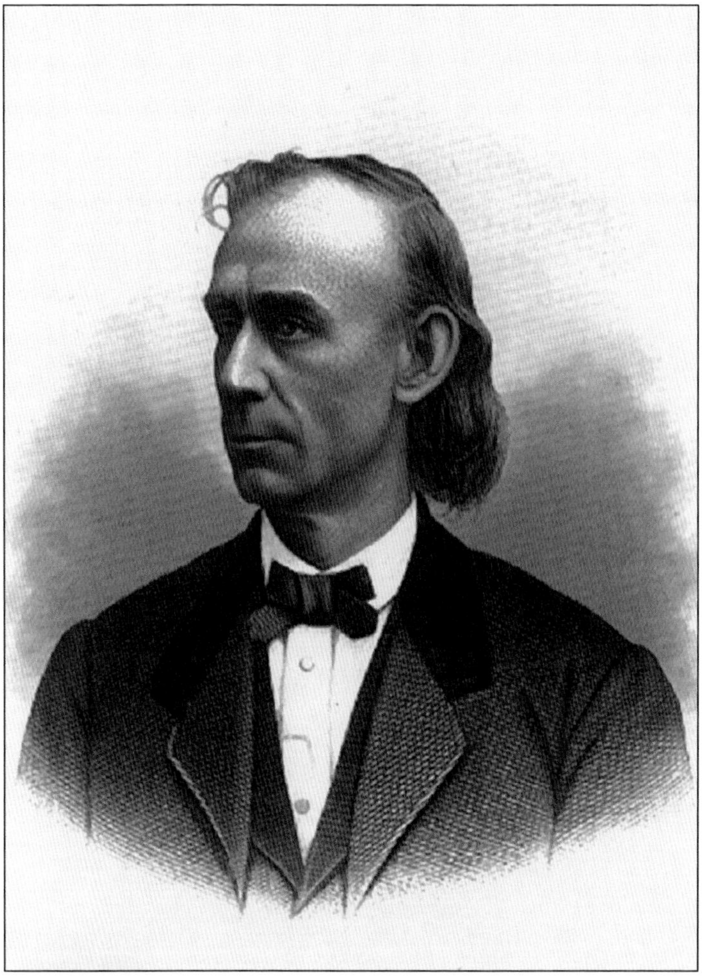

On Sunday, January 13, 1861, Rev. William H. Boole, the staunch abolitionist pastor of the First Methodist Church, preached "Antidote to Rev. H. J. Van Dyke's Pro-Slavery Discourse—American Slavery Has No Foundation in the Scriptures." He argued that the Bible did not approve slavery. It was a brilliant and courageous sermon. Boole proved the strength of his faith by resigning and joining the Union army as a chaplain.

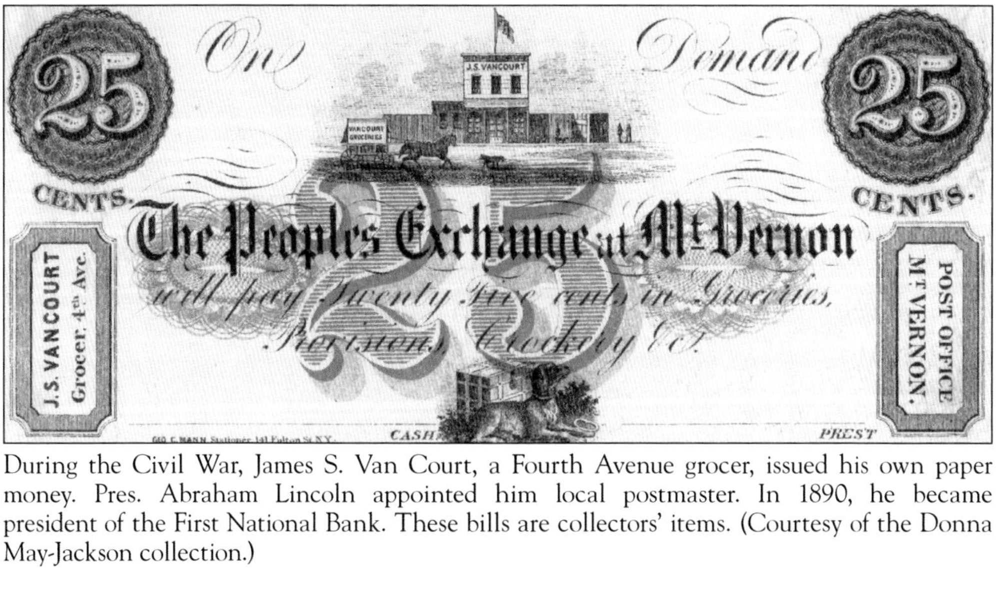

During the Civil War, James S. Van Court, a Fourth Avenue grocer, issued his own paper money. Pres. Abraham Lincoln appointed him local postmaster. In 1890, he became president of the First National Bank. These bills are collectors' items. (Courtesy of the Donna May-Jackson collection.)

In the first decades of the village, traveling amusements were important pastimes. Residents were eager to see what daring acts had come to town. This was especially true when the one-ring circus made its tour. It gave a free exhibition consisting of a tightrope act. Often this took place on Fourth Avenue where the rope was stretched across the street from the tops of opposite buildings. This was usually a teaser act to lure people to visit the circus grounds over by Rich and Lincoln Avenues. The evening performances were 25¢.

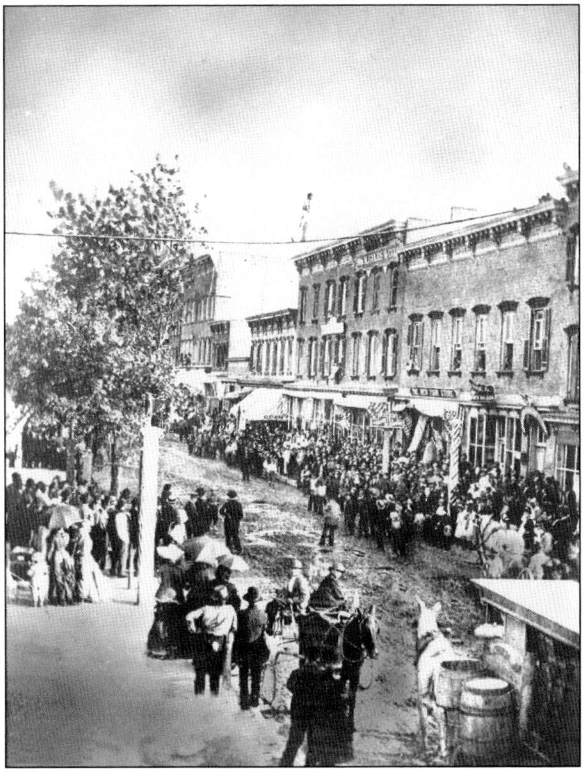

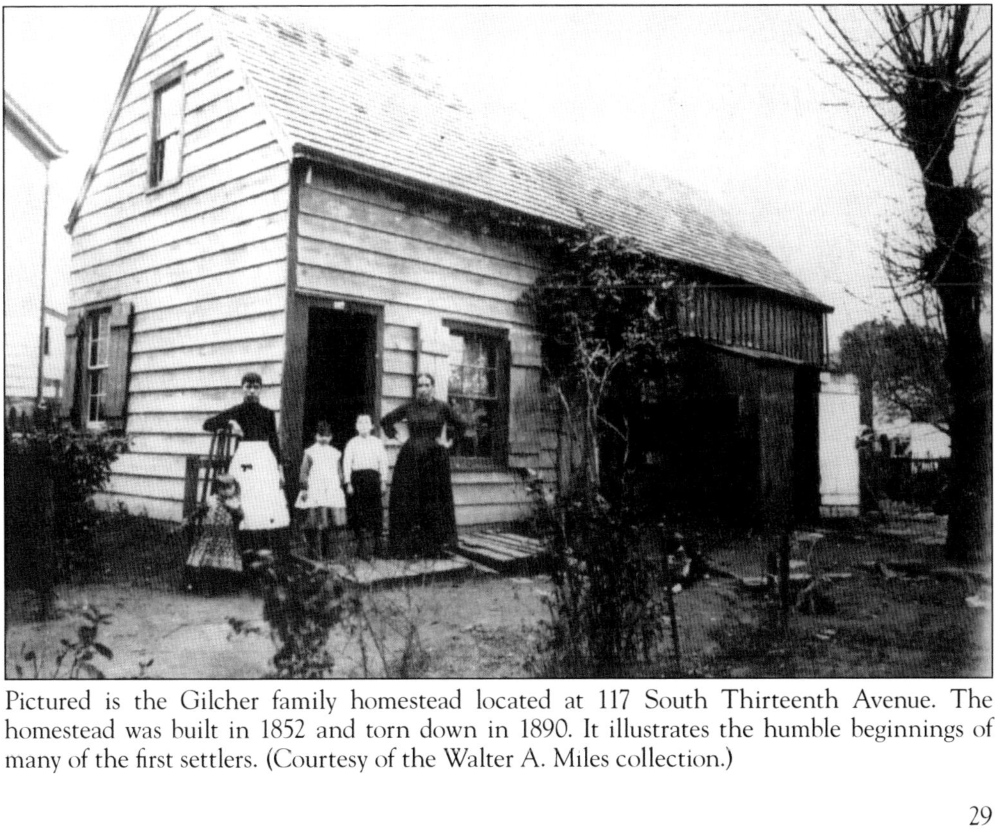

Pictured is the Gilcher family homestead located at 117 South Thirteenth Avenue. The homestead was built in 1852 and torn down in 1890. It illustrates the humble beginnings of many of the first settlers. (Courtesy of the Walter A. Miles collection.)

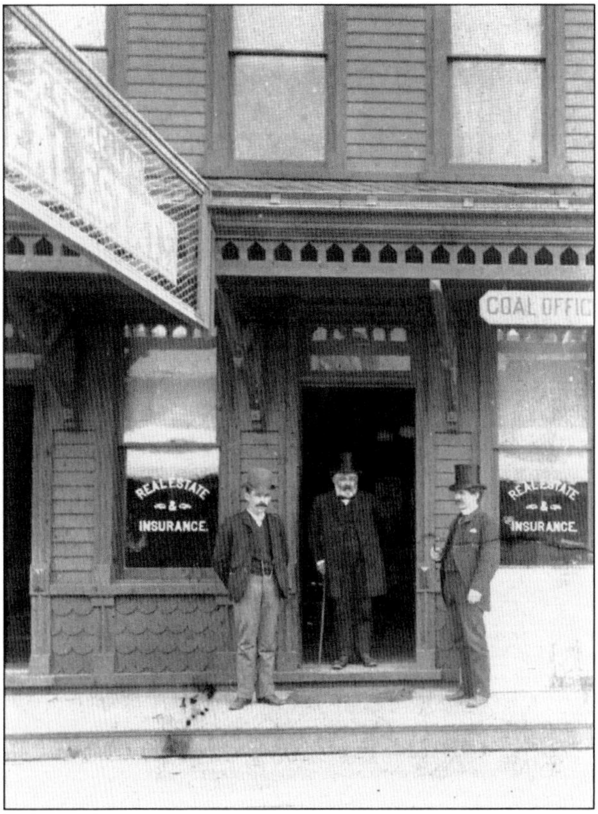

This is the C. S. McClellan building located at First Street near the southeast corner of Fourth Avenue. Standing in the door is Pelham McClellan. He is the father of Clarence S., standing to his right. They were leaders in real estate, insurance, and banking. They began in 1878 and are still in business. The First National Bank, currently the Chase Bank building on First Street at the corner of Fifth Avenue, was built by C. S. McClellan. It was the city's first "skyscraper." This photograph was taken in the 1880s.

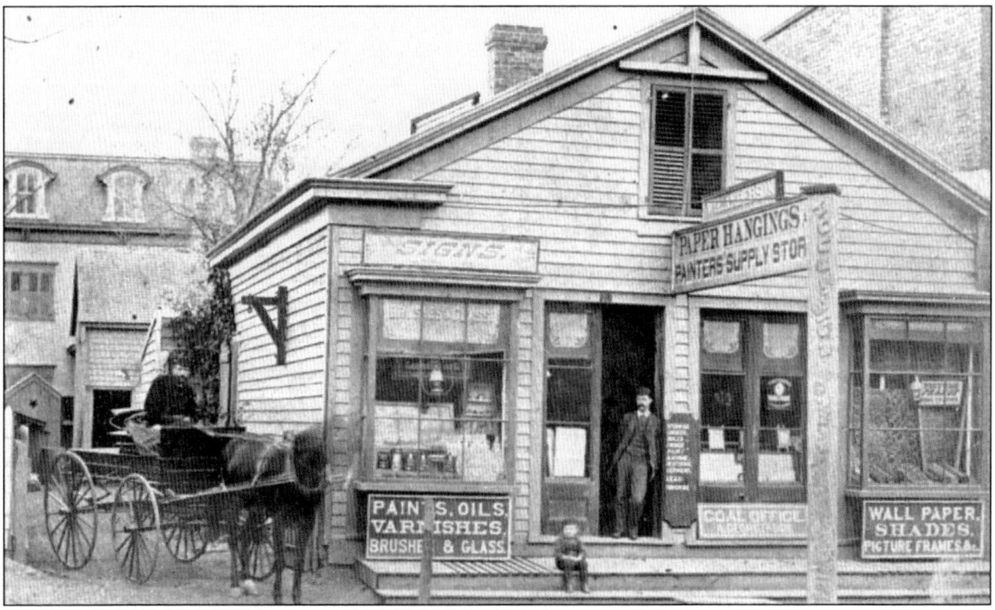

This is a photograph of the Anderson building at 68 South Fourth Avenue, near the corner of Second Street. Many of the earliest businesses on Fourth Avenue were affiliated with home construction and decorating. Today a clothing store is at this location. This photograph is from around 1880.

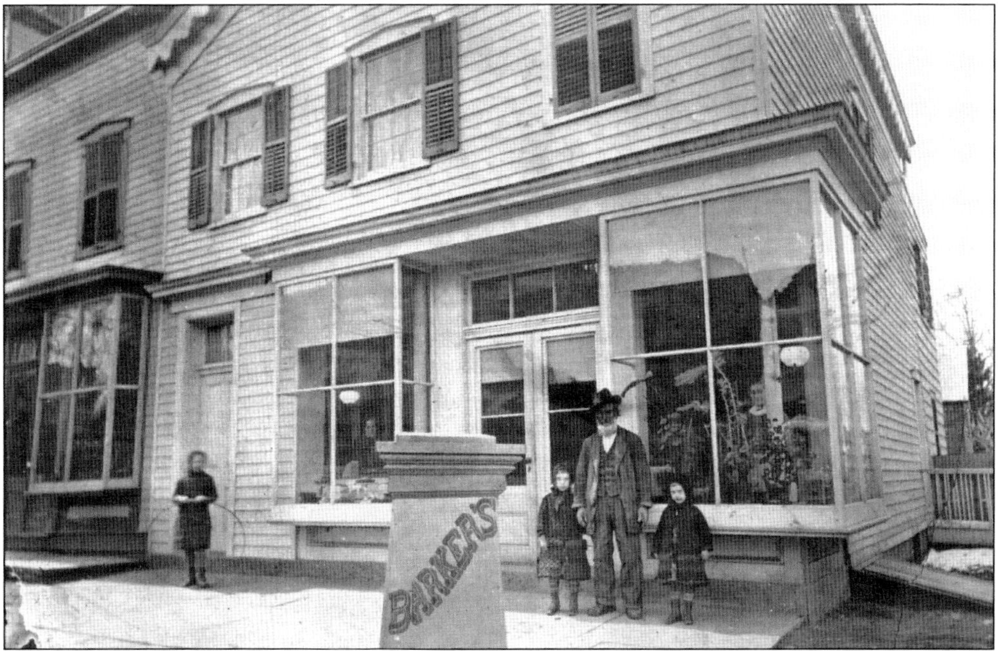

Between 1868 and 1873, the center of business was at the corner of Fourth Avenue and Third Street. The 1879 image above shows Sanford Hallock's Bakery, which was on the southwest corner. It was the first in the village. Below is the same location in 1948.

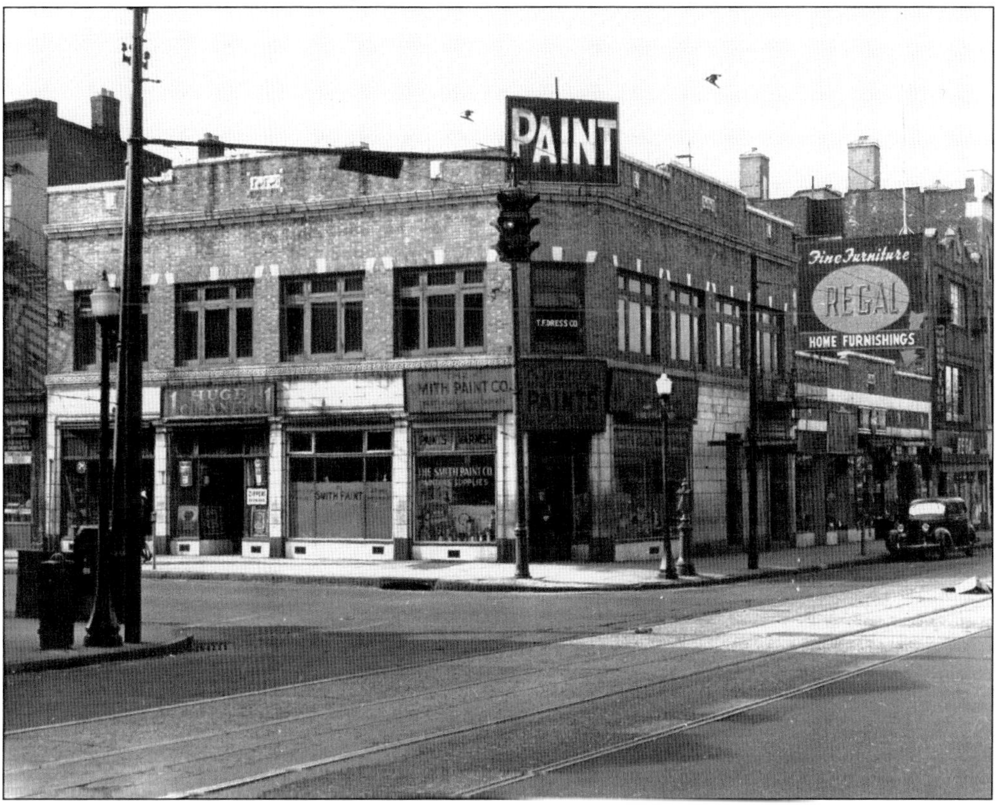

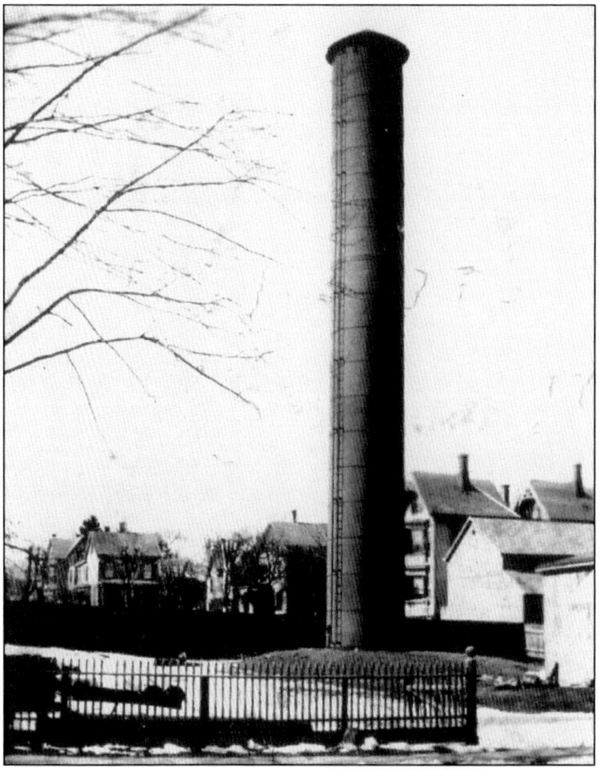

This 1882 photograph of the Mount Vernon Water Company shows where it bored an artesian well, 500 feet deep, and developed a flow of 72,000 gallons of drinking water per day. It was Mount Vernon's first effort to supply its own water. It was on the south side of Third Street, between Seventh and Eighth Avenues, where today the Benjamin Levister Towers building at 70 West Third Street stands.

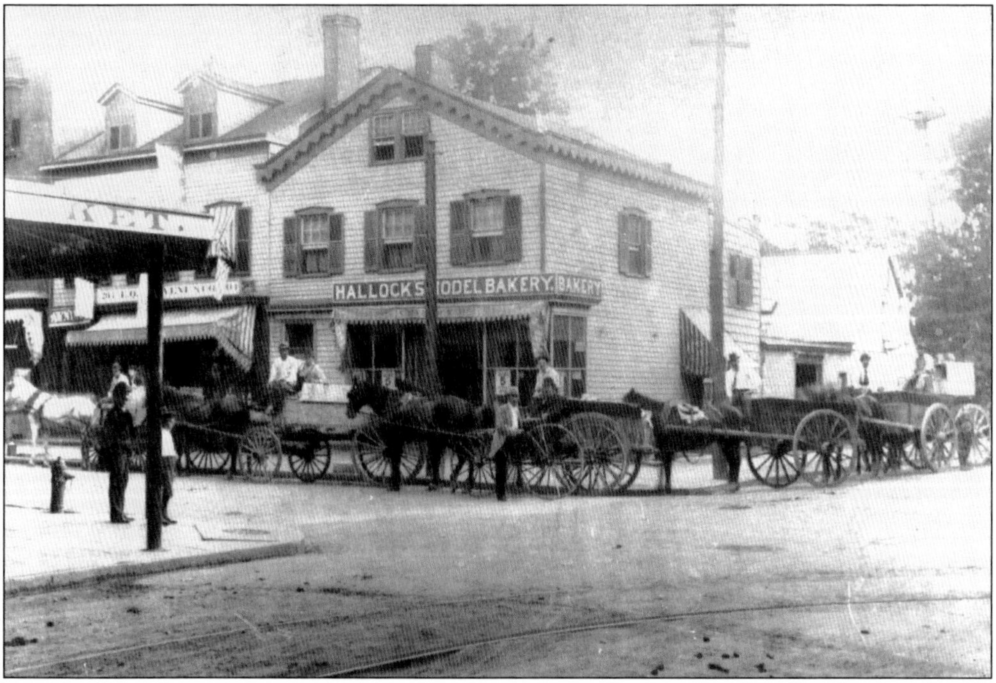

This is an 1878 picture of the Department of Public Works and Sanitation. These wagons are collecting refuse at the southwest corner of Third Street and Fourth Avenue. Hallock's Bakery is in the background.

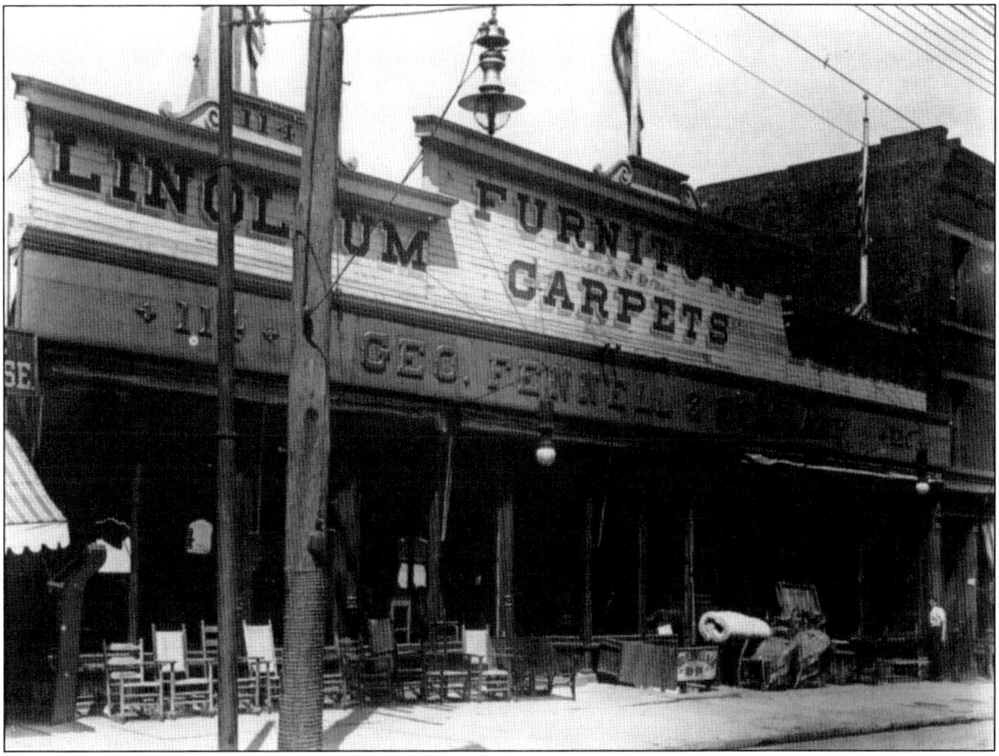

George Fennel's furniture store was founded in 1879 and remained in business at 110 South Fourth Avenue into the 1950s. For over 60 years, it was the leading outlet for home furnishings. Today it is a hardware store.

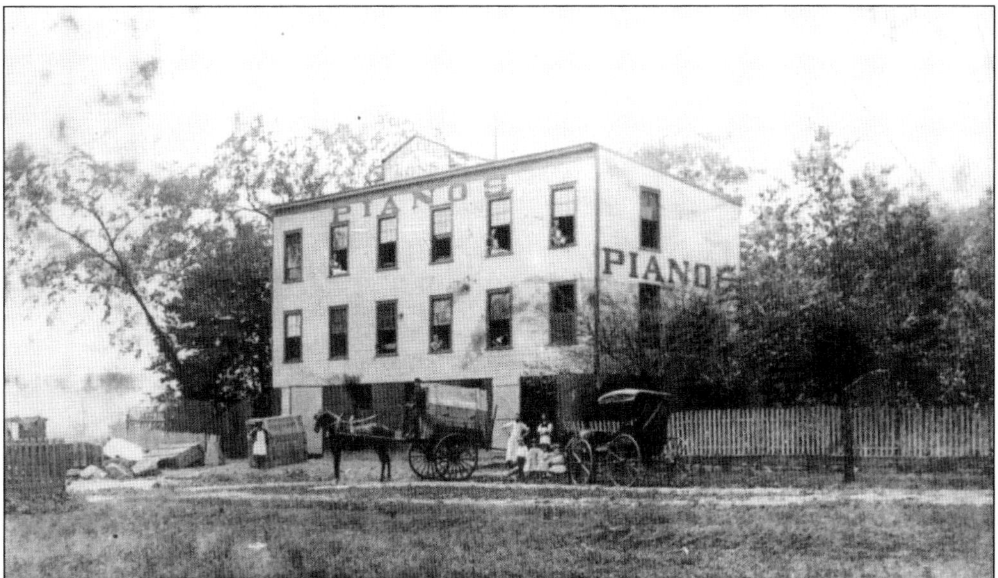

The base economy of the village and city was retailing and manufacturing. Above is the Schleicher and Son piano factory located on Fourteenth Avenue just south of West Third Street. This photograph is from around 1885.

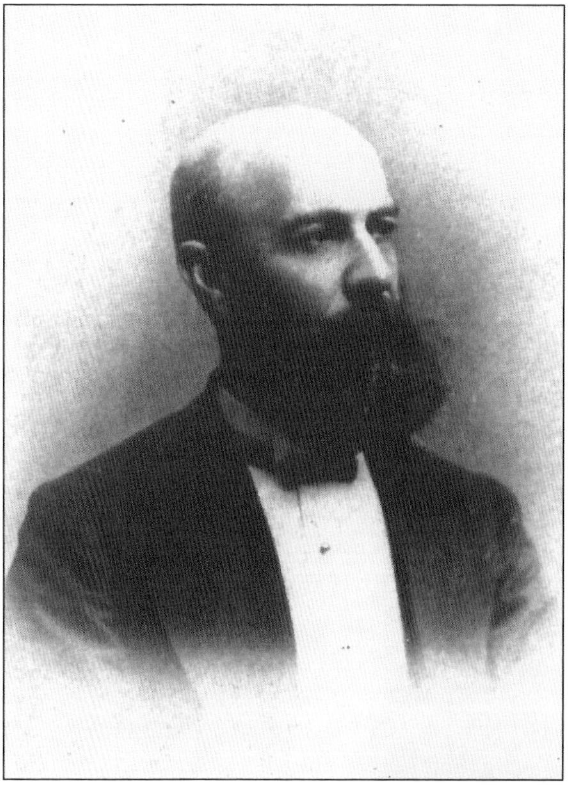

In 1864, Joseph S. Wood, educator and politician, came to Mount Vernon. He retired as school principal in 1875. In 1898, he became president of the newly consolidated school districts and built new schools. The high school and night school were established, and the network of playgrounds currently affiliated with local schools was constructed. He helped obtain $50,000 from Andrew Carnegie to build the public library. Although Wood and his wife were the epitome of early-20th-century successful and influential citizens, the picture below of an anonymous family found among the files of the Westchester Woman's Club speaks to the quality of life for many residents in the 1880s and 1890s. The powerful women's organization was founded in the Wood's home. In 1932, the new state-of-the art concert hall adjoining Washington Junior High School was named Joseph S. Wood Auditorium.

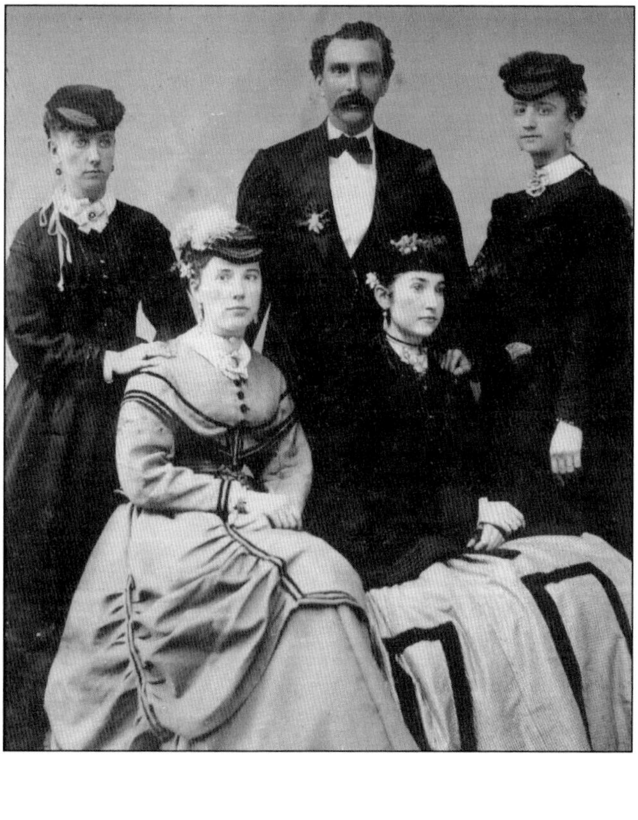

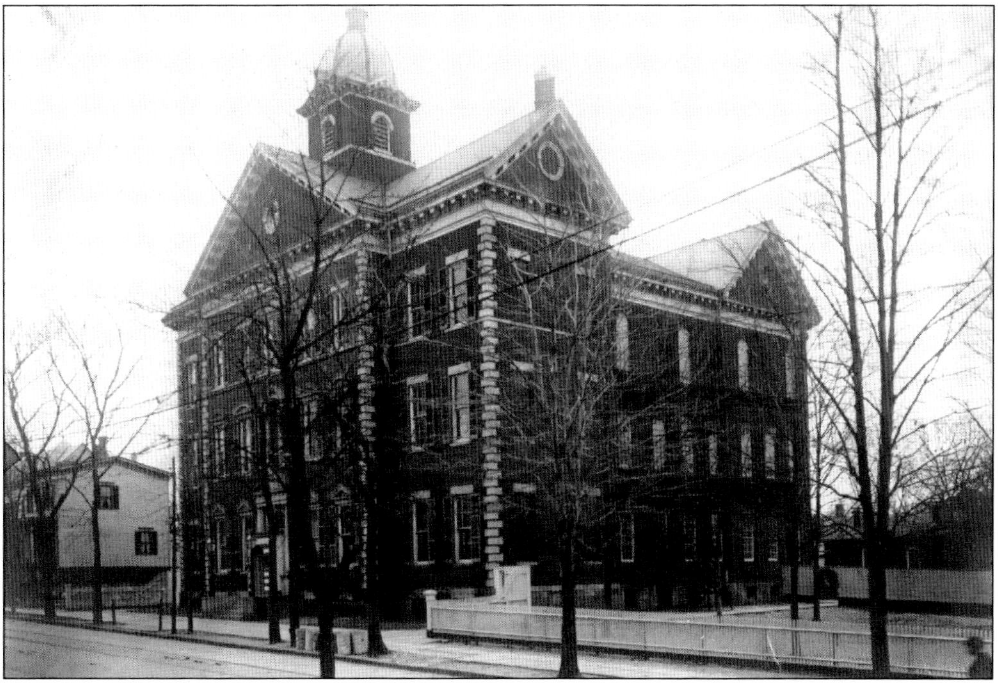

The building above is school No. 1, on Fifth Avenue near the corner of Second Street, and was erected in 1877. It later became known as Washington School. Below is the new Joseph S. Wood Auditorium, built in 1932. In the background is Washington Junior High School. The entire complex is fronted on South Sixth Avenue and Second Street. Today it is called Nellie Thornton School.

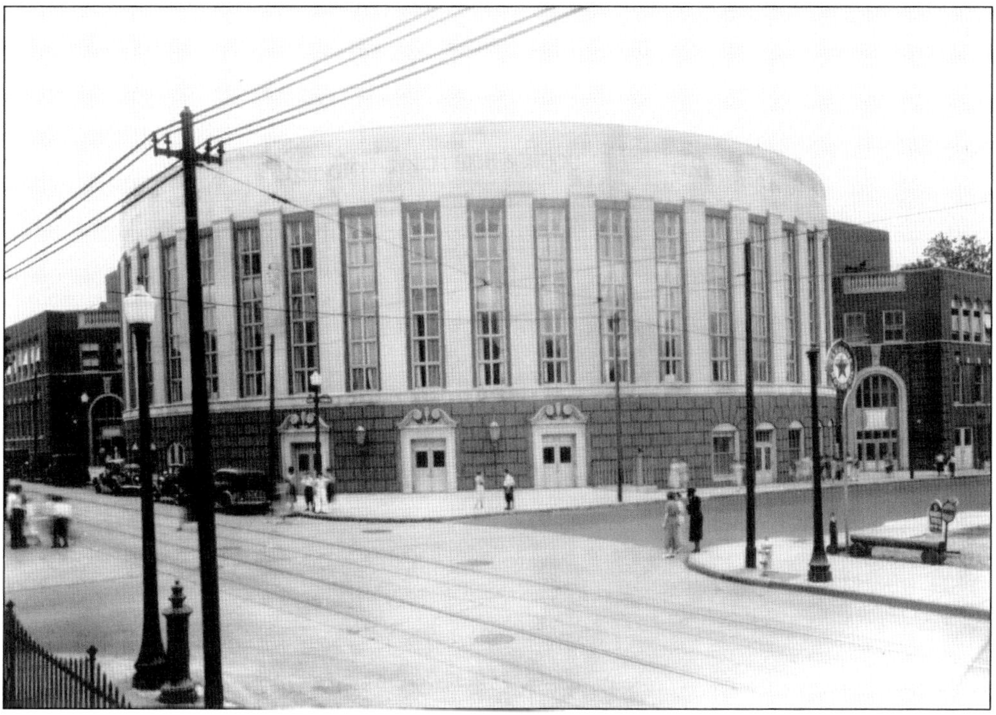

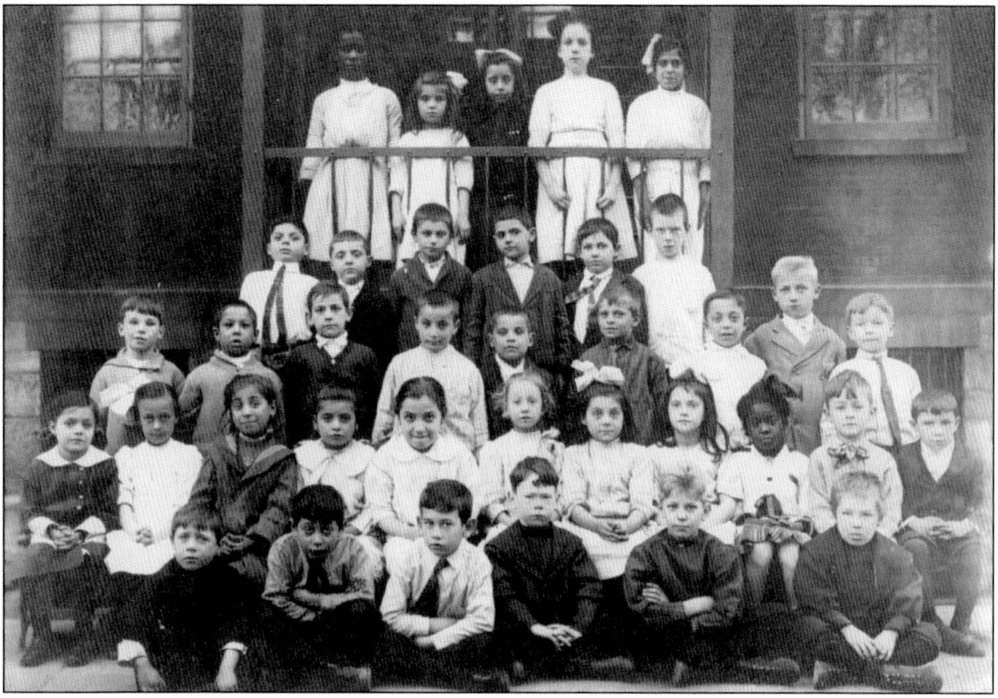

In the 1890s, school No. 1 (Washington School) served many immigrant children. Their parents came to Mount Vernon to experience the American dream of upward social mobility through free and public education. The family names of students from the two photographs are ancestors of many current residents. Perhaps some names are recognizable: Colarusso, Mosca, Depalo, Campanelli, Deleno, Albis, Corrado, Impara, DeAngelis, Spero, Imbrogno, Orsenigo, DeFillpe, Blenniss, Bernstein, McCaffery, Munas, Wilkey, Becker, Mullhausser, Grebstein, Emmeluth, and the like.

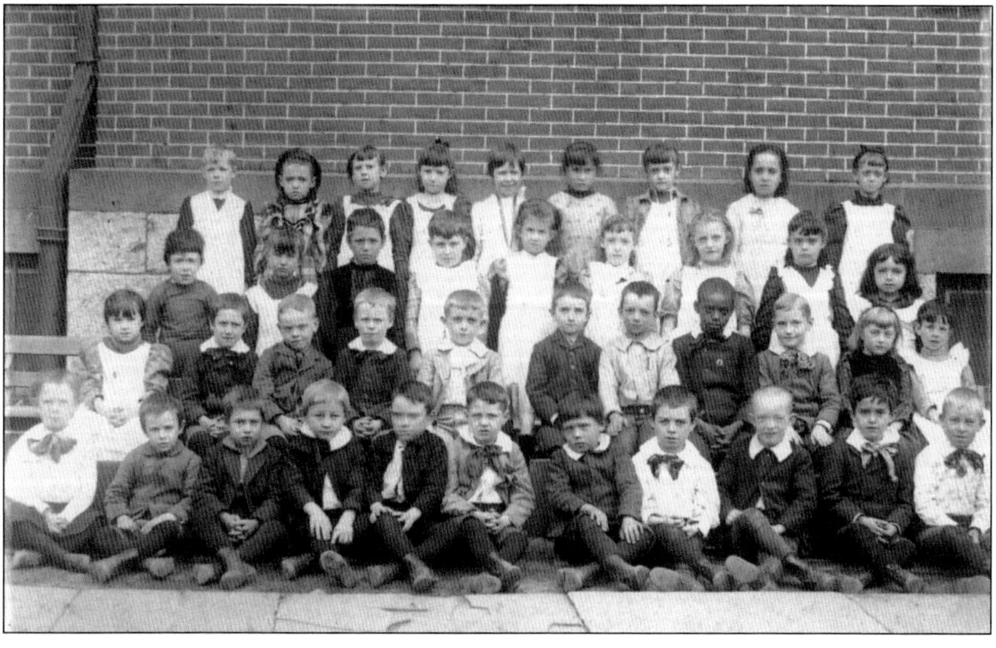

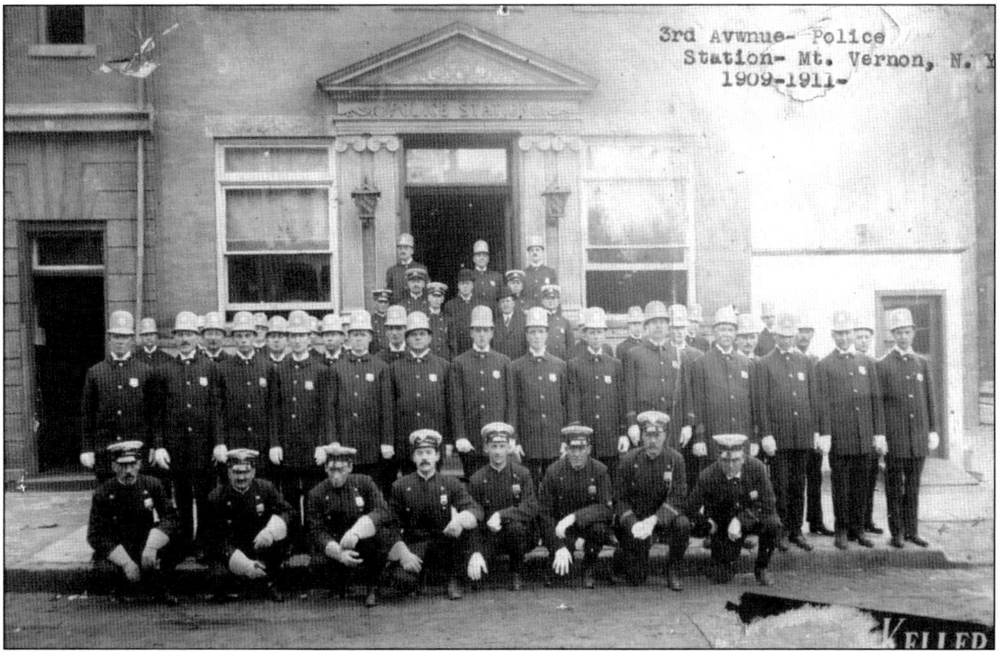

In 1892, Capt. Joseph Marz and policemen Frederick Van Garral, Matthew Bennett, Joseph Gagg, and James Fallon were the Mount Vernon police force. During the first half of the 20th century, Chiefs George Atwell and Michael Silverstein were the pioneer leaders of the modern police department. In later years, Silverstein was known as the unofficial "Mayor of Mount Vernon."

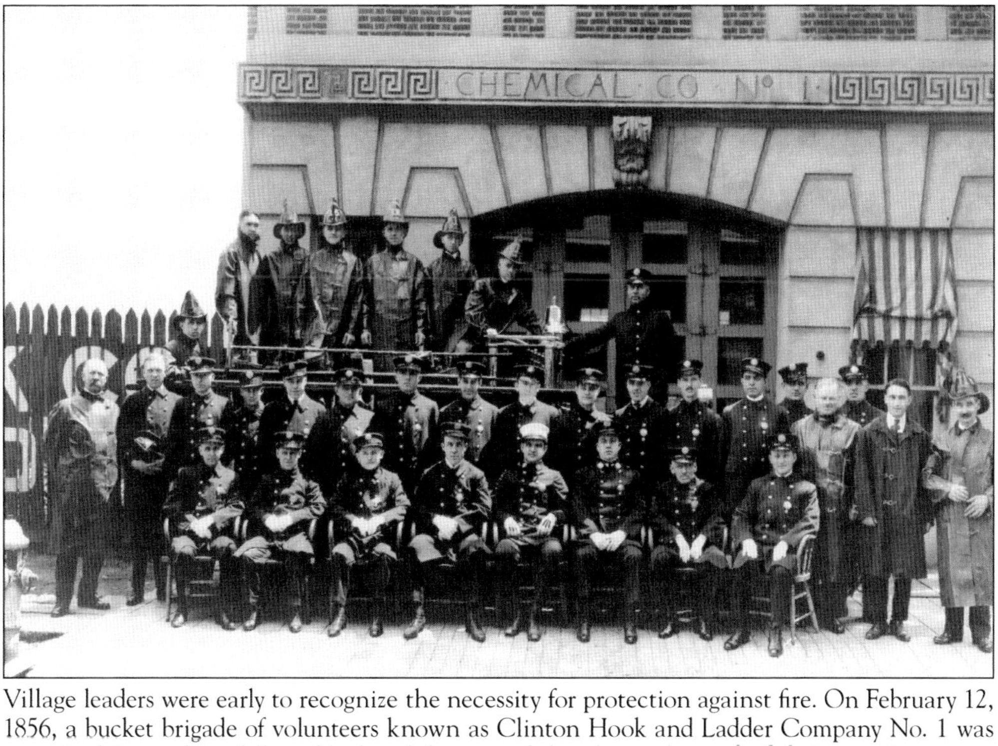

Village leaders were early to recognize the necessity for protection against fire. On February 12, 1856, a bucket brigade of volunteers known as Clinton Hook and Ladder Company No. 1 was organized. It was later followed by hand-drawn and then horse-drawn firefighting equipment.

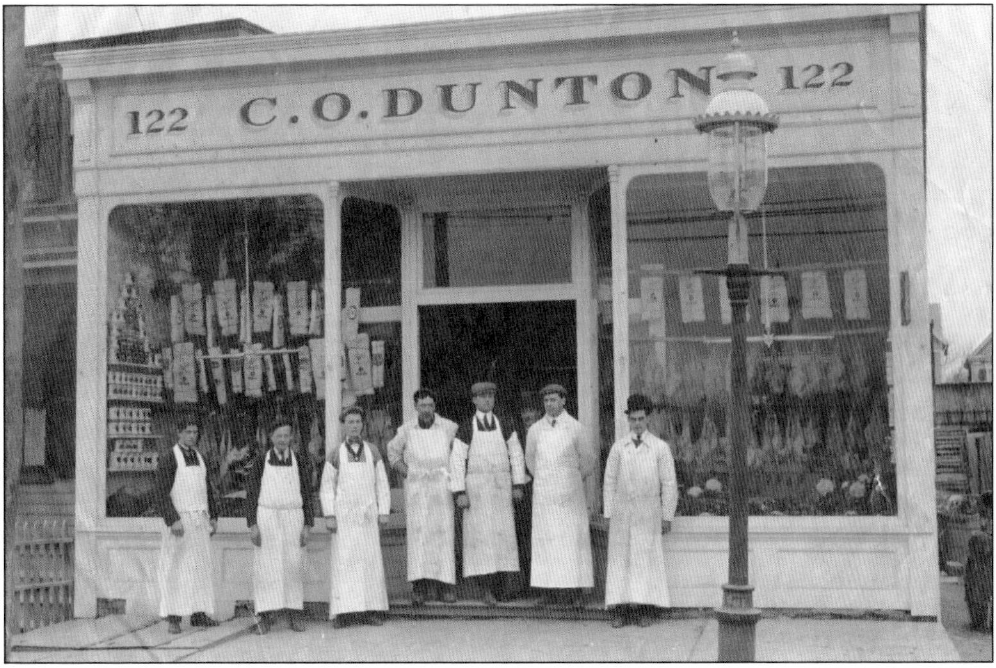

Claude O. Dunton, a meat butcher, was located at 122 East Third Street. South-side shops were busy and prosperous. His residence was near his business at 8 Martens Place. This image is from around 1915. (Courtesy of the Donna May-Jackson collection.)

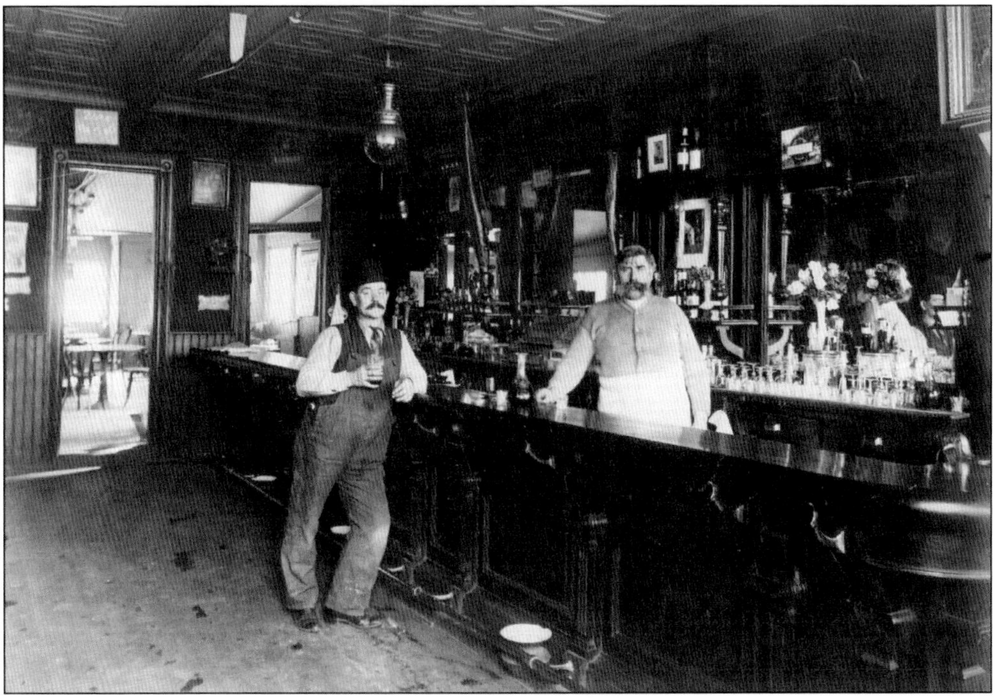

Mount Vernon had an active temperance movement. This was one of many saloons. Joseph Schaeffer was the proprietor of this saloon at 8 East First Street, seen in 1914. His residence was 9 Wilson Place. (Courtesy of the Donna May-Jackson collection.)

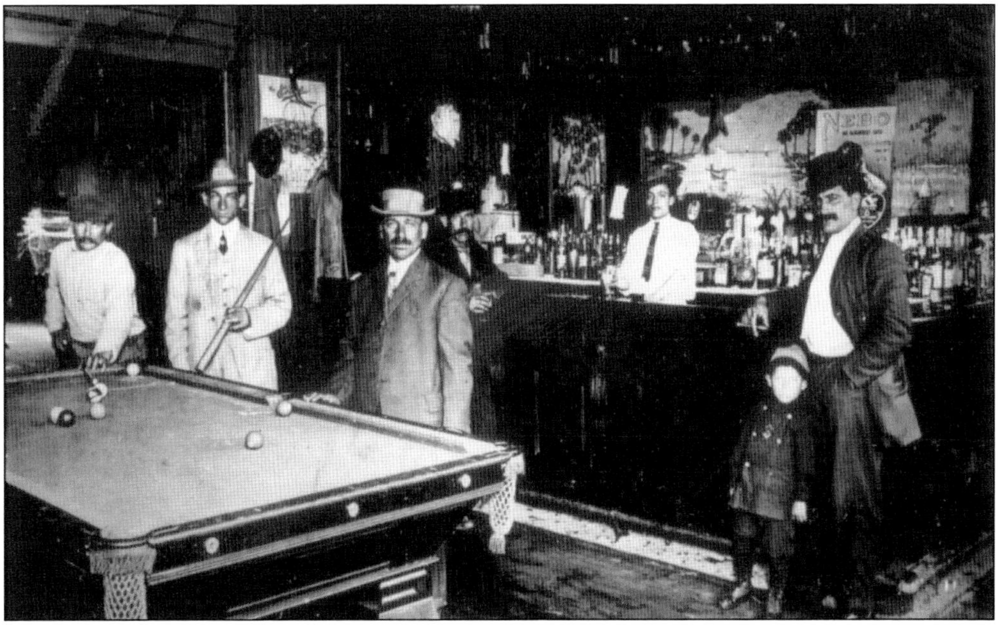

At the beginning of the 20th century, the heart of the Italian immigrant community was the southwest side of the city. Pictured above is Anielo Tucci's saloon located on Seventh Avenue between Second and Third Streets. The bartender is Filippo Quaranta, also known as "Mr. Forty." He is the father of Salvatore Quaranta, the longtime leader of the chamber of commerce. As more African Americans settled the south side, the establishment became Harris's Bar. (Courtesy of Salvatore Quaranta.)

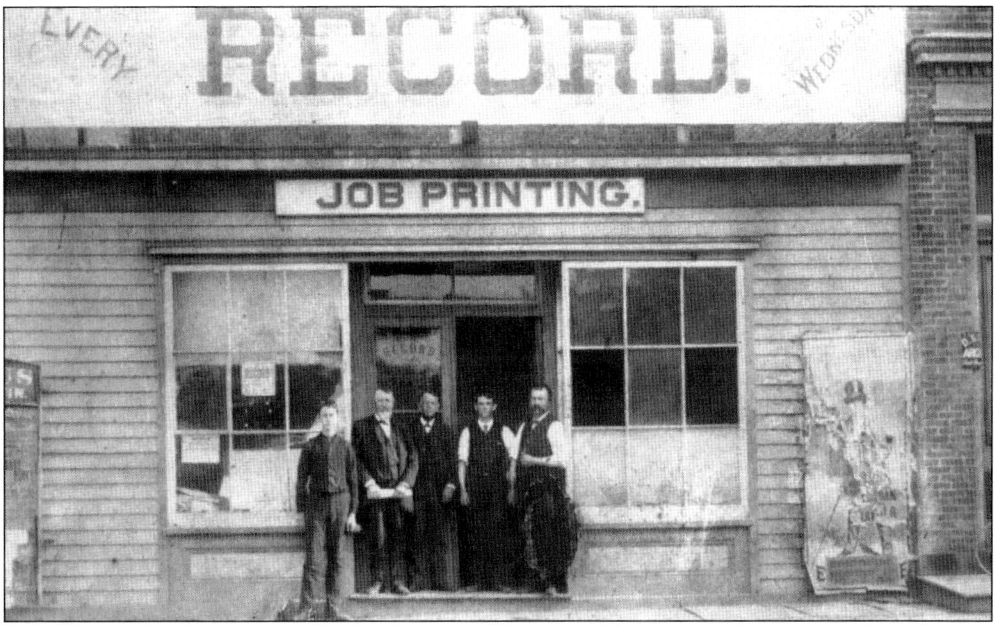

As the village of Mount Vernon grew, so did the number of newspapers. Before the *Argus* became a daily newspaper in 1892, there were several weekly newspapers. They were usually partisan outlets for one of the political parties. The *Westchester County Record* was located on First Street between Fifth and Sixth Avenues. This photograph is from 1888.

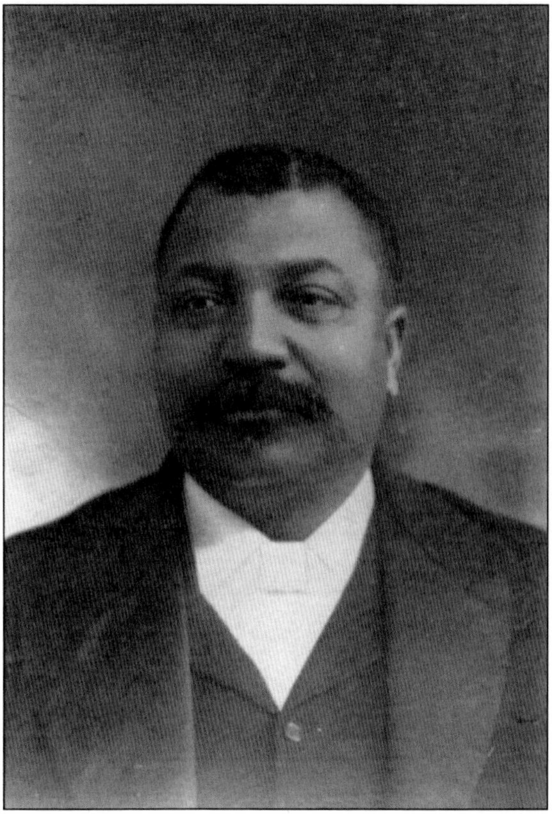

Pictured is Rev. Granville Hunt, the second pastor of Grace Baptist Church. He served from 1898 to 1913. He was the most ambitious and politically active of the city's early African American clergy. Educated, articulate, and charismatic, he was a willing spokesman for the growing African American community. The Hunt family and former city councilman James Finch are descendants. This photograph is from 1905.

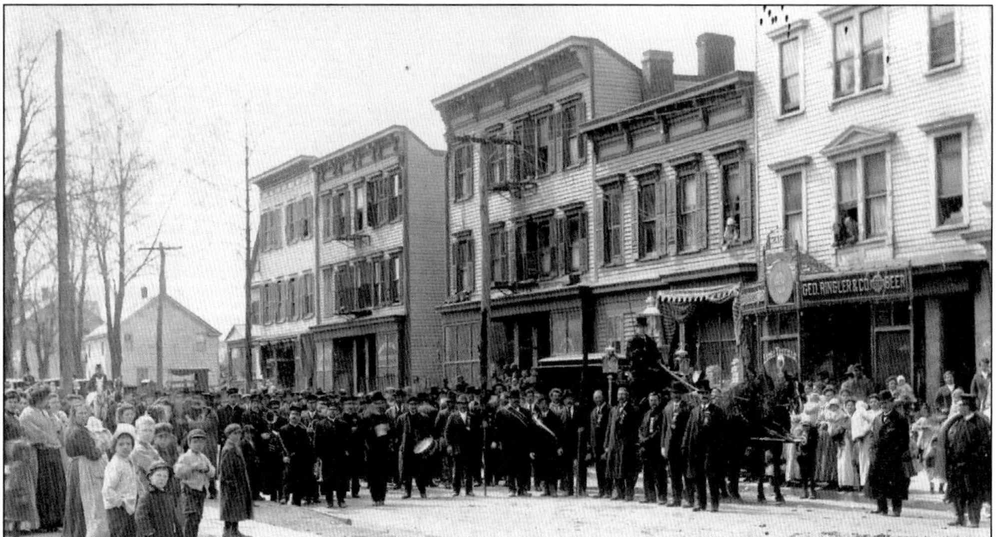

The above is a rare 1905 photograph of a gathering and processional at the corner of South Seventh Avenue and West Third Street. This southwest sector of the city was the center of the Italian immigrant community and later the African American neighborhood. This solemn photograph appears to be a funeral.

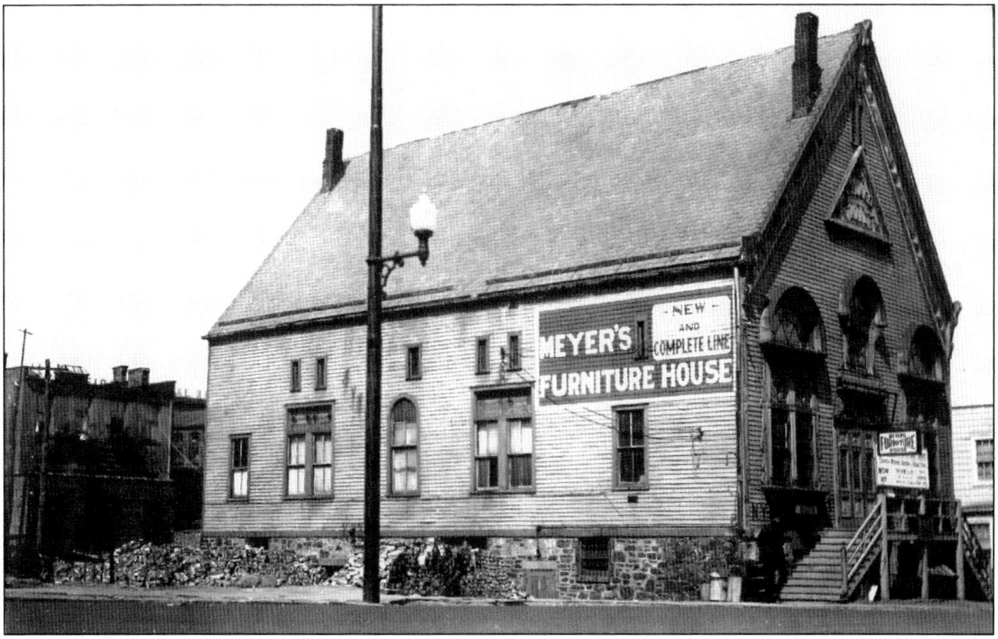

The photograph above is Willard Hall, at 28 South Third Avenue, built by the Westchester Temperance Union. The cornerstone was laid on February 21, and it was dedicated on May 31, 1891. In the 1890s, the African American Baptist congregations began the work that led to the establishment of Grace Baptist Church. This photograph is from around 1924.

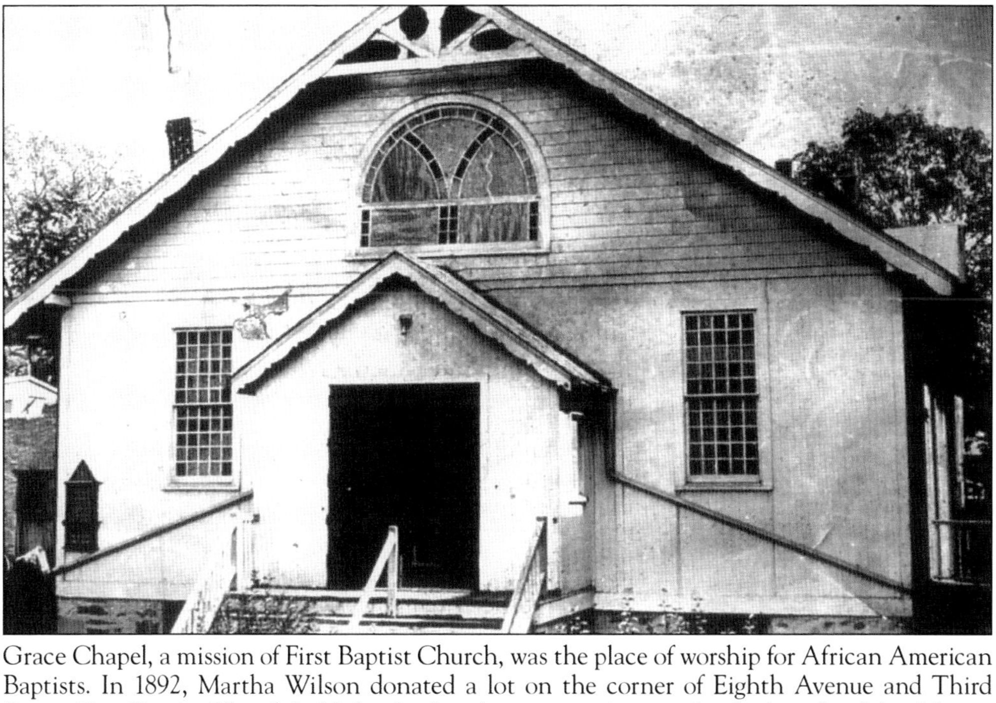
Grace Chapel, a mission of First Baptist Church, was the place of worship for African American Baptists. In 1892, Martha Wilson donated a lot on the corner of Eighth Avenue and Third Street. First Baptist Church held the deed to the property in trust for the benefit of the African American mission. The structure above was moved and is now White Rock Baptist Church at Fifth Avenue and Fourth Street.

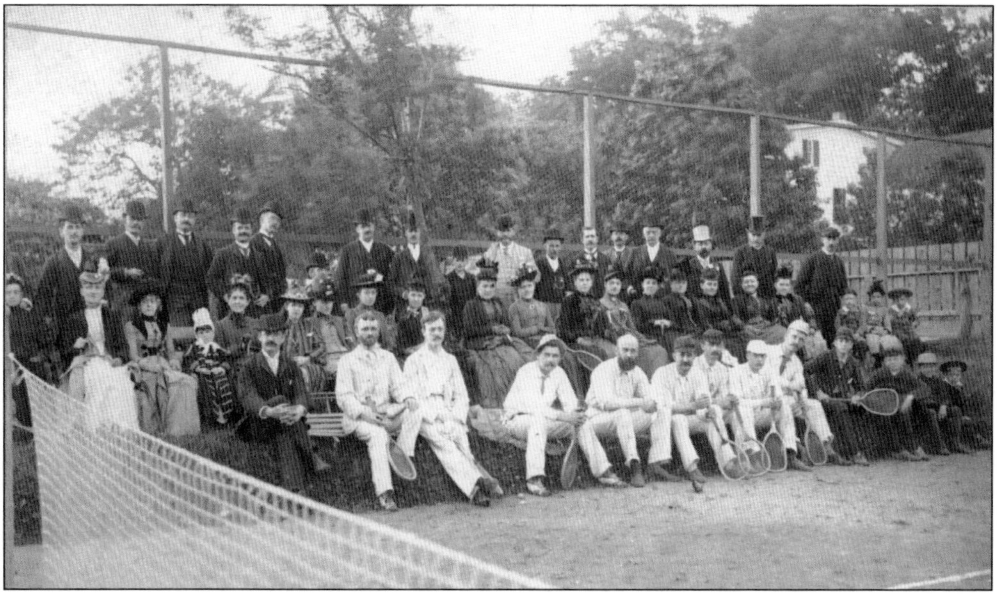

This is a tournament day at the Crescent Lawn Tennis Club. Well into the 20th century, Mount Vernon had strategically placed tennis courts in nearly every neighborhood. The photographer was G. B. Maynard. It is from the Burr Davis collection at the Mount Vernon Public Library Virginia Moskowitz Local History Room.

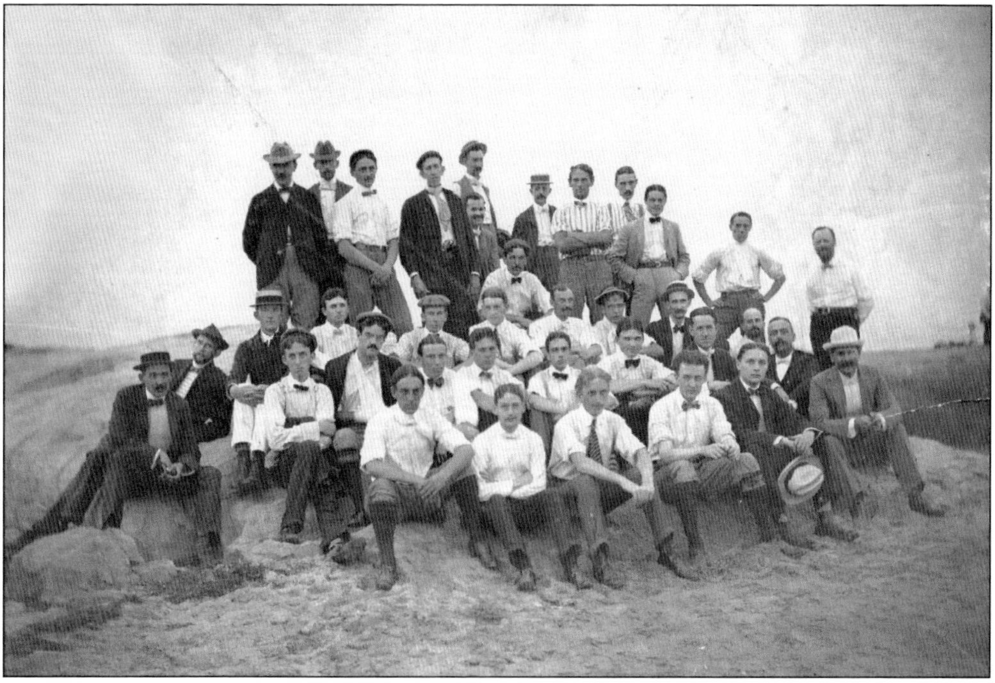

In 1896, a social group called the Westchester County Wheelmen was founded. Cycling was an athletic phenomenon for middle-class men. It was not long before the club grew to over 150 members. They wore colorful green outfits trimmed with gold braid, and the club's emblem was prominently displayed on their caps. Whenever they rode up county to compete, they routinely brought at least one of the trophies back to Mount Vernon.

At the beginning of the 20th century, William Stratten was one of the wealthiest men in Mount Vernon. He lived in the exclusive Chester Hill section on Summit Avenue. He was the president of Westchester Lighting and Power. His offices were in the Fairfax Hall at the southeast corner of First Avenue and First Street. It was the precursor to the Con Edison building currently at the same location.

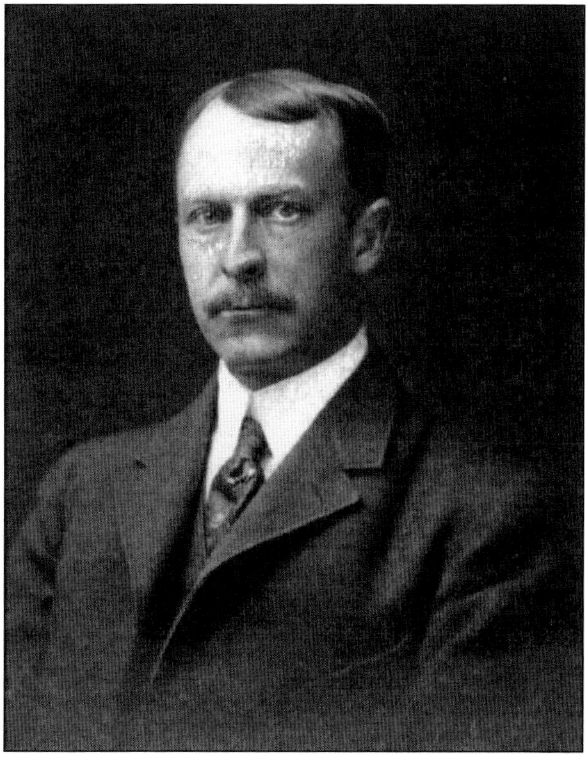

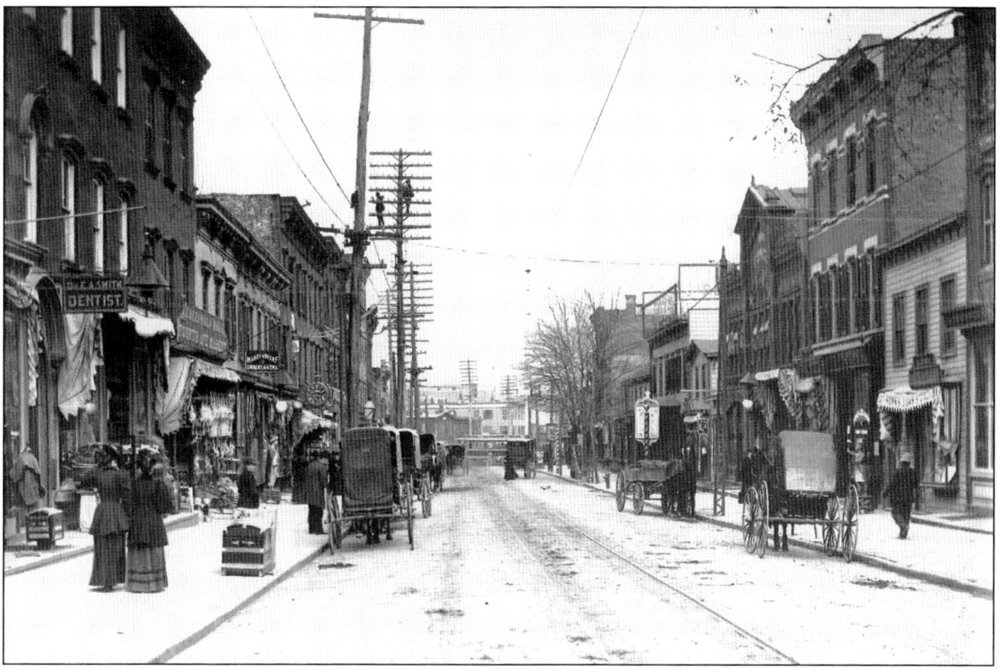

This is a view from 1888 looking north on Fourth Avenue between First and Second Streets. Notice the carriages, trolley tracks, New York-New Haven Railroad train (far background), and electrification lines. Mount Vernon was getting ready for its official status as a city. This photograph was taken by Henry Sihler.

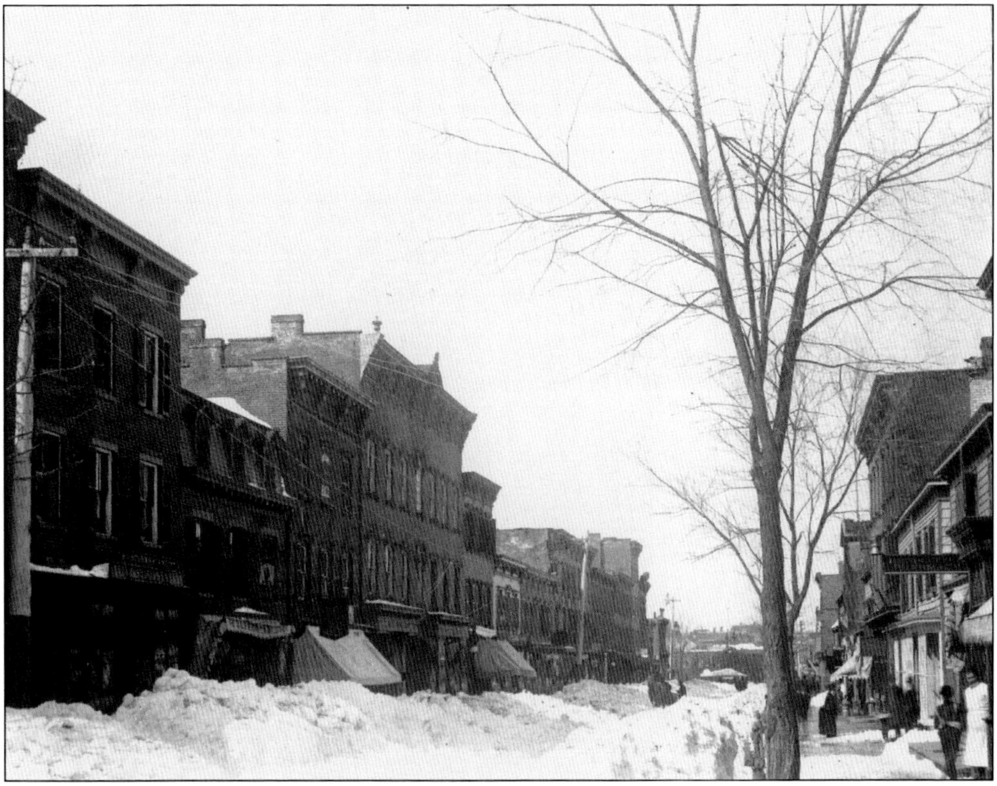

No one could ever forget the blizzard of 1888. All trains were stalled and passengers from New York up through Connecticut were stranded in Mount Vernon for three days. The railroad station, armory, and public schools were turned into motels. All the stores were depleted of food. Many local residents opened their homes for the hundreds of travelers fleeing the trains for shelter and safety.

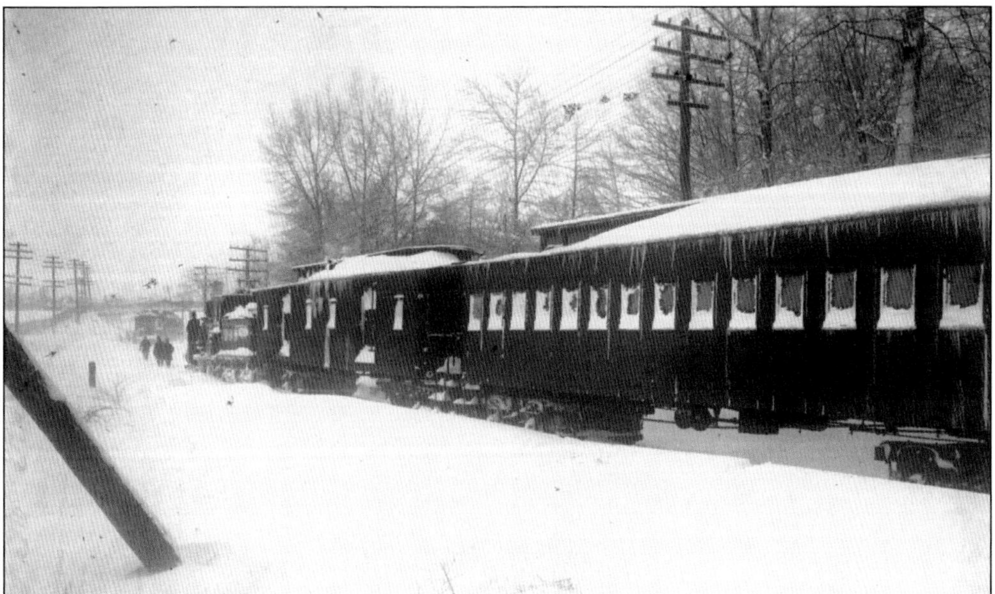

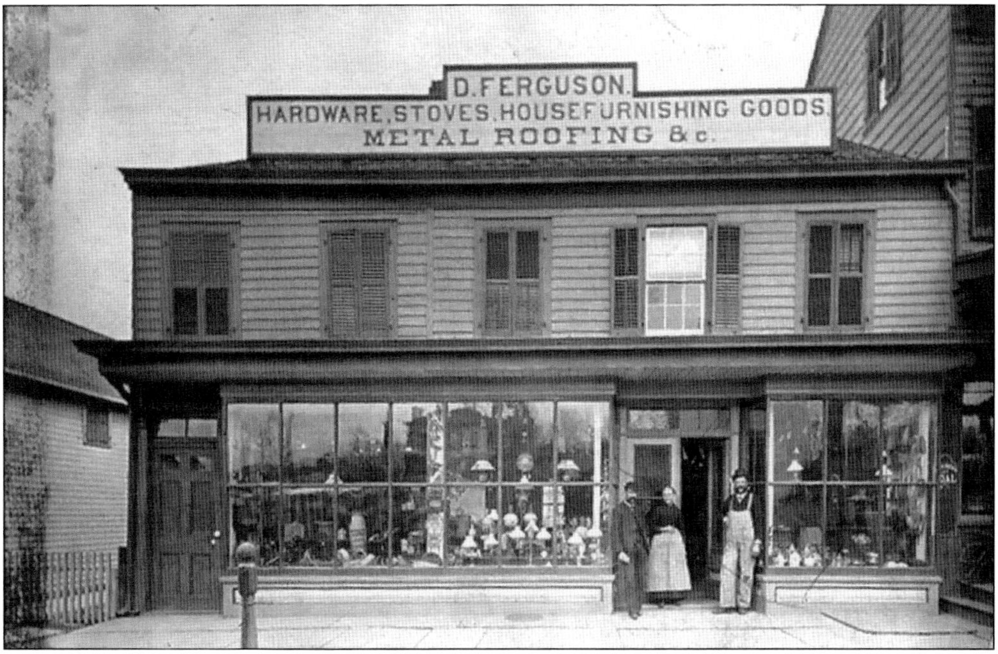

Donald Ferguson was a founding member of the Stevens Home Industrial Association No. 1. In 1852, he built a home at 250 South Fifth Avenue, where most of his family was born. It was also where the village's first hardware, plumbing, and tinning shop was located. His son, George D. Ferguson, became an important leader in preserving Mount Vernon history, writing a comprehensive series of newspaper articles, and led city tours in the 1920s.

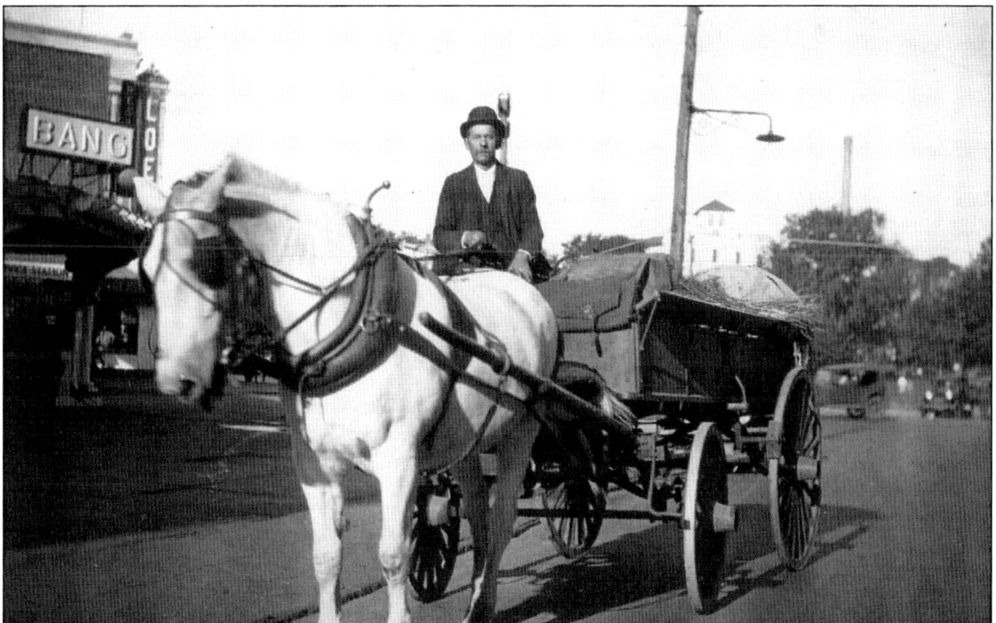

As late as the 1920s, Valentine Kloepfer continued to sell fresh vegetables from his Union Corners garden out of his horse-drawn wagon. In this photograph, he is going south across the Fifth Avenue bridge. Loew's Theater is to the rear and left.

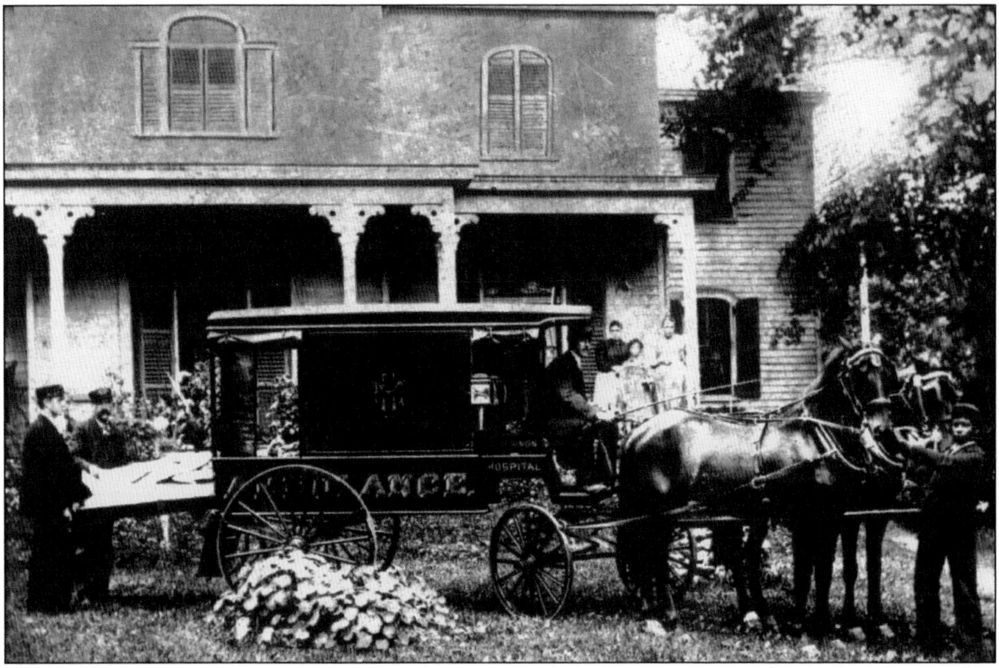

Mount Vernon's first ambulance service was initiated by popular subscription on July 22, 1893. Mount Vernon Hospital is in the background of the photograph. Dr. Archibald Banning, police and ambulance surgeon, promoted the service. From left to right are Banning, Fred Davis, James Fitzpatrick (driver), and Arthur Keeler (holding the horses).

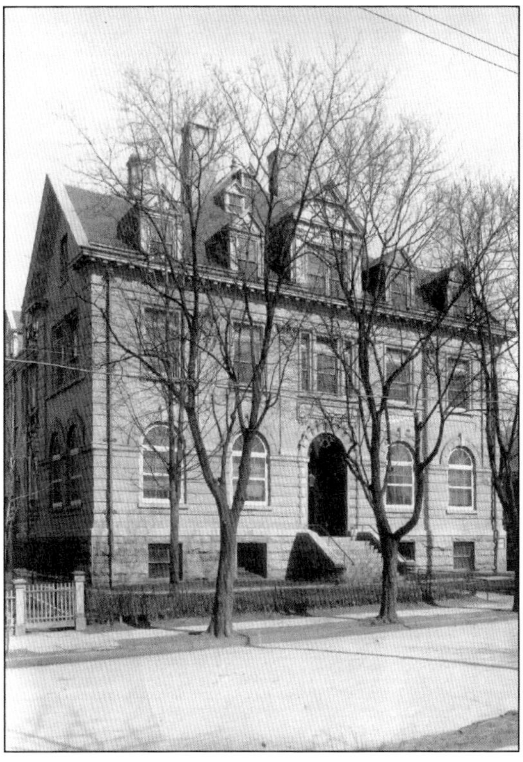

In January 1895, the state legislature passed a bill consolidating the city school districts and authorized Mount Vernon to organize a high school. Classes were started in the Chester Hill School (now Lincoln). Abial B. Davis was named principal. On May 19, 1896, the school board authorized $60,000 to build a high school at South Fourth Avenue near Fourth Street. In less than 10 years, the number of students outgrew the building. In the 1960s, it was destroyed by a fire and torn down.

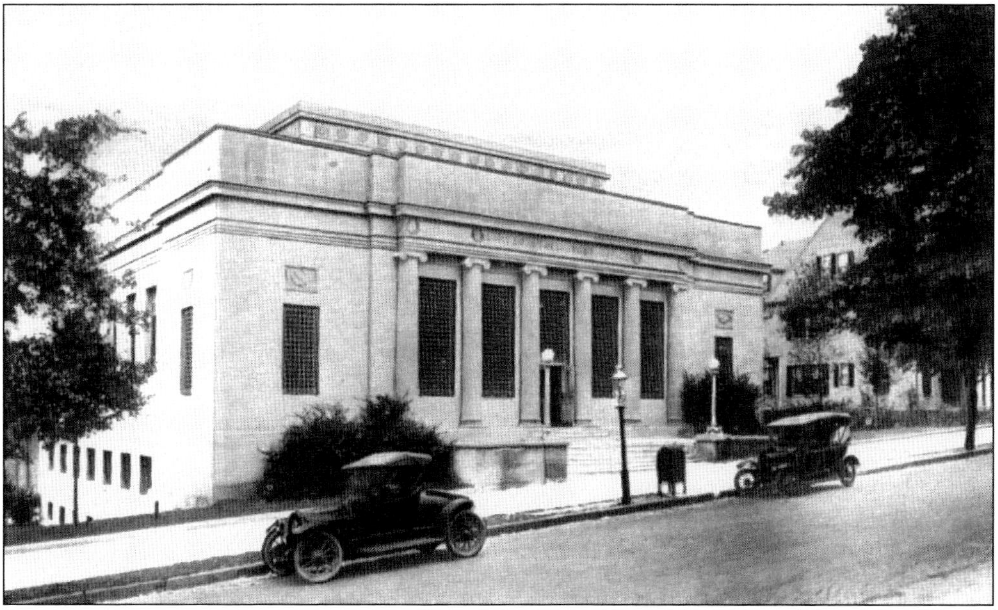

The post office was established in 1851 at Hunt's Bridge. It was later operated at the Mount Vernon Hotel. In 1892, it was moved to the Martens Building on East First Street and later another site at Prospect Avenue, near North Second Avenue. On August 15, 1902, it moved to its present site on First Avenue near First Street. The current post office was built on December 8, 1917.

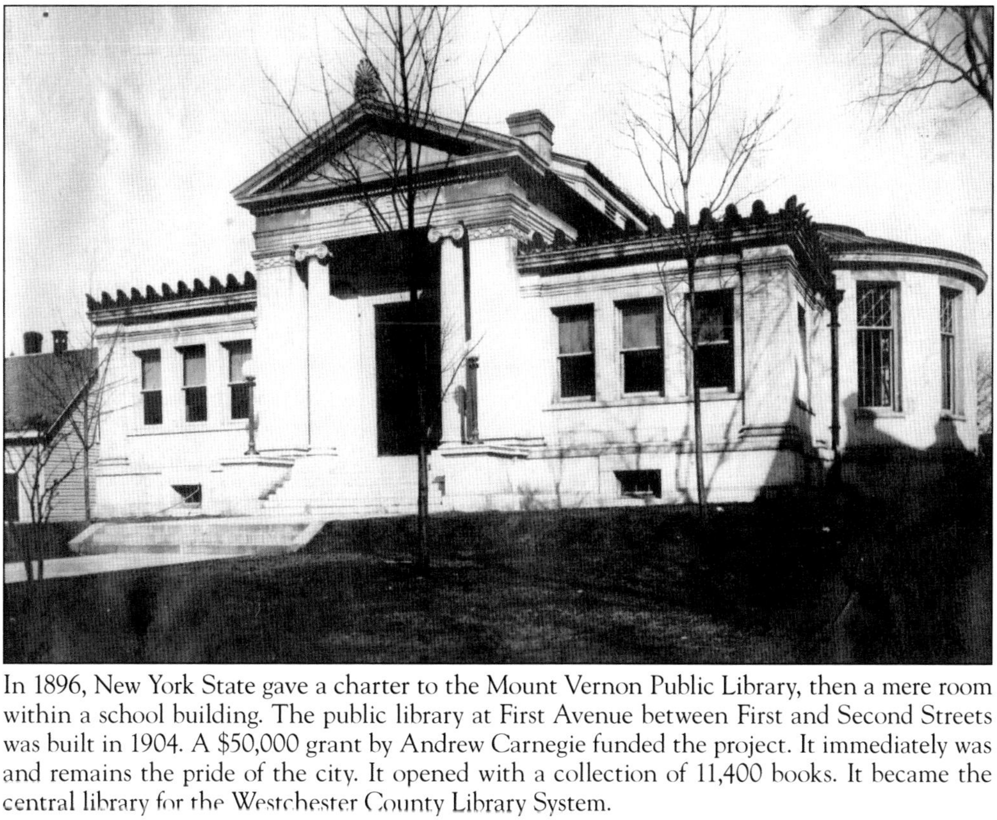

In 1896, New York State gave a charter to the Mount Vernon Public Library, then a mere room within a school building. The public library at First Avenue between First and Second Streets was built in 1904. A $50,000 grant by Andrew Carnegie funded the project. It immediately was and remains the pride of the city. It opened with a collection of 11,400 books. It became the central library for the Westchester County Library System.

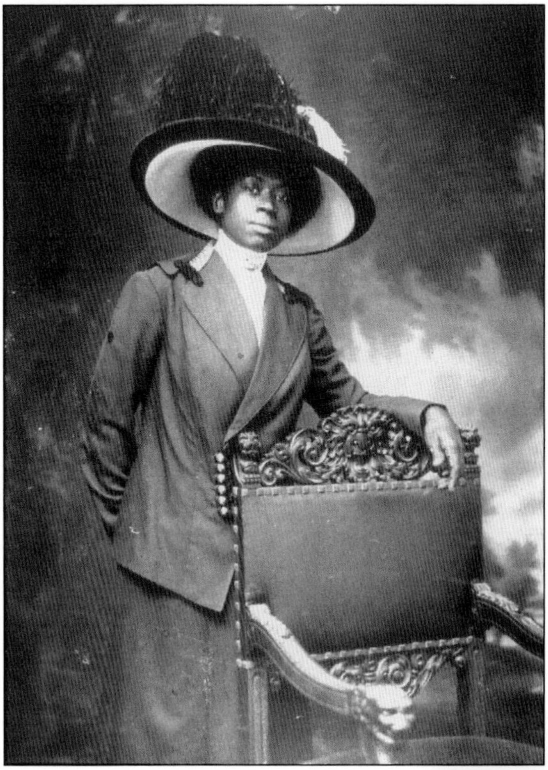

On the left is Annie Harper Bridges, and below is Sarah B. Bridges, her sister-in-law. Annie came to Mount Vernon in 1906. Sarah's parents, Thomas and Terri C. Bridges, came to the city in 1894. Her father was an artist and businessman. In 1909, Annie's two brothers James M. and Walter established Bridges Real Estate, and for many years, it was run by James's son Lawrence at 22 West First Street. Ludacris, one of the world's premier hip-hop artists, is the son of Wayne Bridges, a descendant of this successful family.

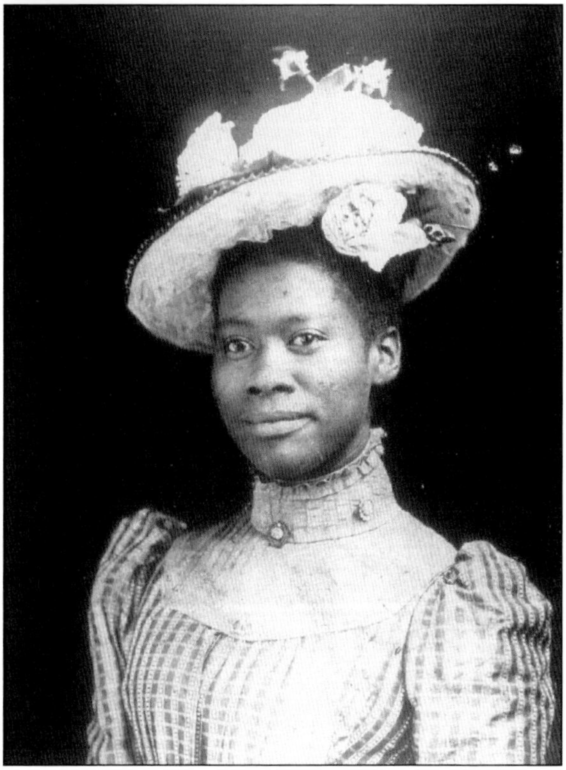

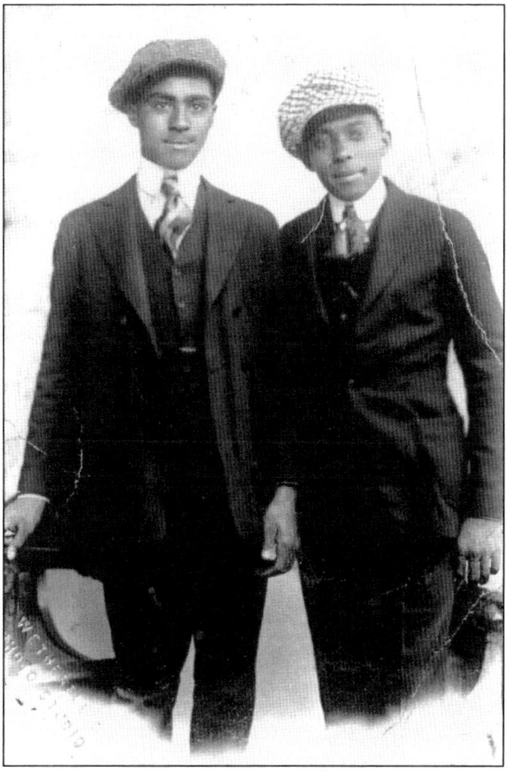

For most of the 20th century, Italian Americans and African Americans called the south side home. They were newcomers suffering from ethnic and racial injustice and looking for economic opportunity. They came from villages, towns, and cities in southern Italy and the southern United States. They gathered as clans and families looking for work, housing, and education for their children. Cultural diversity made the city unique in the county. Pictured below are Filippo "Mr. Forty" Quaranta and Salvatore in front of 425 South Eighth Avenue in 1914. At right are William and Nathan Coleman around 1919.

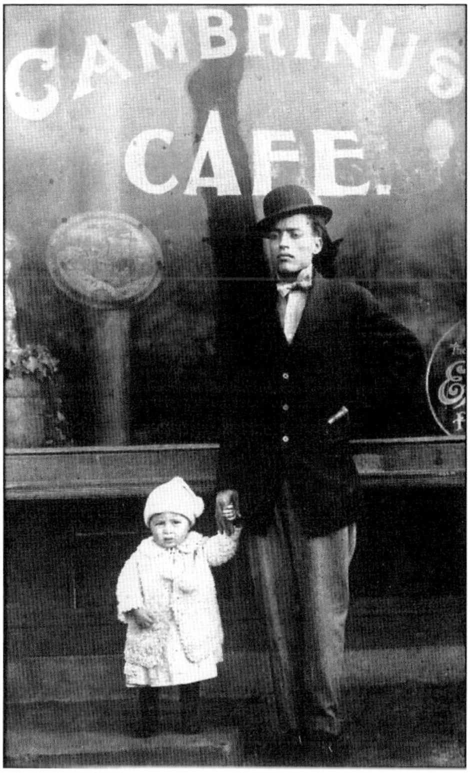

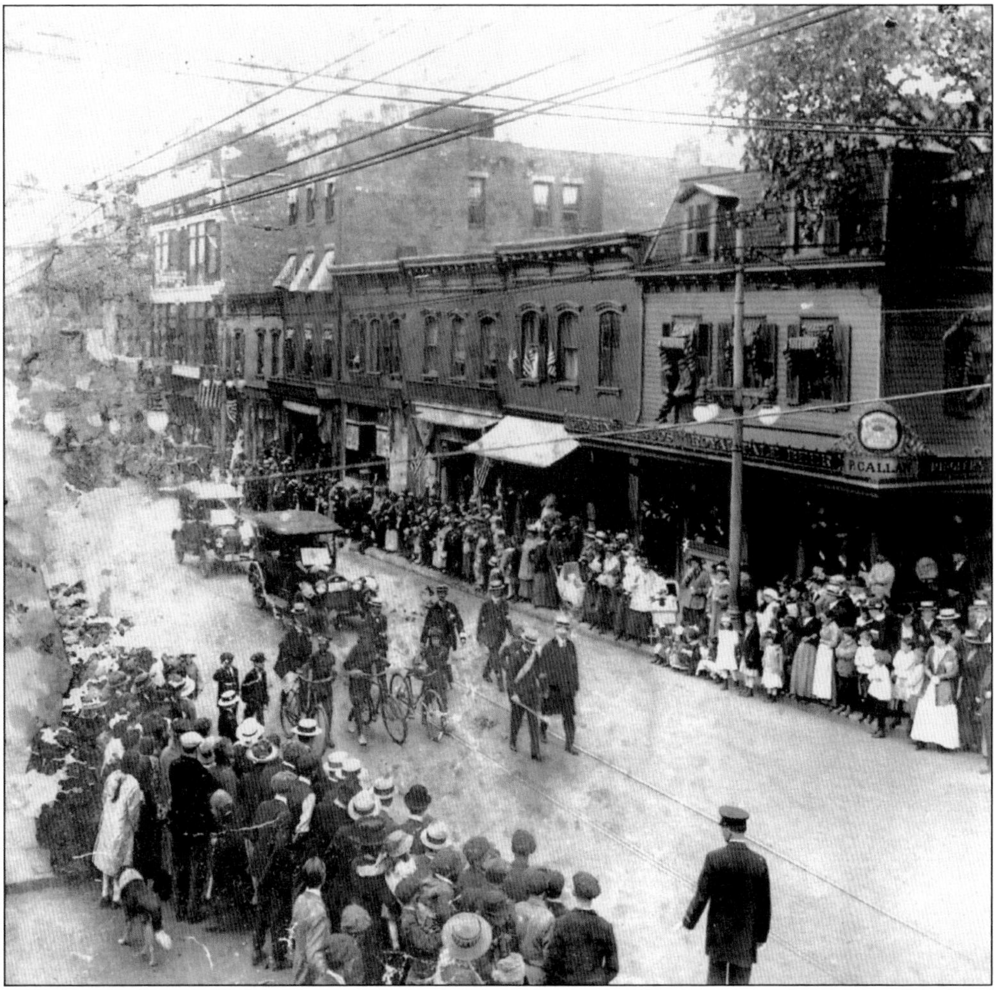

The tradition of parades down Fourth Avenue goes back over a century. Mount Vernon's annual parades were legendary, drawing participation from throughout the metropolitan area. From Memorial Day to school band day parades, to public displays of appreciation of local heroes like heavyweight world boxing champion Floyd Patterson and baseball great Kenneth Singleton, to the many championship basketball teams, the city has always gathered along Fourth Avenue to show appreciation for their notable deeds. Above is a photograph of an early parade at Fourth Avenue and Second Street. This photograph is from around 1911.

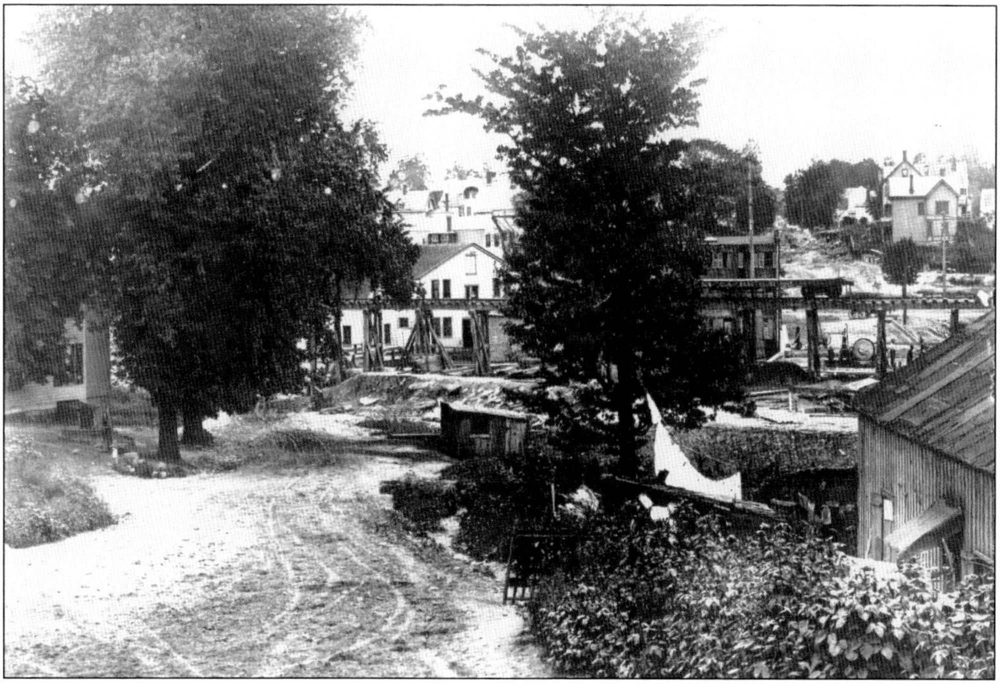

The picture above is a 1910 view of Oak Street looking west down the hill toward the Bronx River and Yonkers. The elevated New York-Harlem Railway can be seen as it was shifted farther away from the river. The image below is the same viewpoint in 1948.

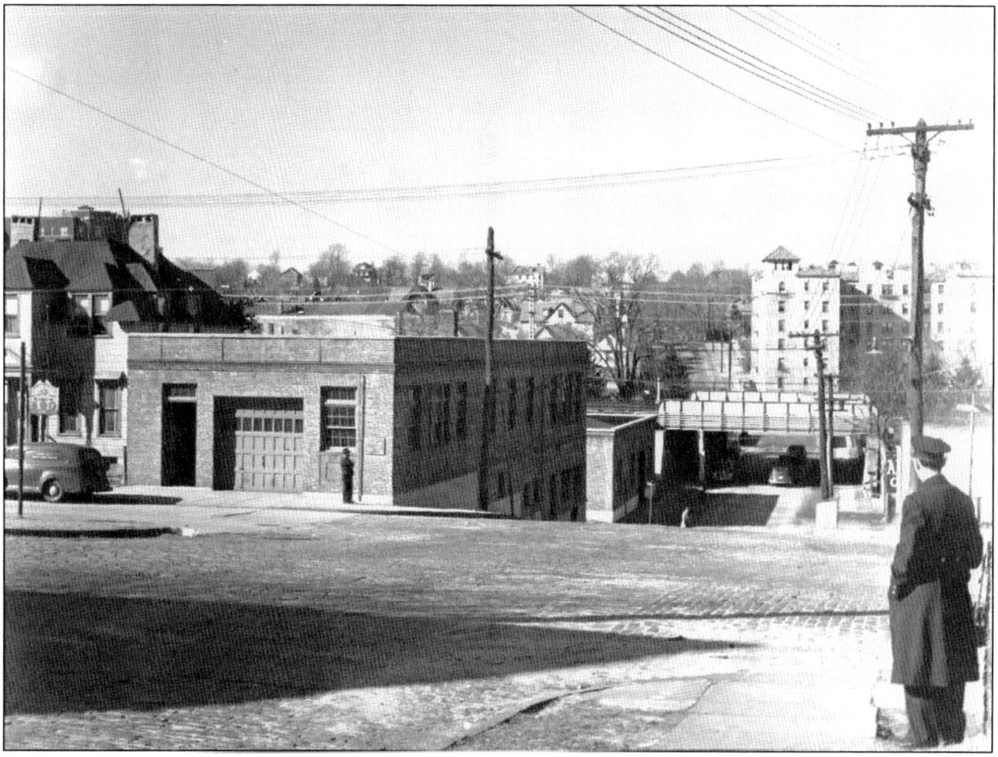

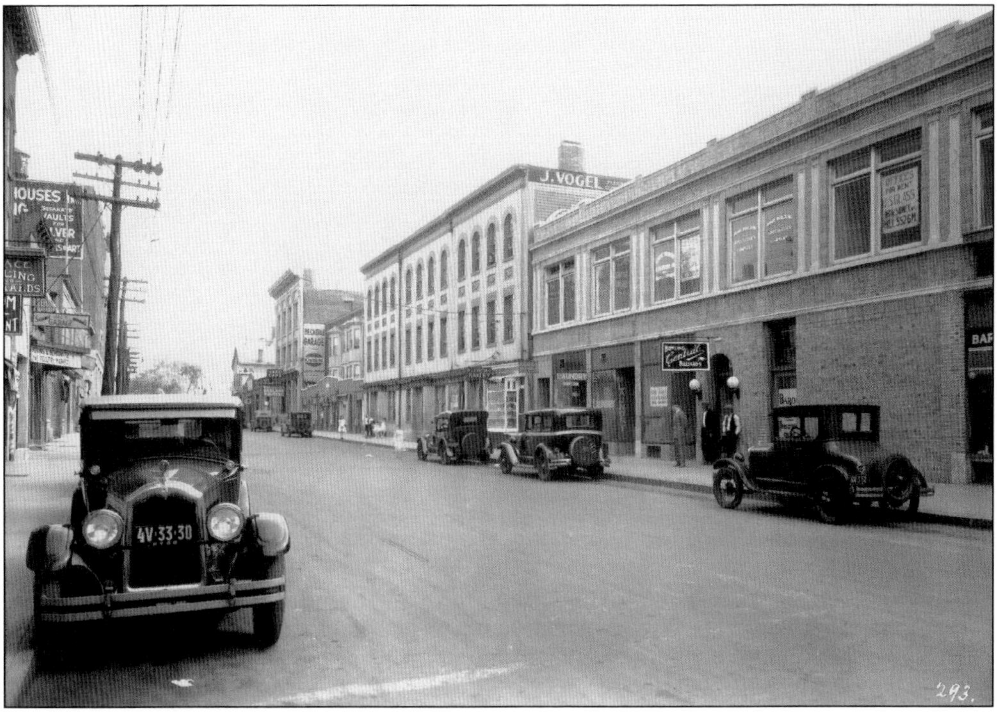

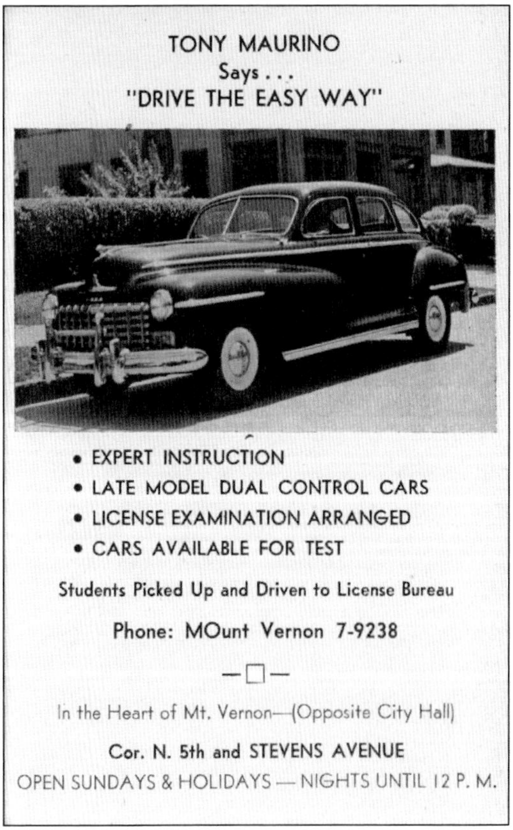

By 1900, railroad technology began to give way to a personal mode of mechanical transportation—the automobile. Trolleys and streetcars inevitably could not compete with the fascination with cars. In 1899, Dr. Thomas F. Goodwin introduced the first horseless carriage to Mount Vernon. Driving down Fourth Avenue or on his way to visit a patient, crowds gathered to see the automobile. Like with its several railways, the city became bordered with parkways, continuing its legacy of perfect location. The 1930 photograph seen above shows South Sixth Avenue near First Street, and the image at left is a 1948 advertisement of the most popular driver education and licensing agency in Mount Vernon's history.

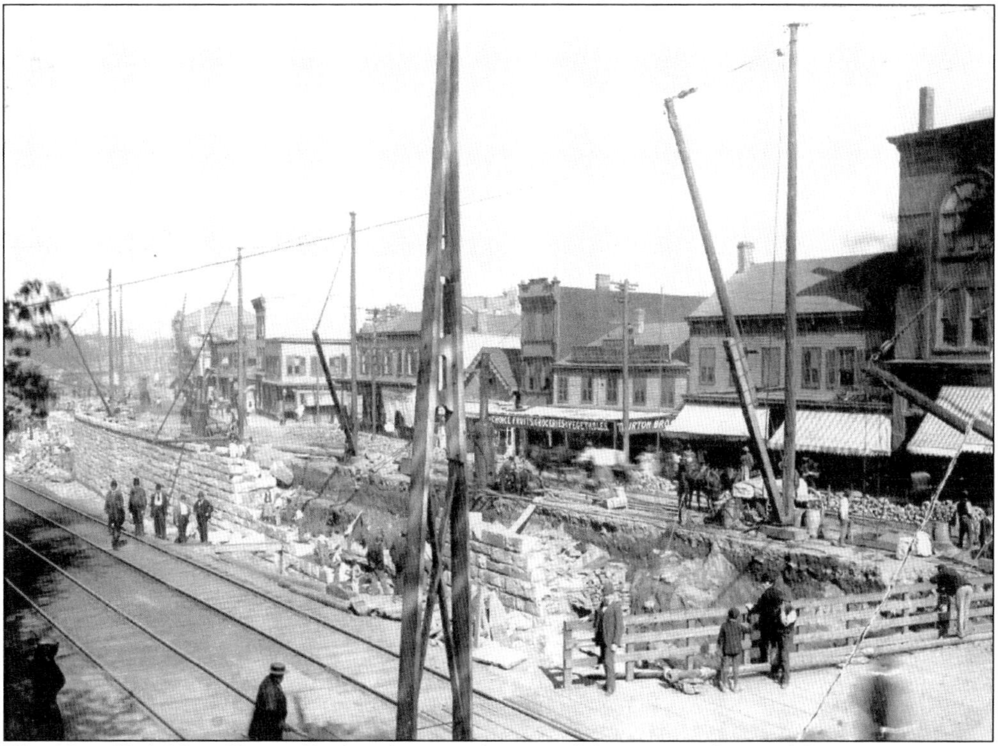

The New York-New Haven Railroad was only one of five major thoroughfares tying Mount Vernon to New York. In 1892, due to numerous pedestrian deaths, it was decided to lower the railroad tracks and build six bridges spanning the "cut." Italian immigrants were used to dig a cut along First Street, across the middle of the city. The cut forever affected people's perceptions of the city. It remains a scar dividing the city north and south.

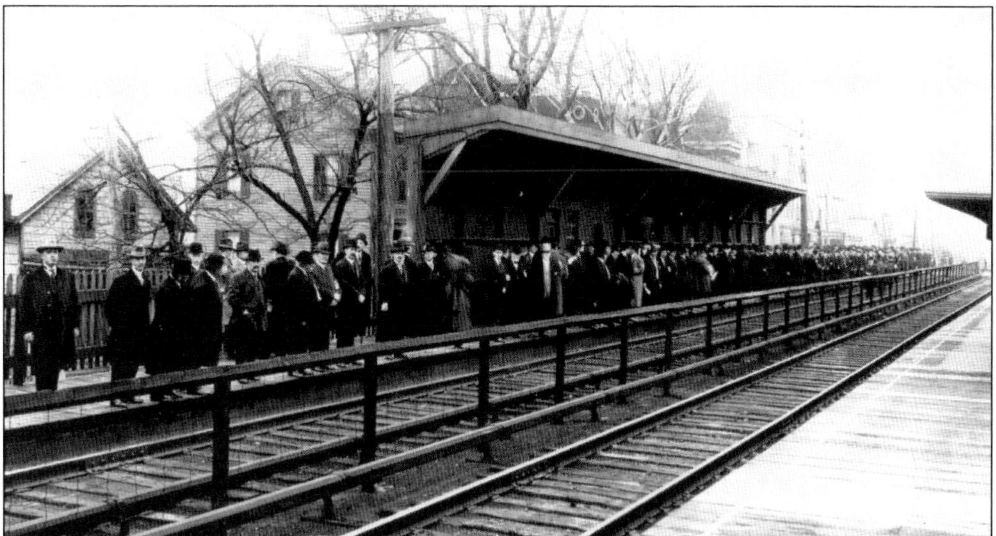

This 1919 picture is of the New York-Harlem Railway station with local officials waiting for a special train to Albany for a legislative hearing on water resources. Today the station is known as Mount Vernon West.

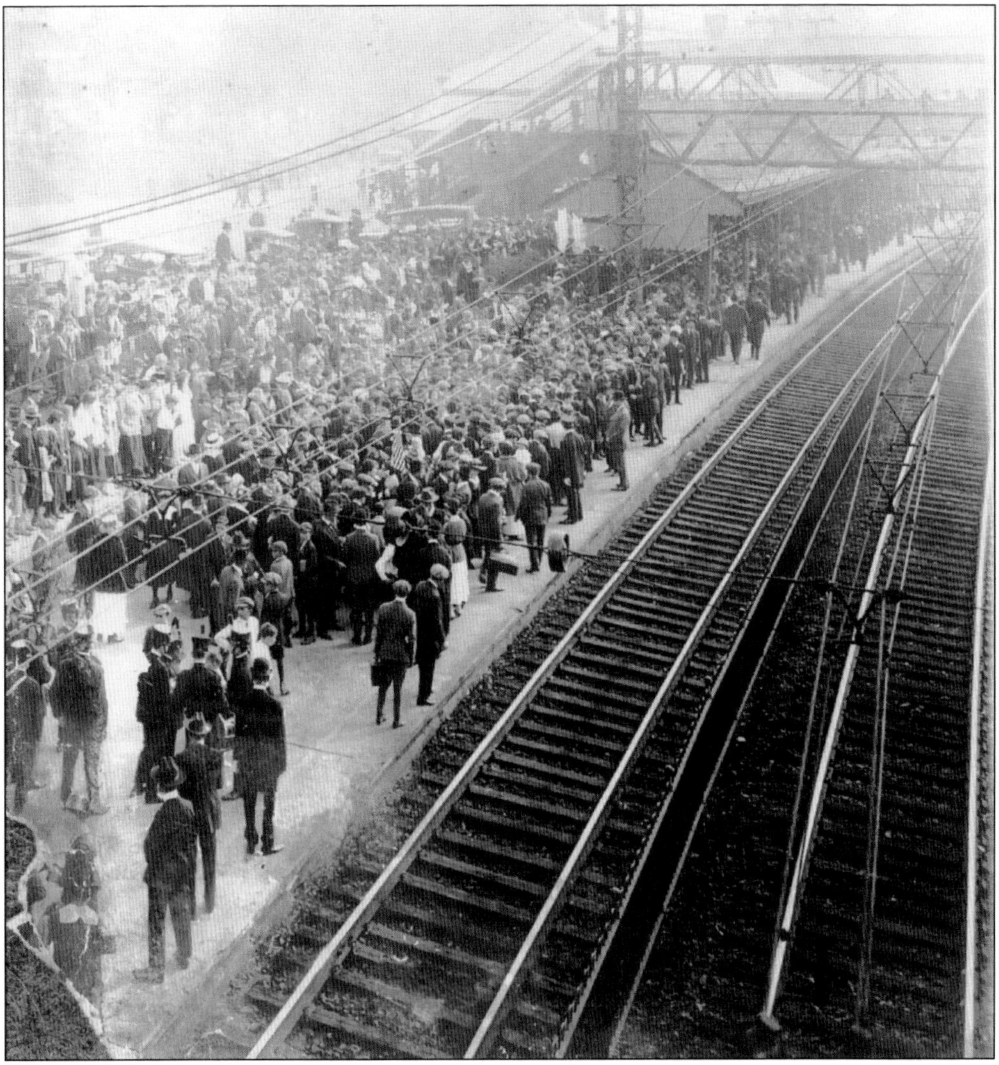

At the dawn of the 20th century, the automobile had not been perfected nor cost-effectively mass-produced. As the population continued to swell, new homes were built, fancy apartment buildings emerged, and the reputation of Mount Vernon's schools, quality of life, and railways continued to make it a desirable bedroom community. The picture above of the Mount Vernon East train station was taken when the trains were electrified through the city, around 1907.

Three

The City of Happy Homes 1892–1953

Twentieth-century Mount Vernon began as modern, progressive, and prosperous. In 1900, the population was 21,228, and its schools were among the nation's finest. Real estate speculators had no problem selling existing houses and new construction projects in the northern and eastern sectors. They emphasized their suburban qualities and, most of all, access to modern transportation. Mount Vernon kept pace with the latest trends from bicycles to trolleys to automobiles. The New York and Boston Railroad (1912) established three stops, and New York City elevated trains (subways) also found their way to the city's southern and western borders. Mount Vernon became an important gateway city.

The most dramatic event was the 1893–1895 lowering of the New York-New Haven Railroad lines from street level, along First Street dividing the city north and south. The cut through the city became the symbol of the gradual loss of civic harmony. Within a decade, city fathers knew it was a mistake. The pick and shovel work was performed by Italian immigrant workers housed on the southwest side. Meanwhile, southern African Americans, looking for jobs as domestic servants, joined the Italians in the southwest sector. Their collective ethnicity and poverty created the proverbial "other side of the tracks." Its effect on real estate values and the status of some schools was devastating. For the rest of the century politicians devised unsuccessful plans to cover the cut.

In 1920, there were 42,726 residents and 61,499 by 1940. Mount Vernon was a city with a spiraling, diverse population. The 1930s Depression and the thousands of unemployed were detrimental to the city's progress. After World War II, the population grew at a staggering rate to reach 71,833 residents. Once again, Mount Vernon was concerned with affordable housing. Expanding south-side slum conditions forced the creation of the Mount Vernon Housing Authority (1945). Its goal was to provide housing for World War II veterans and growing low-income families. It quickly went about clearing dilapidated buildings, the rehabilitation of substandard houses, and the construction of a building complex with five 10-story buildings with 497 apartments, which became known as Benjamin Levister Towers.

Although many of the city's older houses were in disrepair, high-rise apartments were constructed on the north and south sides. At the 1953 city centennial, Mount Vernon still took pride in its reputation as the City of Happy Homes.

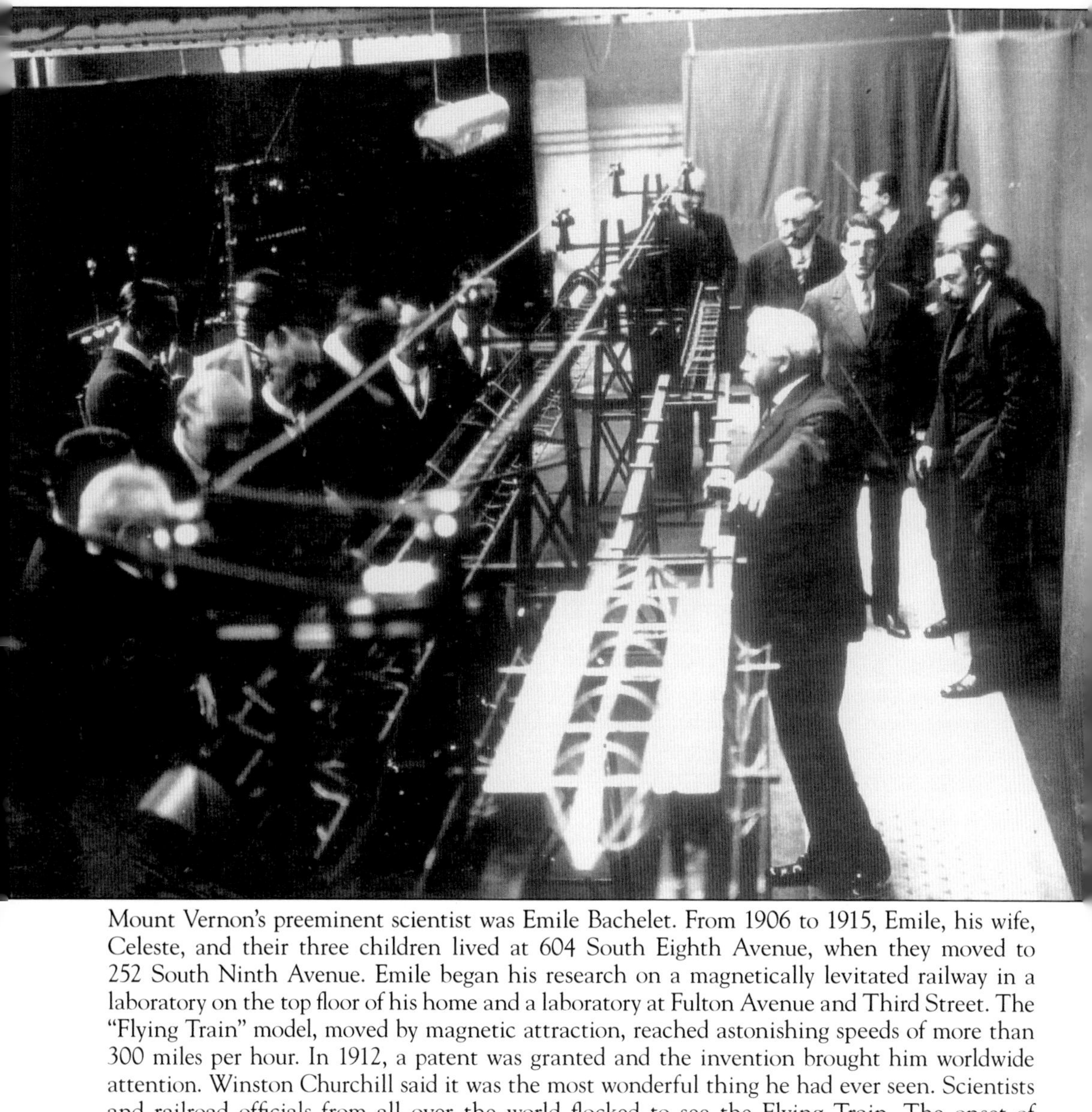

Mount Vernon's preeminent scientist was Emile Bachelet. From 1906 to 1915, Emile, his wife, Celeste, and their three children lived at 604 South Eighth Avenue, when they moved to 252 South Ninth Avenue. Emile began his research on a magnetically levitated railway in a laboratory on the top floor of his home and a laboratory at Fulton Avenue and Third Street. The "Flying Train" model, moved by magnetic attraction, reached astonishing speeds of more than 300 miles per hour. In 1912, a patent was granted and the invention brought him worldwide attention. Winston Churchill said it was the most wonderful thing he had ever seen. Scientists and railroad officials from all over the world flocked to see the Flying Train. The onset of World War I sent the Flying Train into oblivion. In 1946, after many years of trying to fund his transportation system, Emile died. (Courtesy of the Westchester County Archives.)

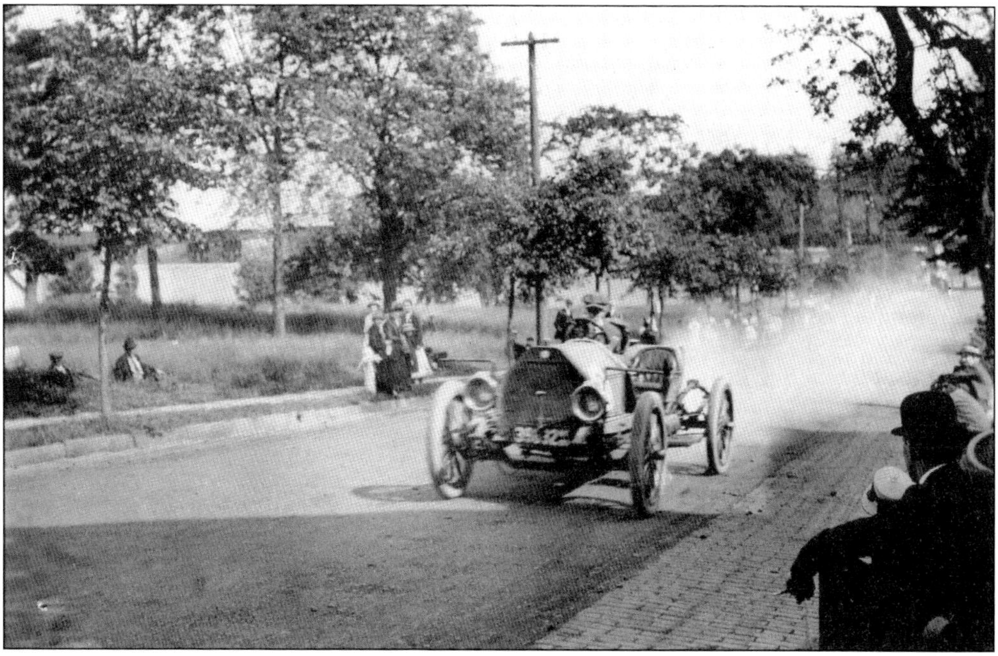

By World War I, all over the city the automobile brought about the end of horse-drawn coaches and hearses, and even stables and barns were converted to garages. The popularity of the local cyclists gave way to 1905 automobile racing up the Columbus Avenue hill (above). The Third Avenue stables of Burr Davis and Son's Funeral Parlor housed shiny black funeral limousines (below).

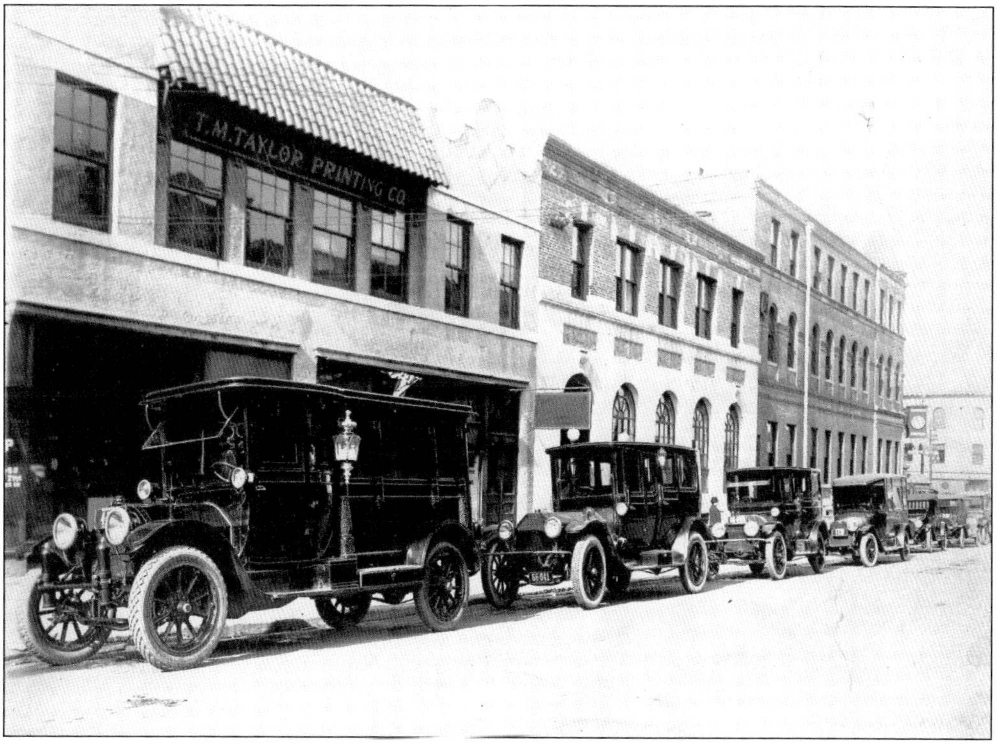

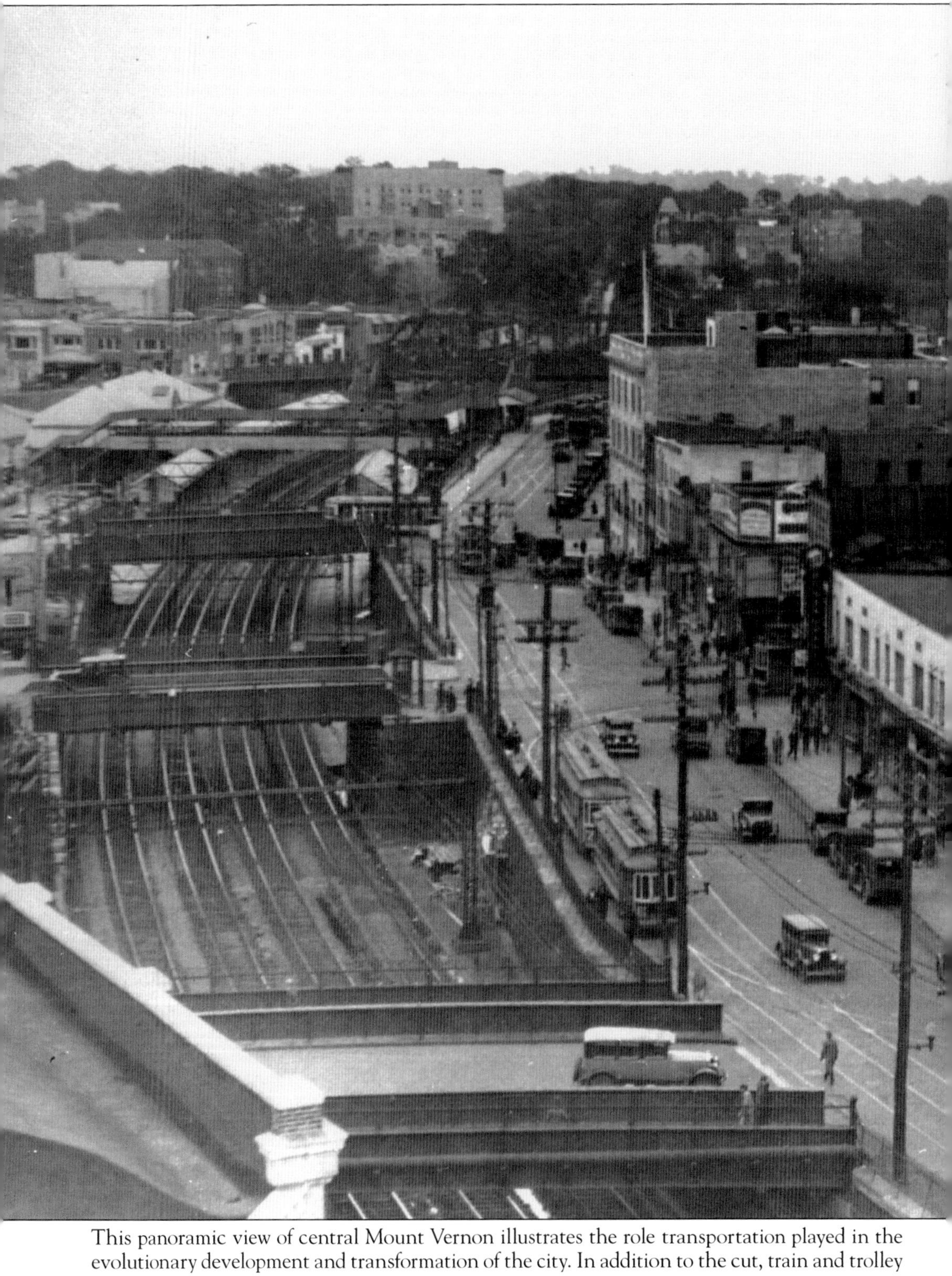

This panoramic view of central Mount Vernon illustrates the role transportation played in the evolutionary development and transformation of the city. In addition to the cut, train and trolley

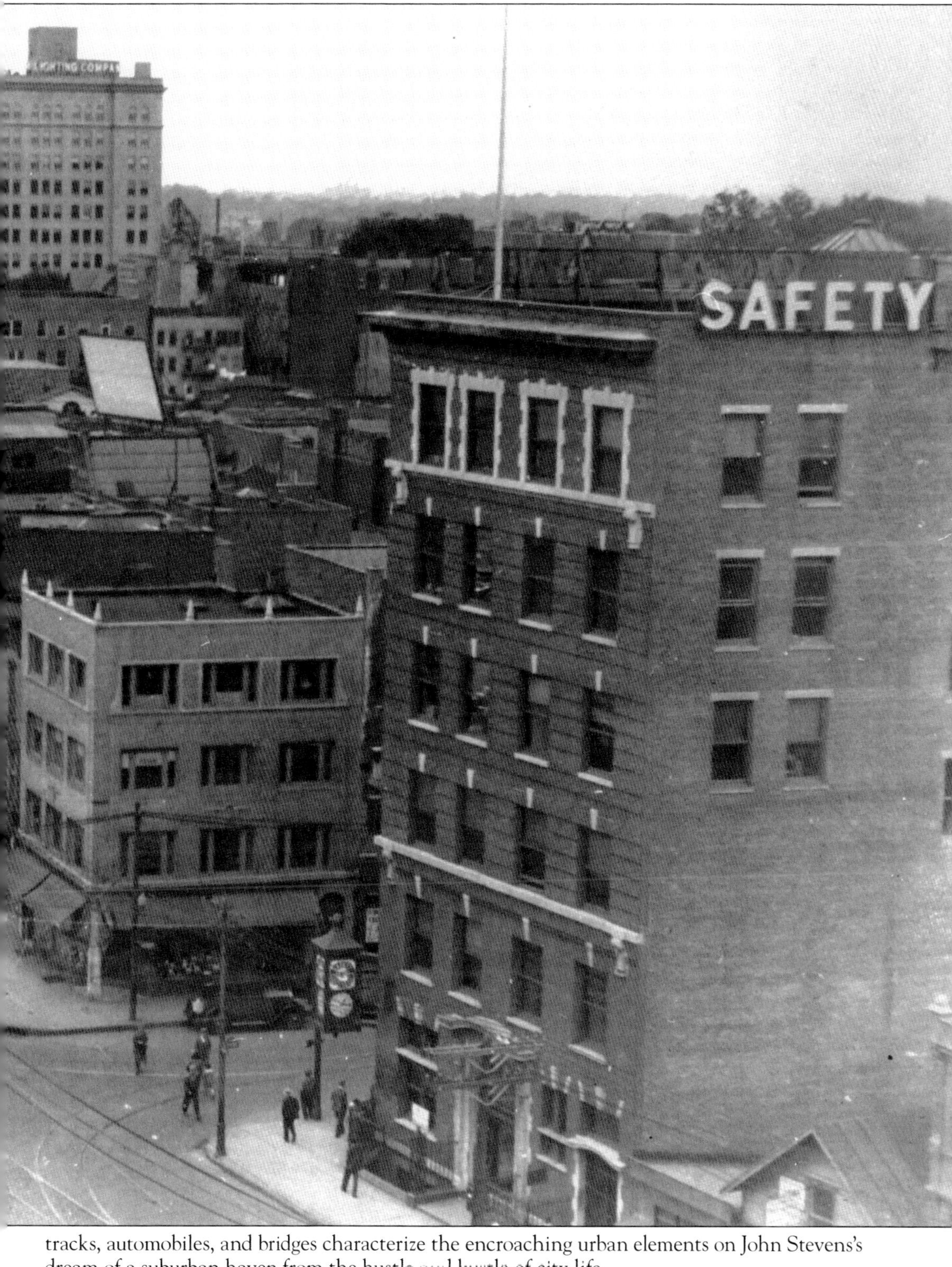

tracks, automobiles, and bridges characterize the encroaching urban elements on John Stevens's dream of a suburban haven from the hustle and bustle of city life.

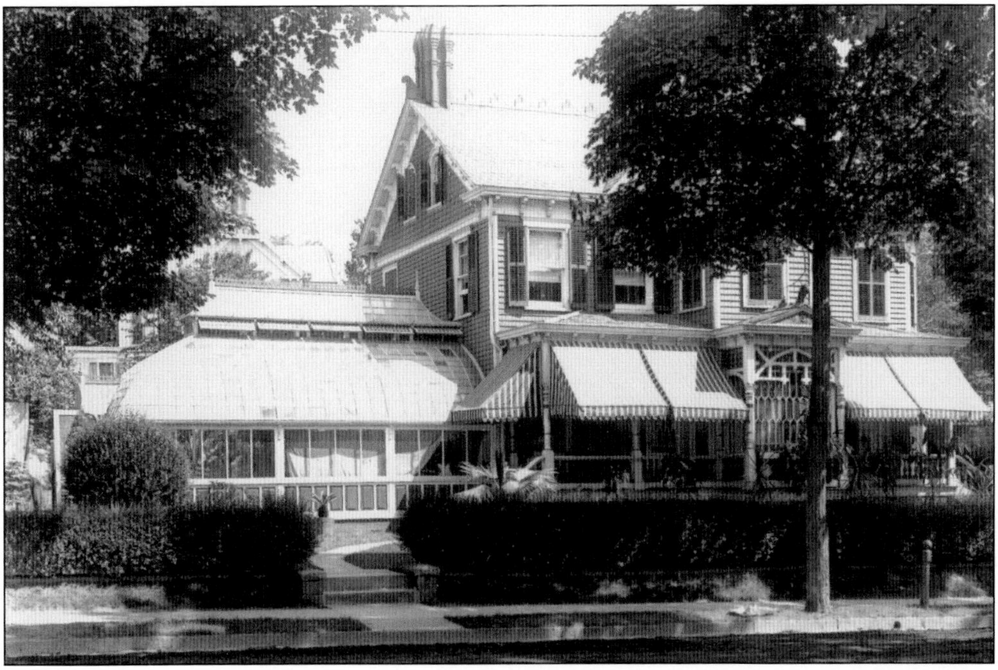

The foundation for the village and city of Mount Vernon was established on the belief that it was important to build homes that residents could be proud. George Crawford, an early political leader, built the residence above at 161 Stevens Avenue. It was one of the city's showplaces. His greenhouse drew people from far and wide. Pedestrians lined the street to view the lemon, orange, and banana trees. There were also numerous varieties of canaries that flew freely about in the greenhouse. The photograph below is the William J. Moore residence. Both photographs were taken in 1911.

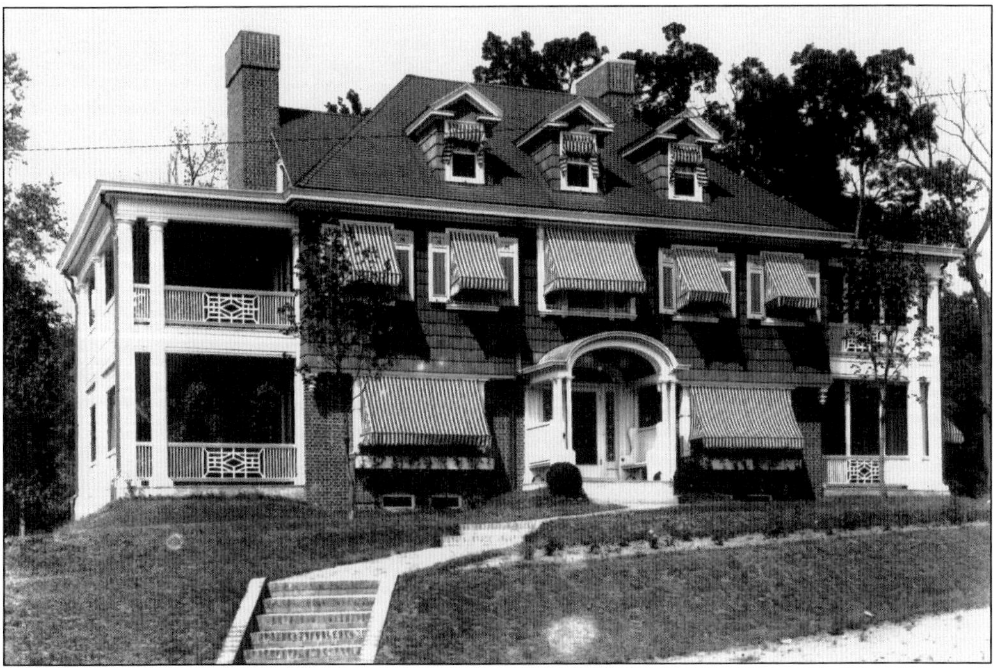

The picture at right is Lulu Glaser, renowned Victorian/Edwardian comedic actress and singer. She was born in 1874 in Pennsylvania and was a highly acclaimed star at the beginning of the 20th century. She appeared in vaudeville and in several nonmusical plays from 1912 to 1915. She was so successful that she had enough wealth to start her own opera company. This was quite rare for a woman of her time. In 1918, at the height of her popularity, she suddenly retired. The 1912 photograph seen below is her home at 262 Primrose Avenue. The photograph was taken by Underwood and Underwood. Her choice of Mount Vernon as a home was not surprising. The city was known for its luxurious homes and, of course, proximity to Broadway. She died in Norwalk, Connecticut, in 1958. (Courtesy of the Donna May-Jackson collection.)

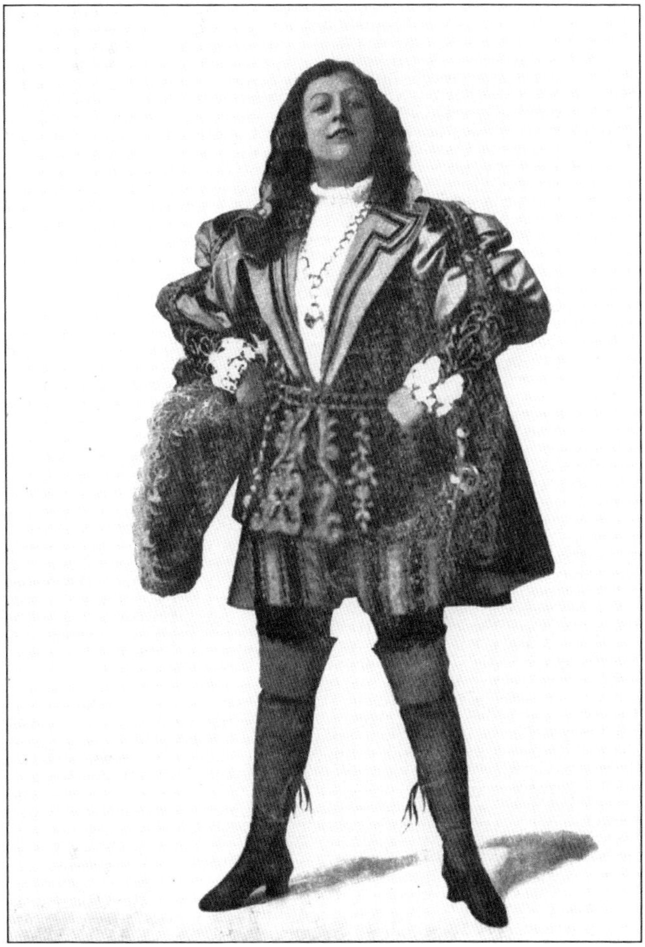

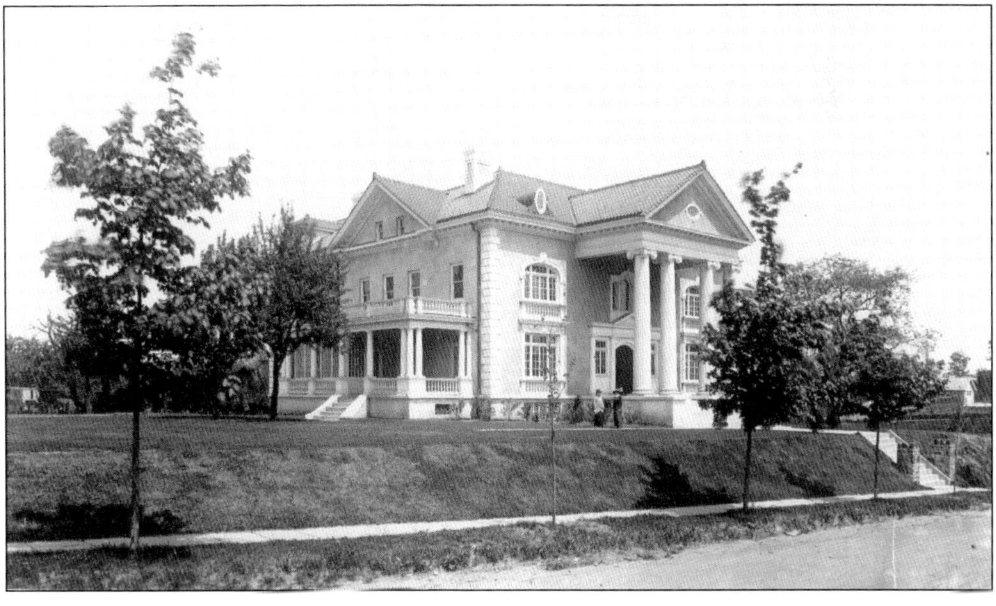

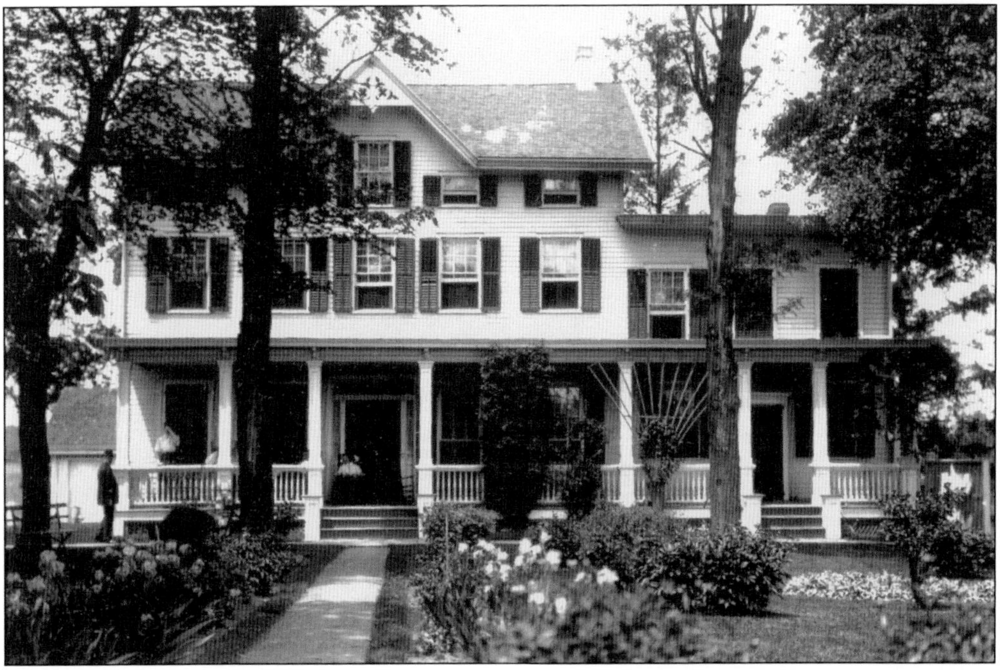

City fathers proudly boasted that Mount Vernon with its tree-lined streets, parks, vibrant commercial district, and esteemed schools warranted its nickname the City of Happy Homes. By 1910, aggressive marketing of the city's real estate led to the construction of homes that rivaled any in Westchester. These Summit Avenue residences belong to Frank Stratten and Robert T. Fowler.

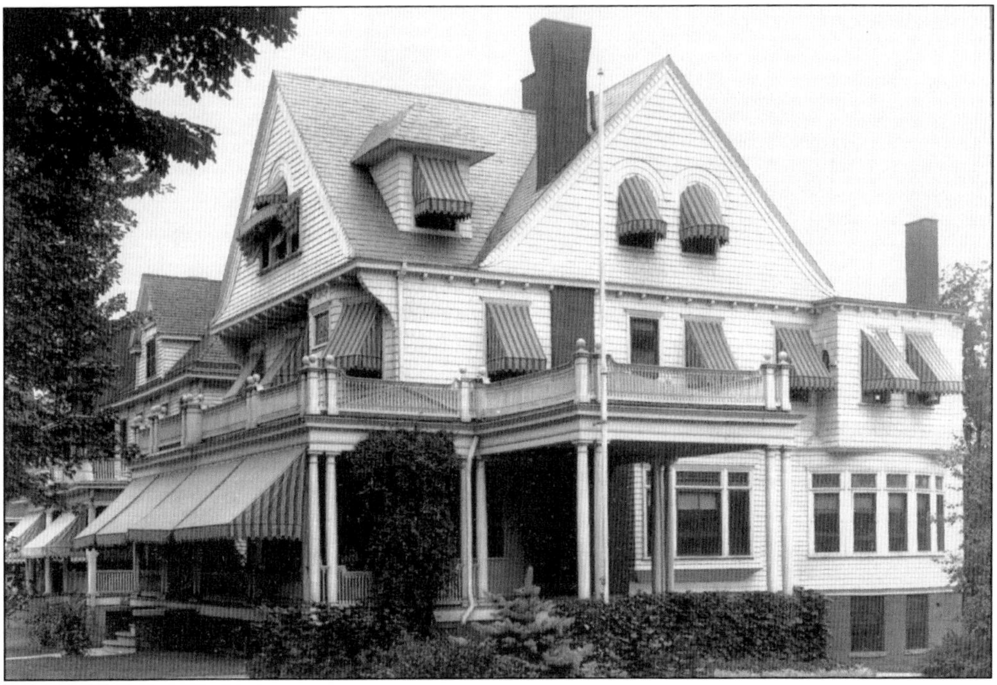

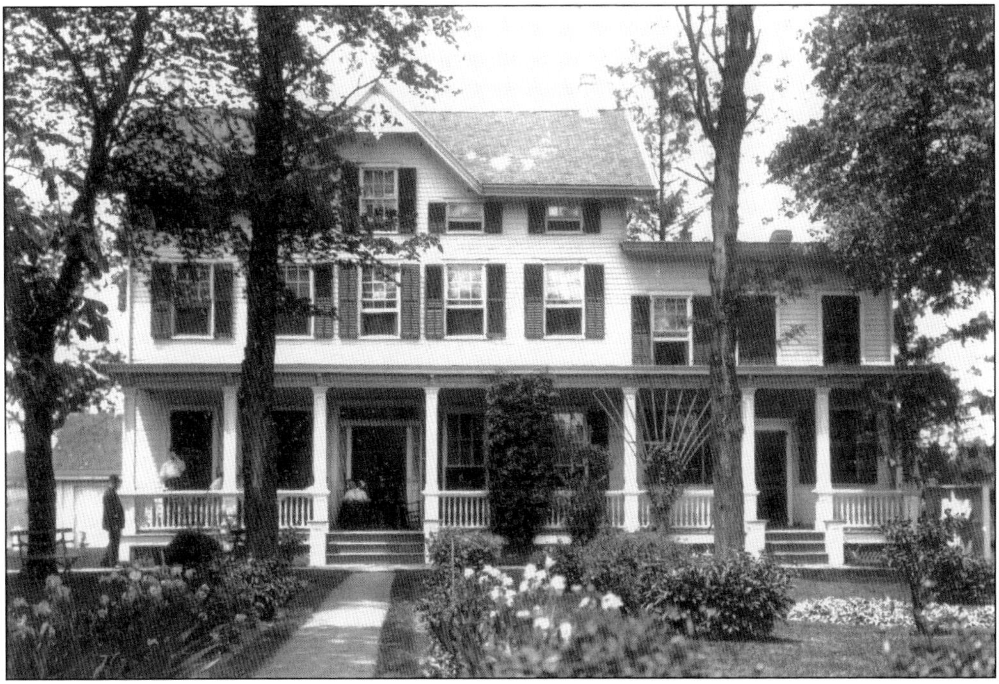

Fleetwood was one of the last sectors to undergo residential development. Much of the area was rural and forests. The photograph above is the Kindlers family residence, 27 Fleetwood Avenue, and is from around 1908. The family's estate was surrounded by a rustic natural landscape called Kindlers' Woods (below).

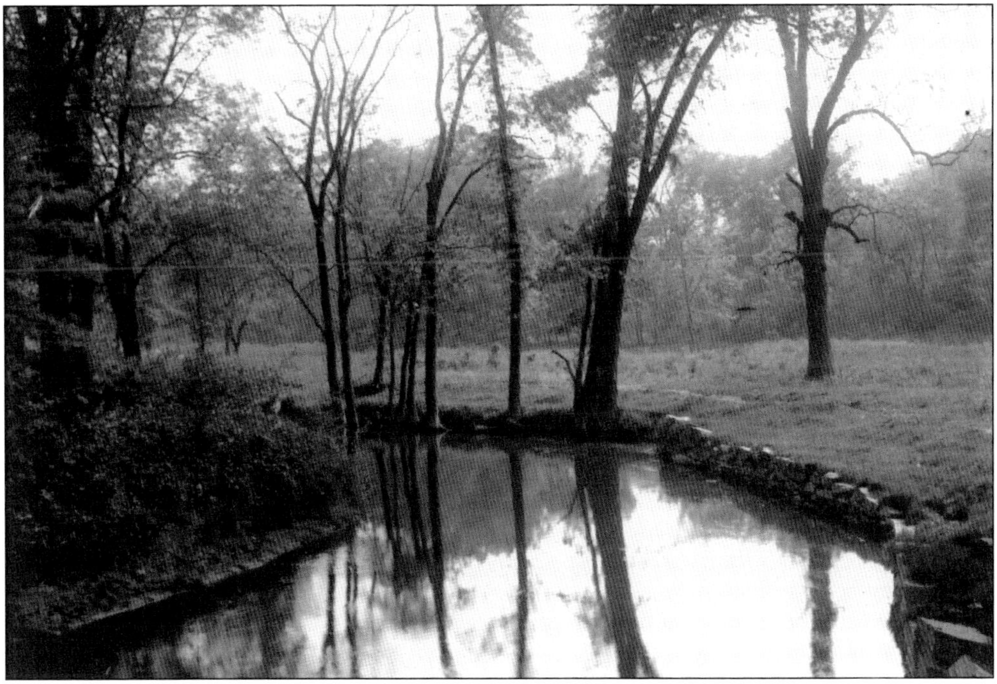

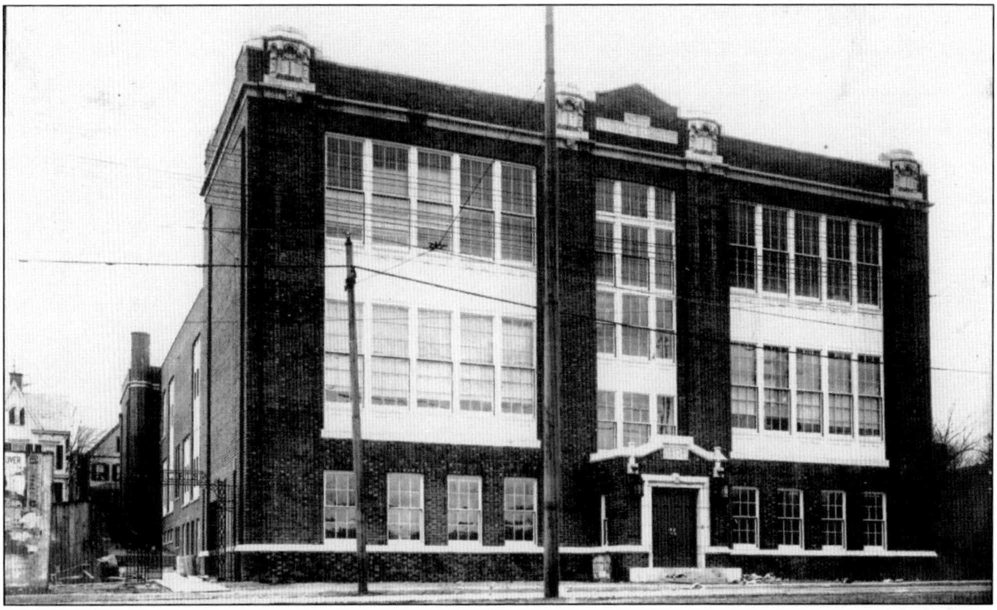

By 1917, Mount Vernon's public schools were exceptional. An assessment of the schools by a national educator was found in *Letters of E. B. White*. He wrote to a friend, "The finest public schools are in Mount Vernon, according to Alice Barrows [Katharine, White's cousin], who didn't spend twelve years in them the way I did. Alice works for the Bureau of Education (Washington D.C.) and says the finest public schools are in Mount Vernon." Ellwyn Brooks (E. B.) White is only one of many graduates to attain national and international success. White became one of America's great essayists and a celebrated author. His children's books *Stuart Little* and *Charlotte's Web* are classics. White was born in Mount Vernon. While living on Summit Avenue, he attended the Chester Hill School (below). Today it is Lincoln Elementary School. The 1904 photograph above is Columbus School on Gramatan Avenue.

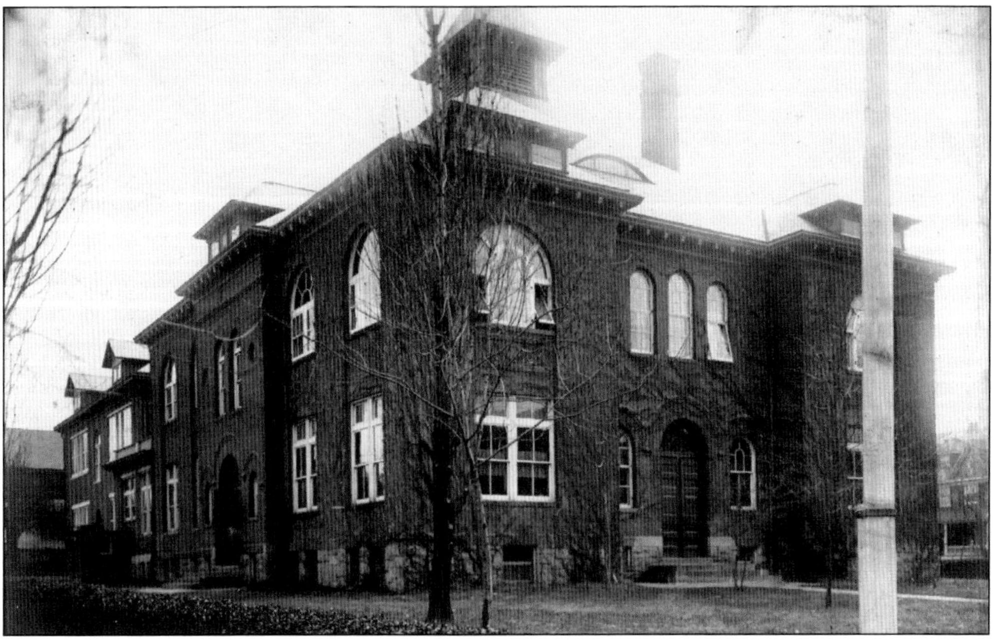

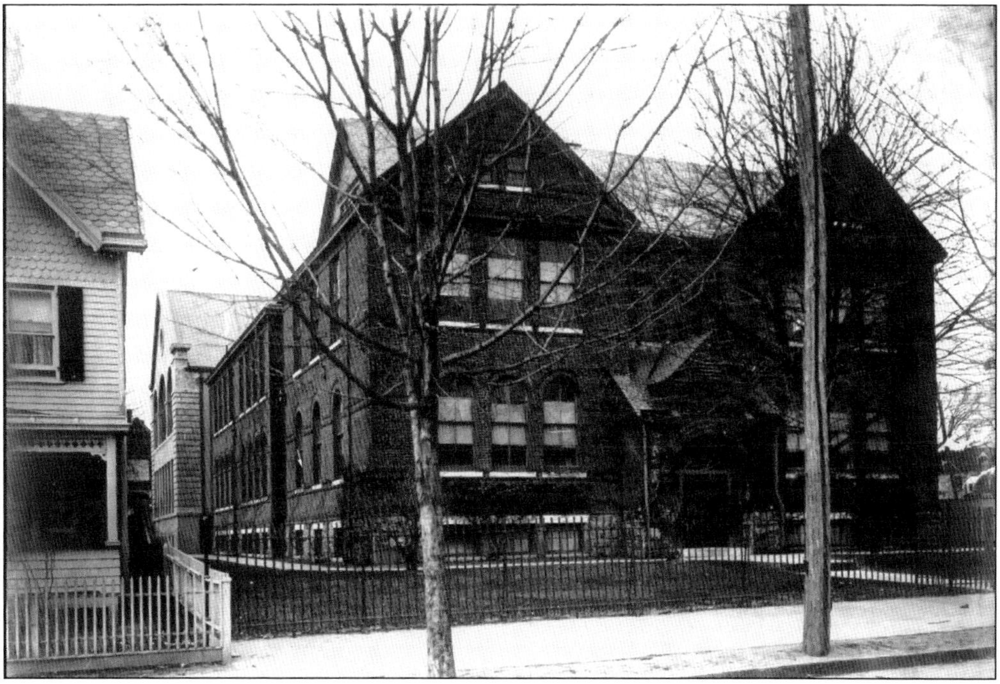

This is the original school No. 4, built in 1888, on Fifth Avenue near the northeast corner of Sixth Street (Sandford Boulevard). By 1927, several additions were made to the building. In 1936, it was torn down and replaced with a new building named Nathan Hale School and is currently known as Cecil H. Parker Elementary School.

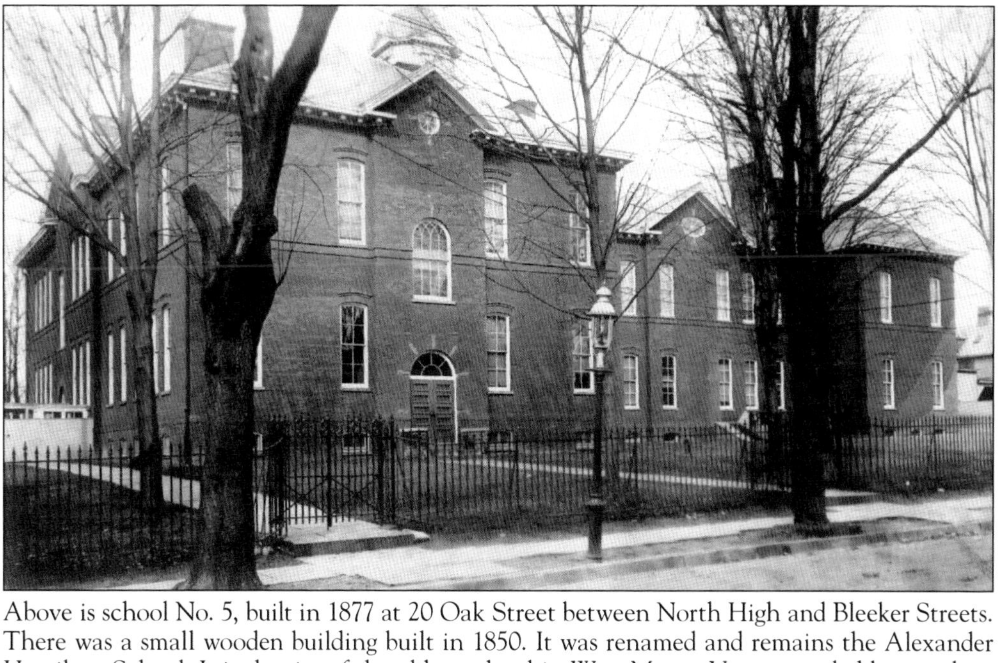

Above is school No. 5, built in 1877 at 20 Oak Street between North High and Bleeker Streets. There was a small wooden building built in 1850. It was renamed and remains the Alexander Hamilton School. It is the site of the oldest school in West Mount Vernon settled by members of the Teutonia Homestead Association, nearly all of whom were German. This settlement was consolidated with the village of Mount Vernon in 1878.

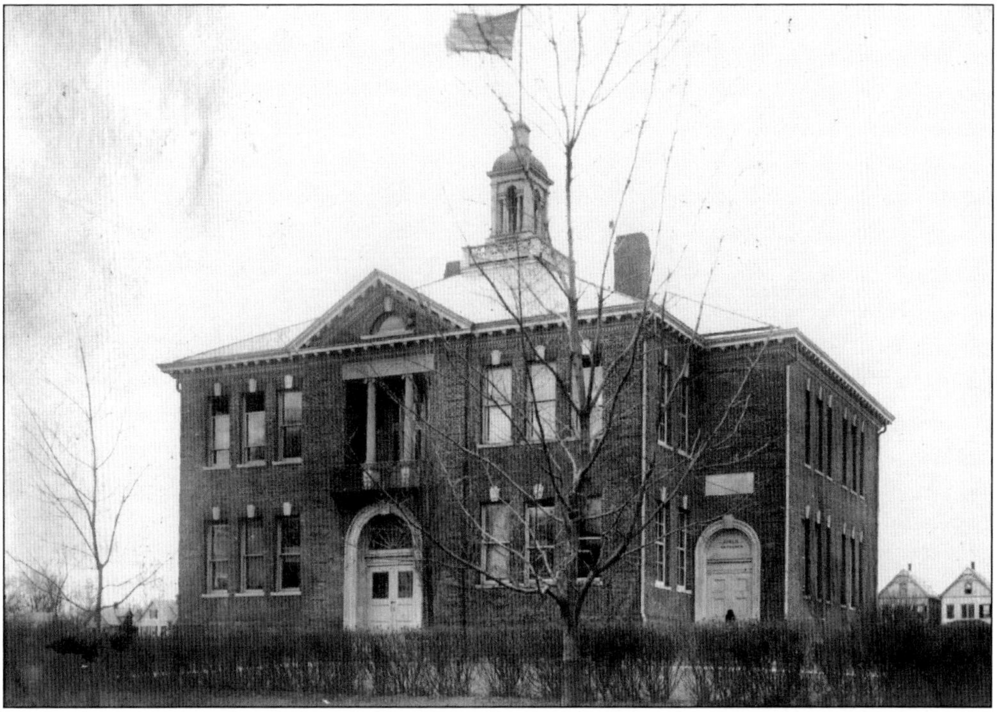

This is the original school No. 2, built in 1893 on Union Lane between Fourth and Fifth Streets. By 1927, several additions had been made. It was renamed Robert Fulton School and is currently the Edward Williams Elementary School.

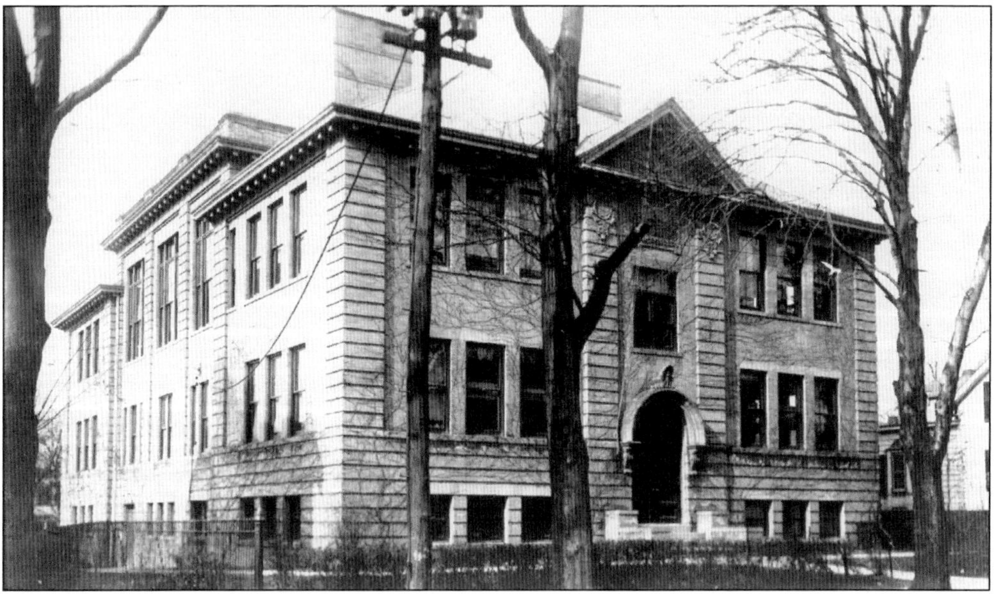

Above is school No. 3, built in 1899 at the northwest corner of Tenth Avenue and Second Street. It was renamed the Thomas Jefferson School and then the James M. Grimes Elementary School. Grimes began his career in the city in 1880 and retired in 1933. It later became the Pennington-Grimes Magnet School, then the Nelson Mandela Alternative School. It was recently torn down and replaced with a new elementary school.

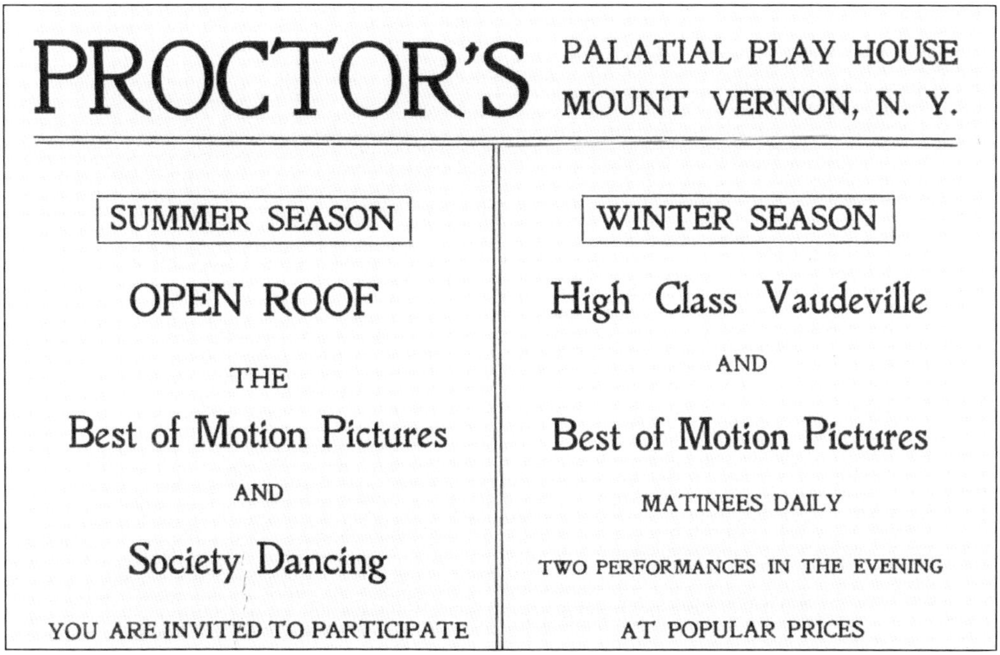

Above is a full-page advertisement in the 1913–1914 Mount Vernon High School yearbook. The Proctor's Theatre building had been recently constructed at the corner of Gramatan Avenue and Fiske Place, where it still stands. It was an impressive entertainment facility for a fast-moving young city. It made a high-profile appeal to the graduates. Mount Vernon High School (below), just up the hill on Gramatan Avenue, was also newly built in 1912. On February 6, 1933, the name was changed to A. B. Davis High School. Its school colors were maroon and white. For over 50 years, it was considered one of the top college preparatory schools in the state. Today it is a middle school.

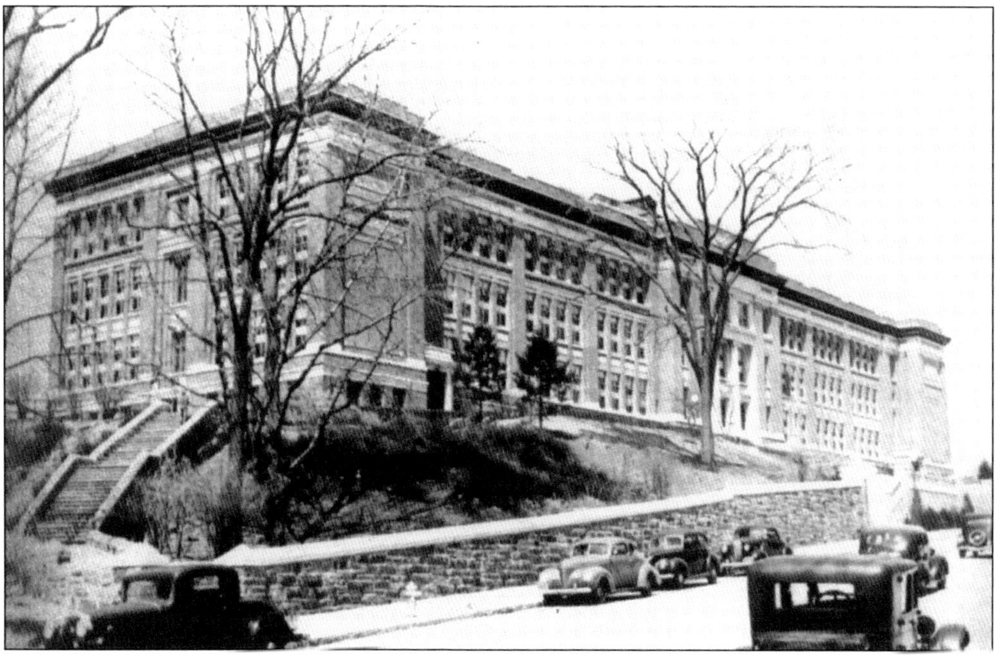

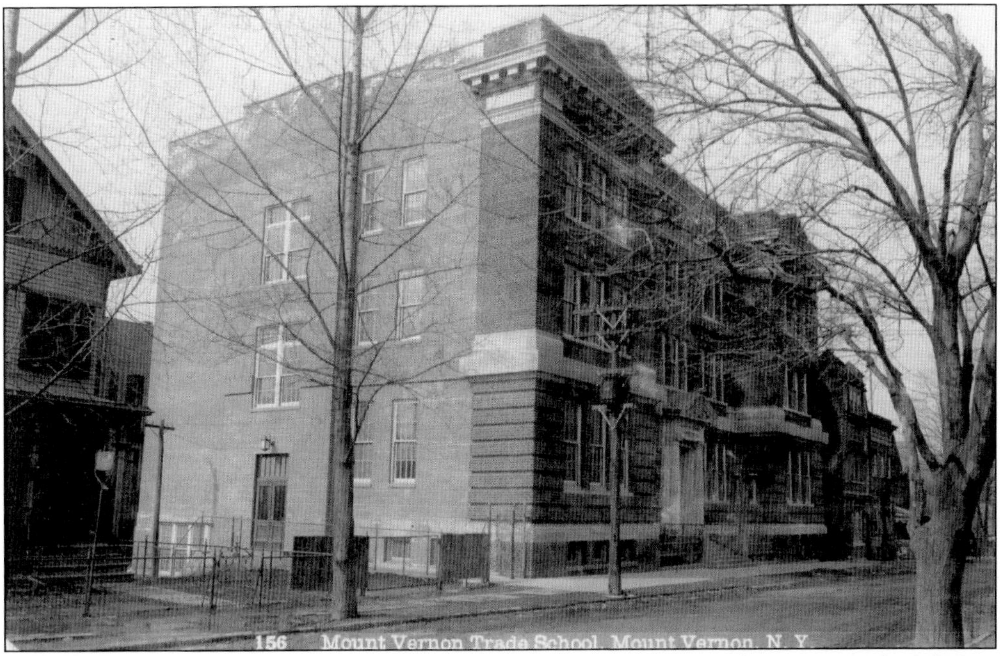

The School of Industrial Arts on South Third Avenue near Second Street was founded in 1910. On December 7, 1931, it was renamed Edison Vocational and Technical High School. Its school colors were blue and gold. In 1963, A. B. Davis and Edison High Schools merged when the beautiful Mount Vernon High School opened on California Road. The colors of the new high school were maroon and gold. For over 50 years, Edison High School trained students for careers generated by the commercial and industrial base of the local economy. Although out of date today, it also trained young women to keep "attractive and worthy homes and rear happy children and upright citizens." In first half of the 20th century, in addition to the college preparatory curriculum at A. B. Davis High School, these were educational priorities.

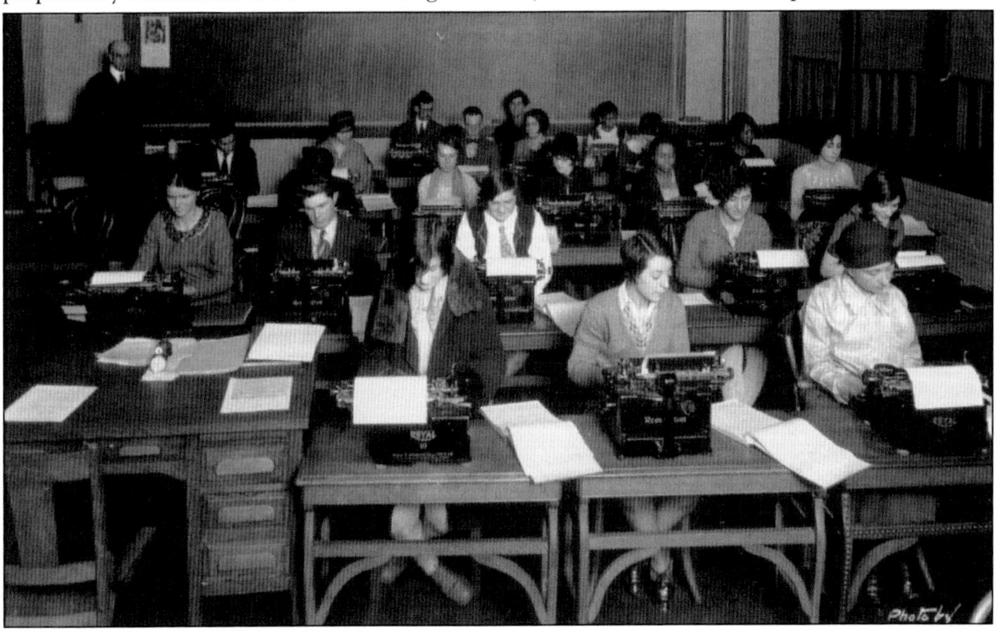

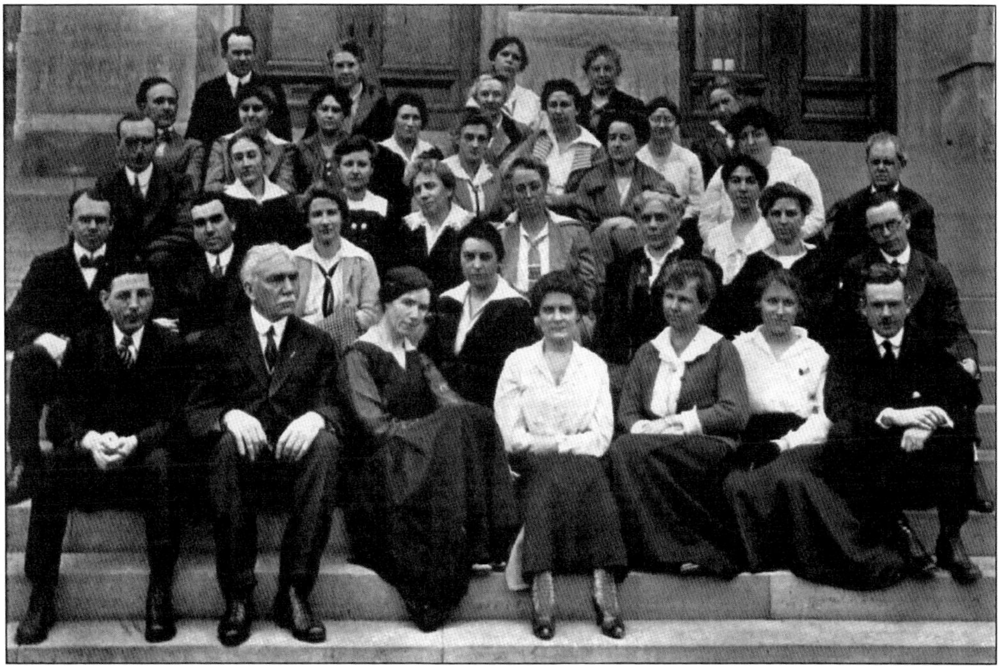

Mount Vernon High School was founded in 1895. By 1917, it had national recognition as one of the finest high schools. Its success was associated with the leadership of A. B. Davis (above, bottom row, second from left) and faculty. Below are the 1917 student leaders of the school yearbook and newspaper, the *Oracle*. Seated in the top row, second from the right, is the editor, E. B. White, born in 1899, the youngest of six children. White grew up in a child's paradise of backyards, skating ponds, bicycles, and pets. He got good grades and won a scholarship to Cornell University. He became an award-winning writer. His popular children's character Stuart Little was born in this city.

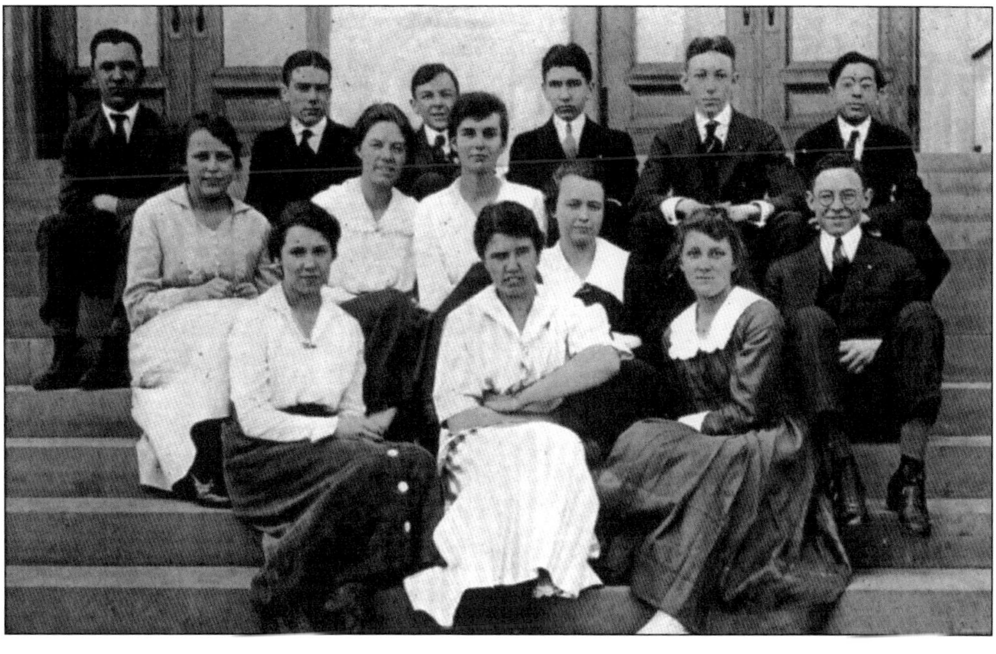

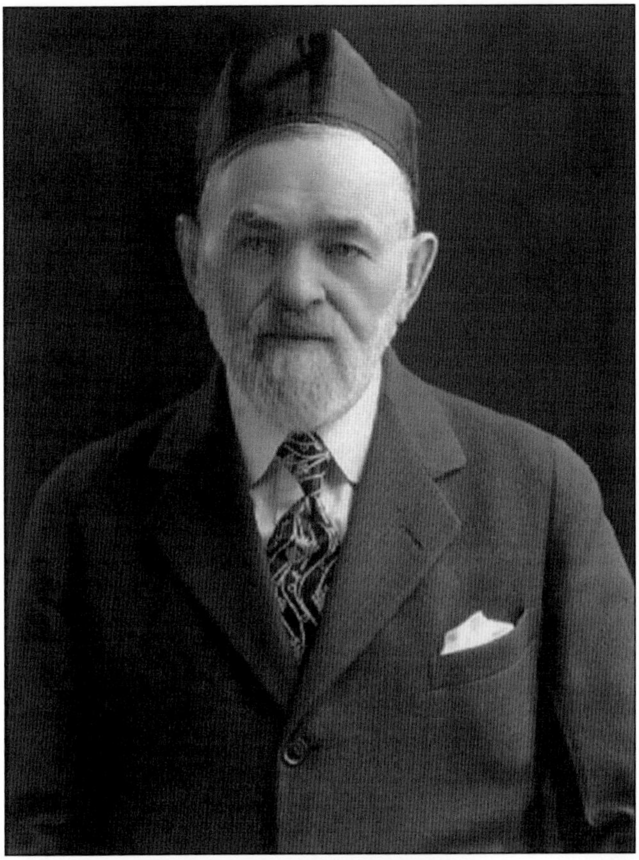

In 1892, Max Yavelow, a Russian emigrant, heard about the prosperity and growth in the new city of Mount Vernon. He invested what little money he had in a peddler's pack, gathered his family, and moved here. He peddled wares among workers lowering the New York-New Haven Railroad below street level. He managed to save $50 and opened a clothing store on Fourth Avenue. By the end of World War I, his original investment grew into a $50,000 business. In 1942, at the age of 91, Yavelow died at his Bedford Avenue home. In 1948, after 59 years, Max Yavelow and Sons closed its doors at 128 South Fourth Avenue. (Courtesy of the Yavelow family archive.)

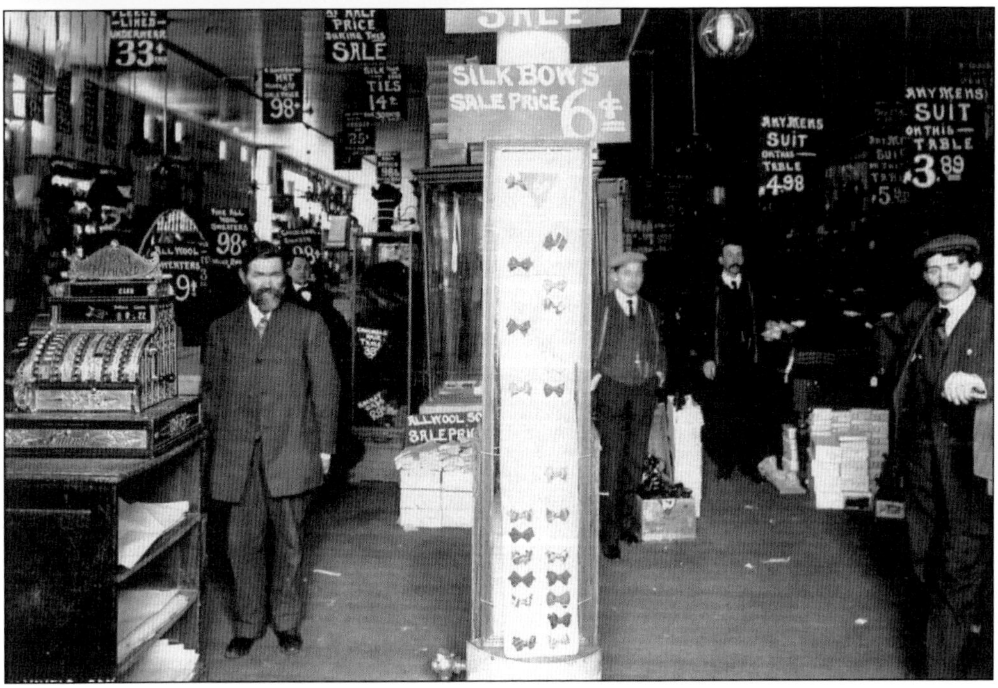

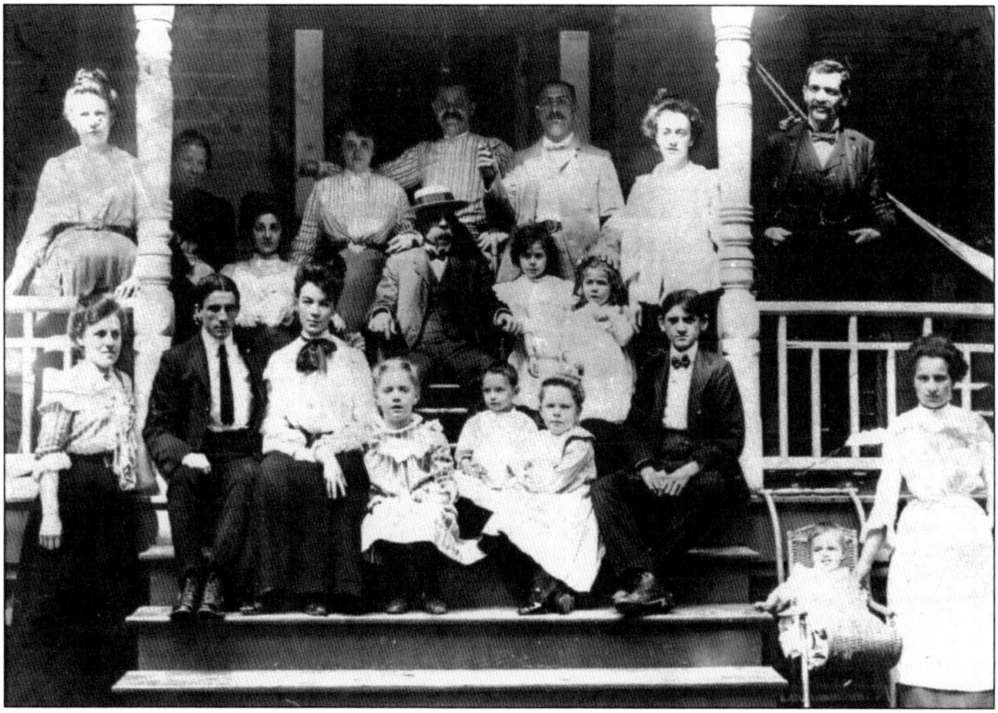

The Yavelows were an upwardly mobile new American family. Max Yavelow's extended family lived in a large house, which later came to be known as the Knolls Inn. It was on the north side of the New York-New Haven Railroad between First Street and Fulton Avenue. The Lion's Club met there for many years. Yavelow was a founder of Congregational Brothers Synagogue on South Eighth Avenue near First Street. The residents of the Jewish faith flourished in Mount Vernon. Yavelow children and grandchildren became medical doctors and professionals. (Courtesy of the Yavelow family archive.)

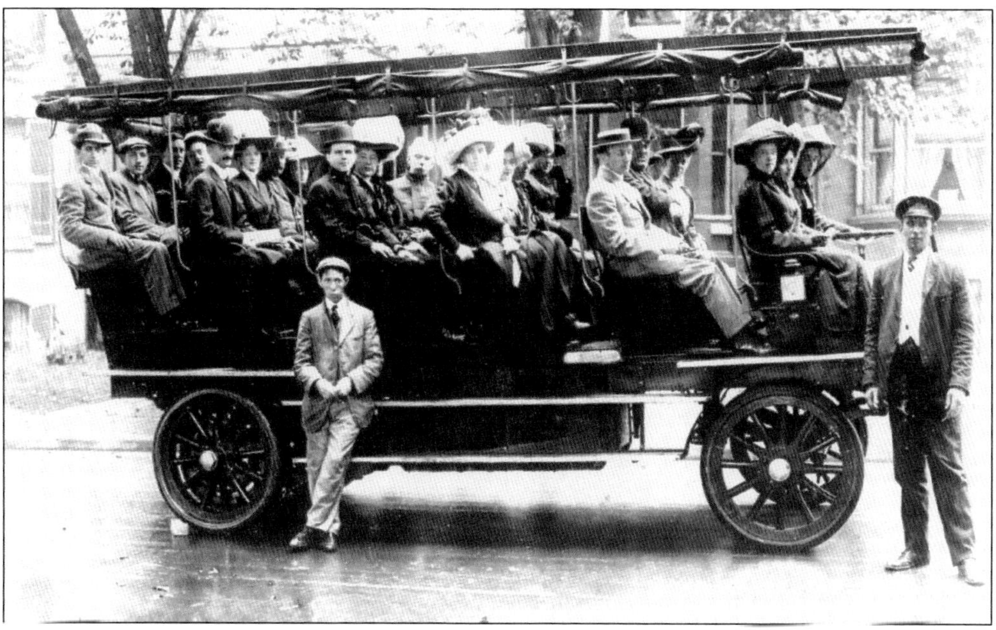

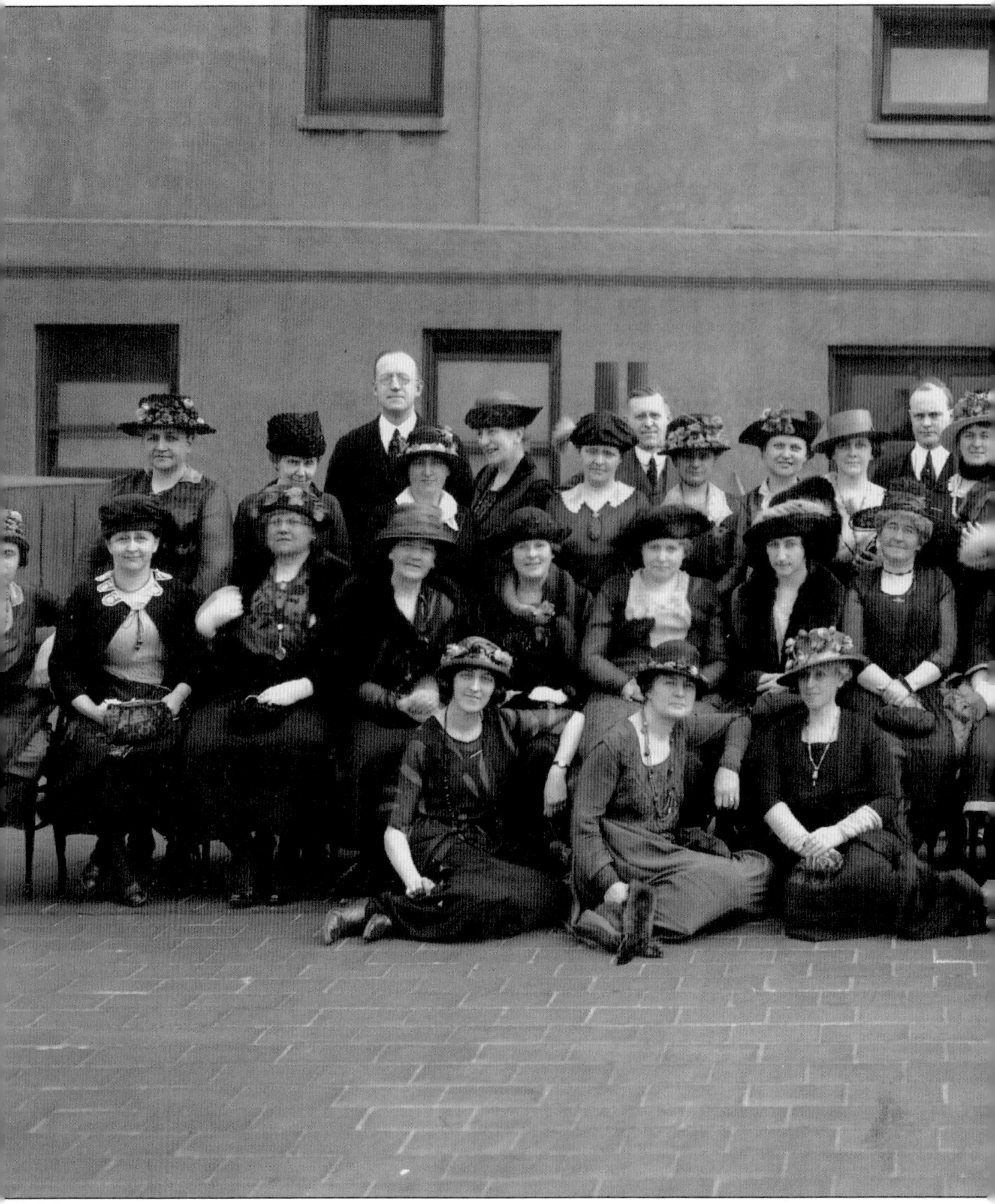

In 1894, 25 women organized the Westchester Woman's Club. These civic-minded women represented the leading and most influential families. They played an extraordinary role in furthering Mount Vernon as a desirable city. Their objective was "to further the education of women for the responsibilities of life, to encourage all movements for the betterment of society and to foster a generous public spirit in the community." They immediately began to make

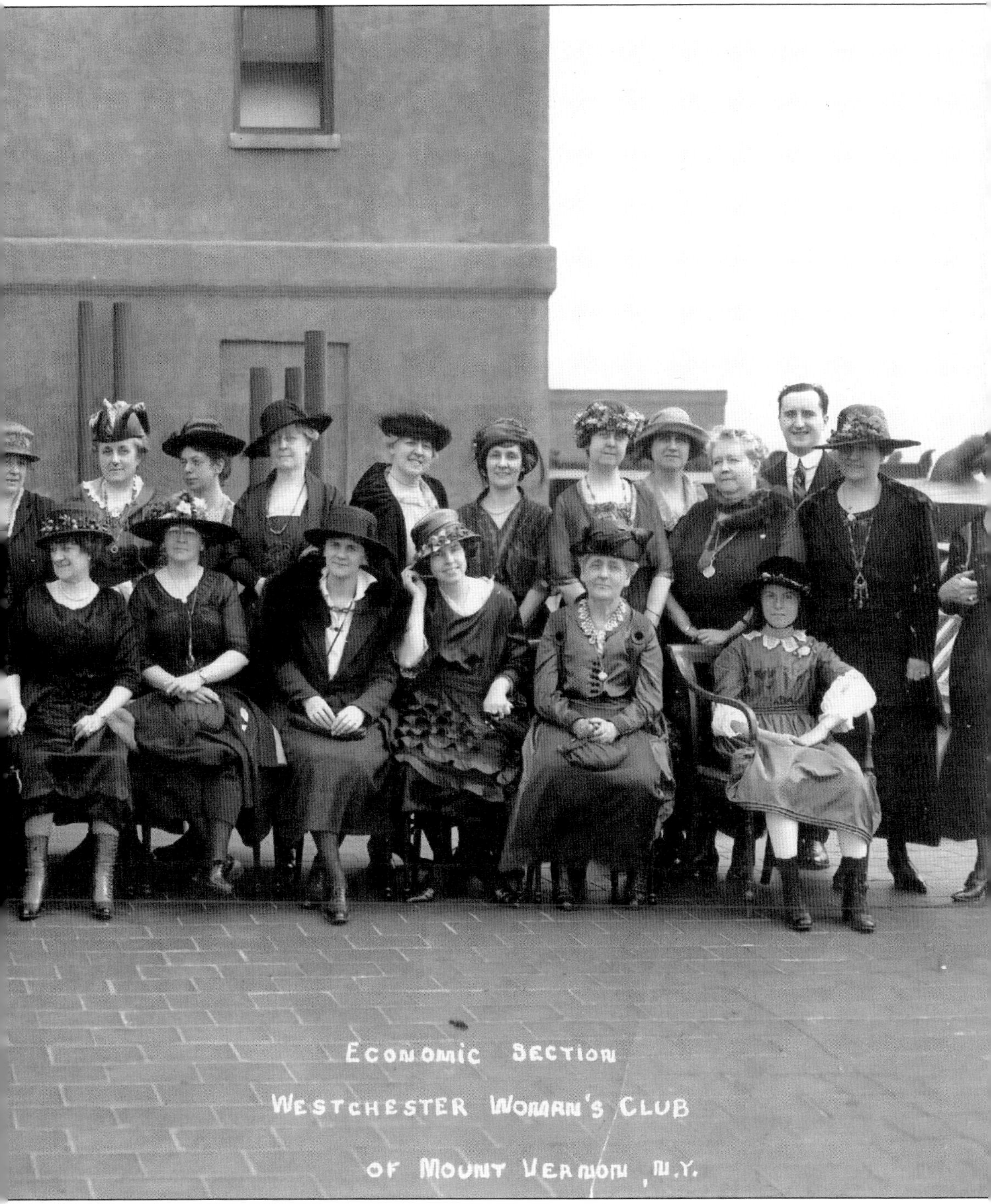

remarkable improvements. They initiated kindergartens in the schools, the first high school, a school for industrial and domestic training, new parks, the network of citywide playgrounds, the city's first water system, the public library, and later the refurbishing of the Depression-era downtown district. In 1910, they built the Westchester Woman's Club facility and auditorium on Crary Avenue (later demolished for the Lefrak cooperative apartments).

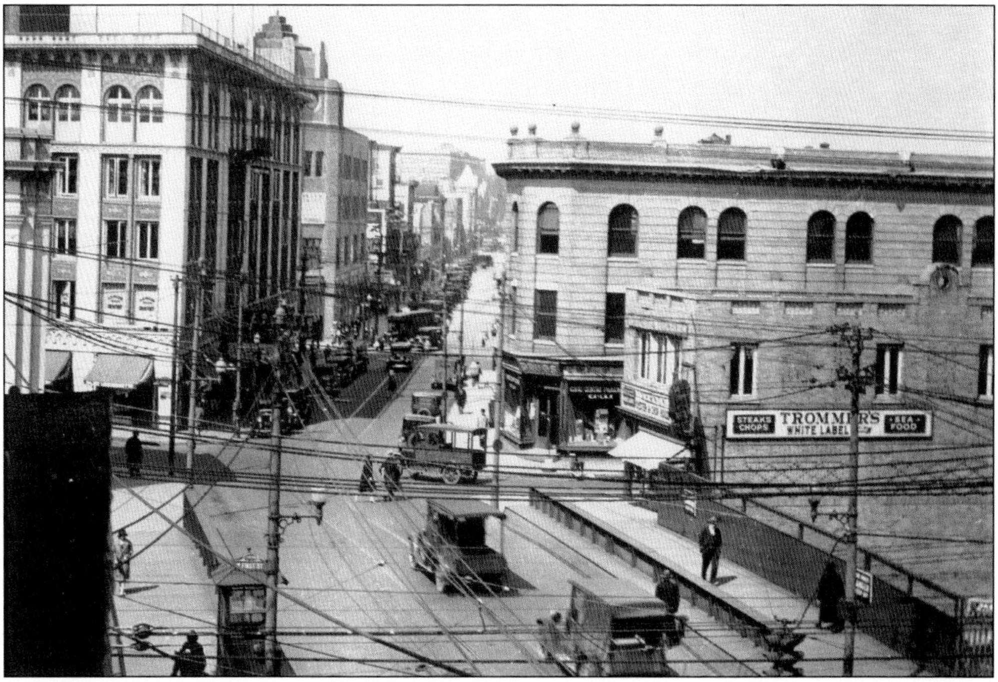

These two pictures of the bridge over the train tracks from South Fourth Avenue looking northward down Gramatan Avenue illustrate the transformation of the strip between 1924 (above) and 1949 (below). The two-story Lucas Building at the corner of Fiske Place and Gramatan Avenue (above right) served as city hall. The current one on Roosevelt Square was completed in 1929. By midcentury, storefronts were modernized, the streets were widened and repaved, and poles and wires were removed. Two floors were added to the Lucas Building.

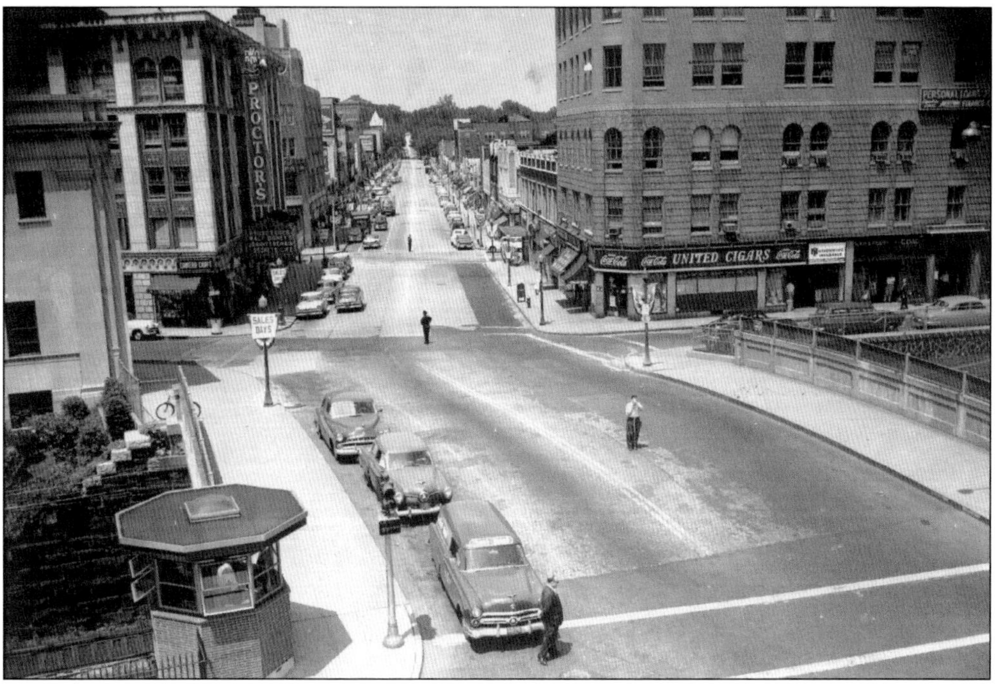

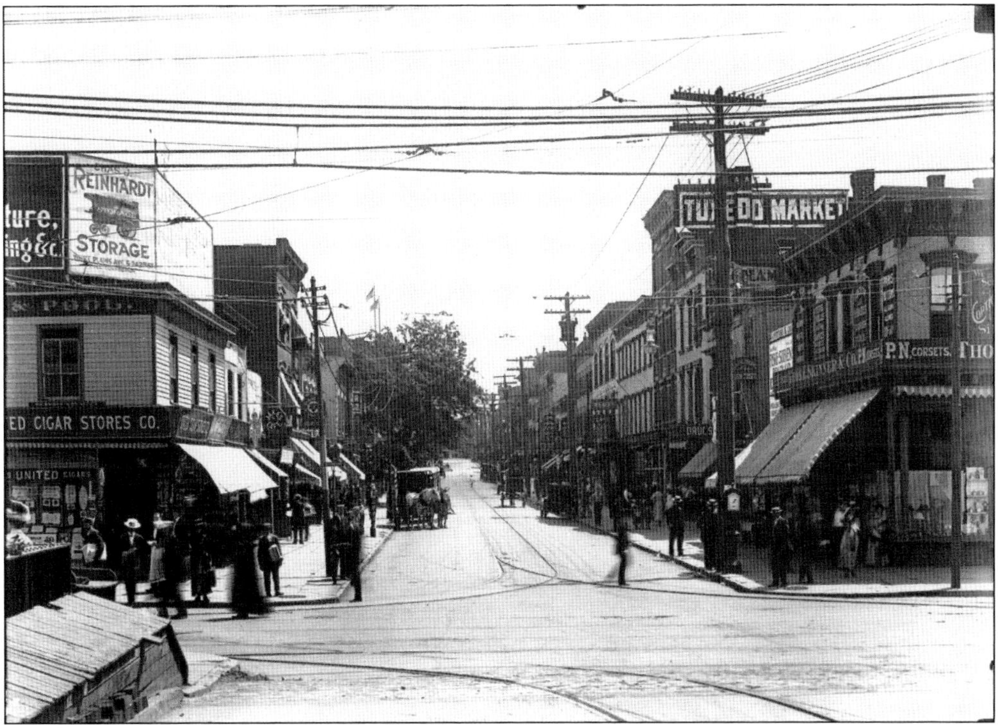

The corner of Fourth Avenue and First Street is Mount Vernon's historic center city. It divided the commercial district north and south and was the traditional location of the depot. The view above is looking southward down Fourth Avenue from the Gramatan Avenue bridge in 1911. Below is a panoramic view of East First Street between Third and Fourth Avenues.

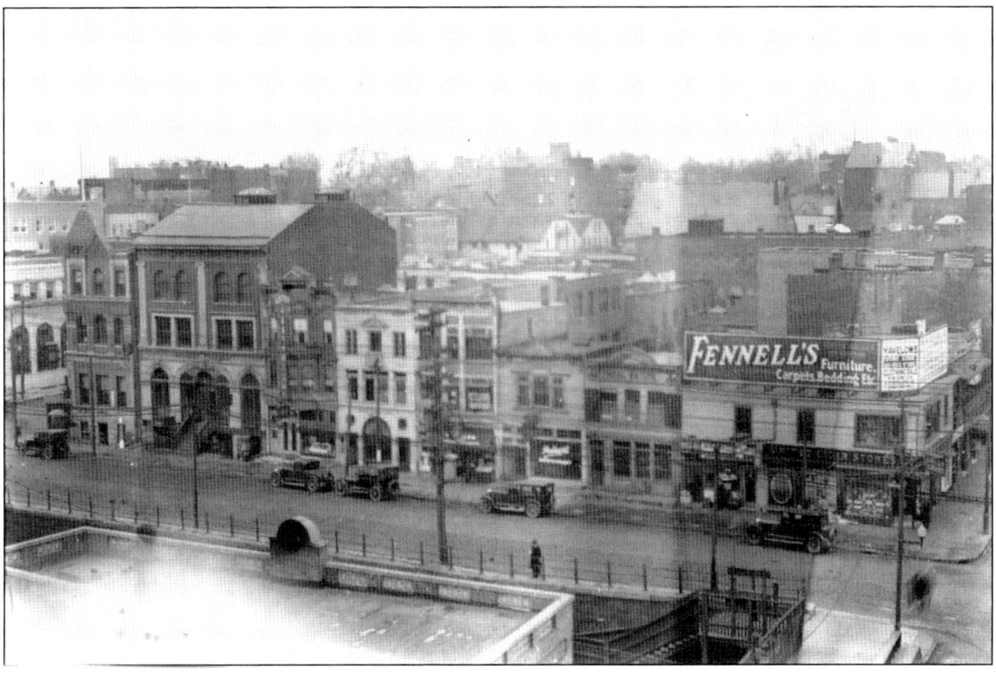

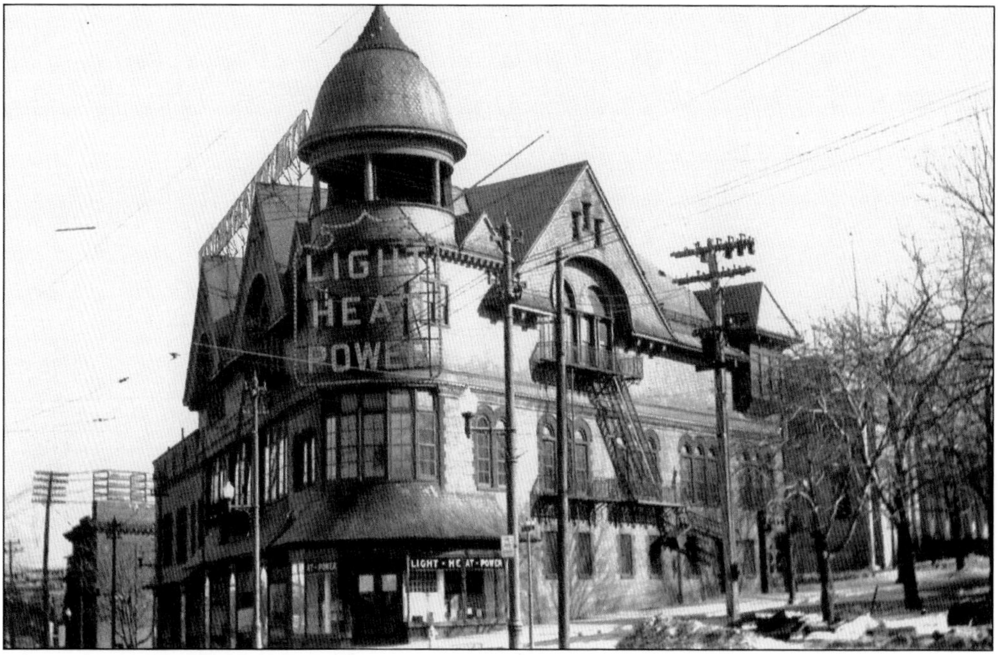

This is a 1911 picture of the Light, Heat and Power Building at the southeast corner of First Street and First Avenue. It was torn down and the Consolidated Edison Tower erected. It is currently a Westchester County government office building.

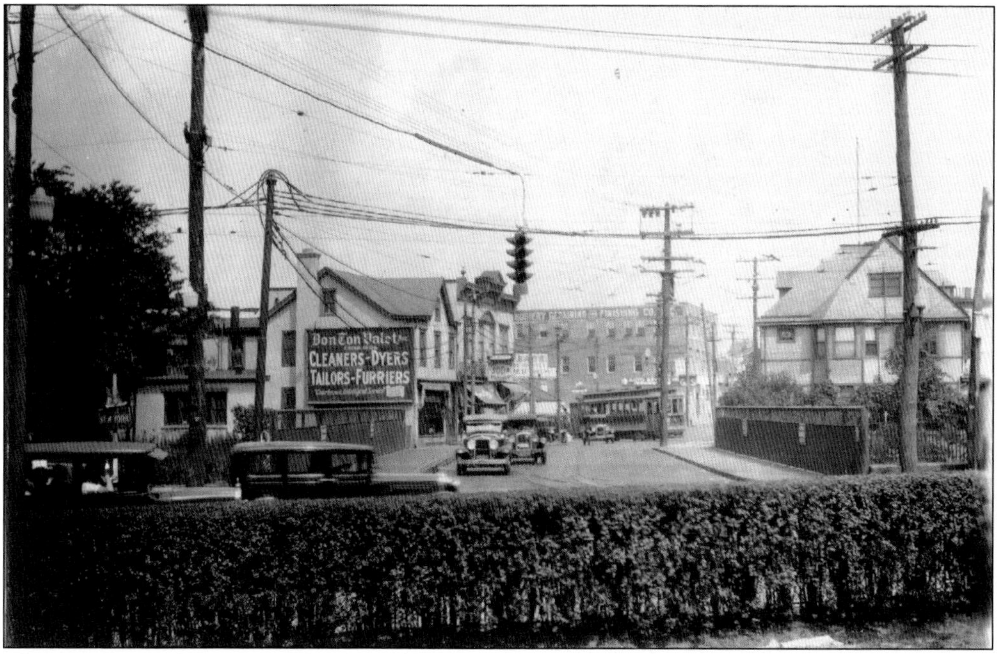

This is a view of Scott's Bridge from Eleventh Avenue and First Street. In the background is Lincoln Avenue as it crosses Mount Vernon and Stevens Avenues. The fourth light in the overhead traffic light was used at that time as an "all red" signal during fire or police emergencies. It was later used as a "flashing blue" to call police to their nearest telephone call-in station. This photograph is from 1925.

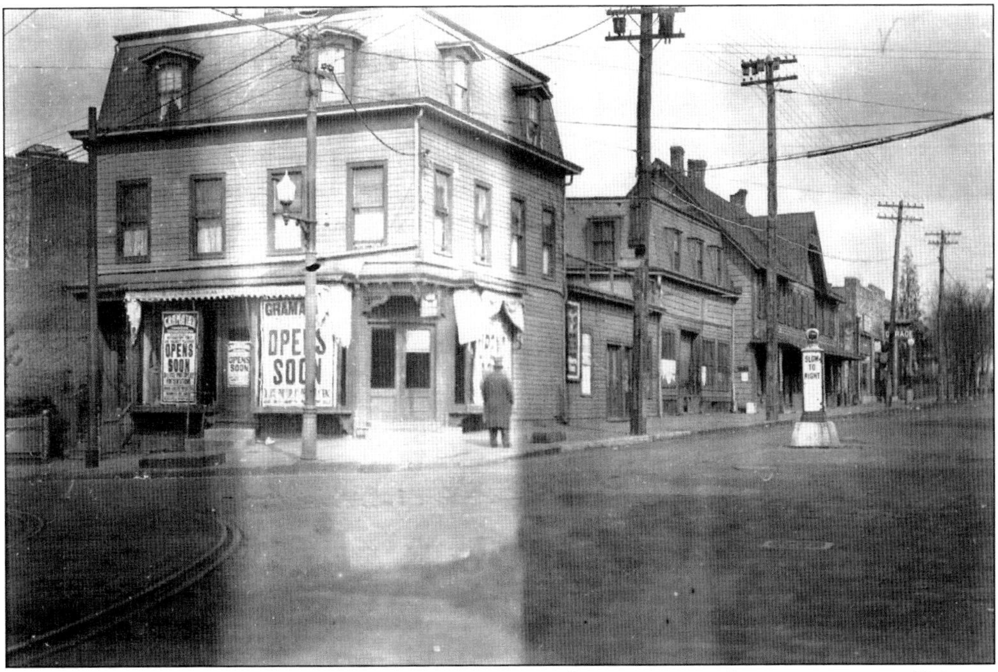

The photograph above is looking eastward on Lincoln Avenue at the intersection of Mount Vernon and Stevens Avenues in 1924. The picture below is the same location in 1948. Initially a German community, today West Mount Vernon is the center of the Portuguese and Hispanic communities.

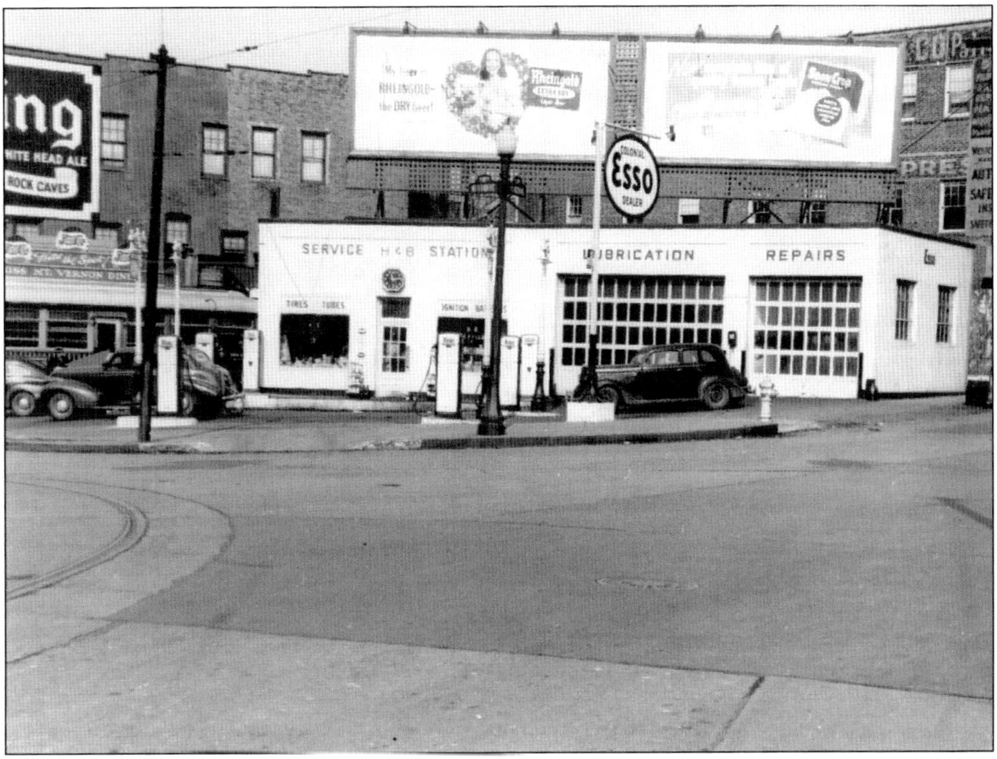

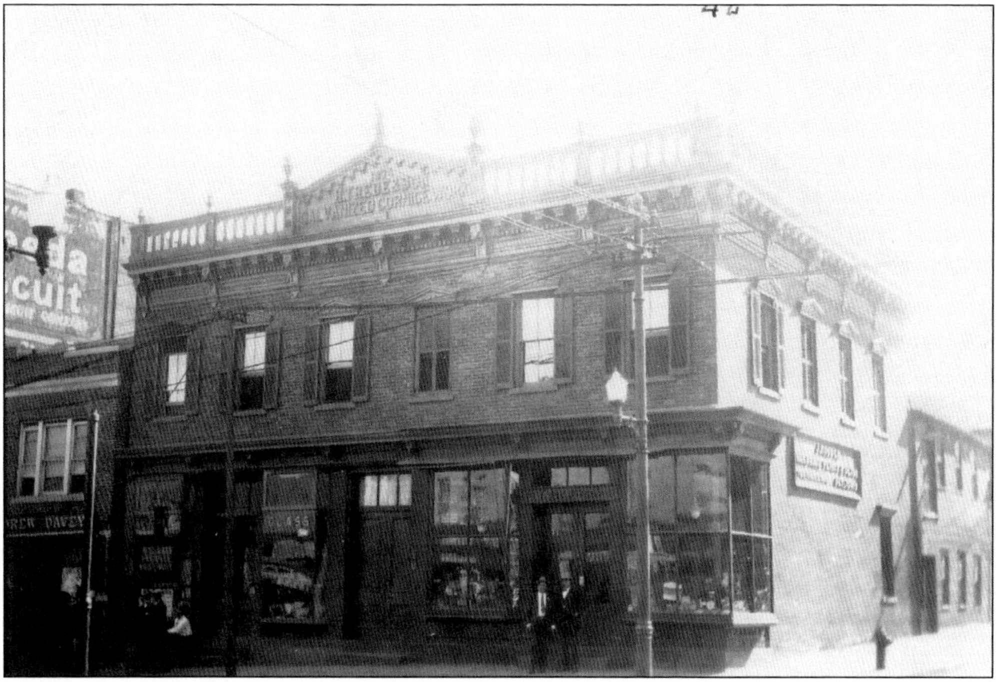

The history of West Mount Vernon mirrors the earlier John Stevens organization and settlement. Mount Vernon Avenue runs westward from Lincoln Avenue down across the New York-Harlem Railway line and the Bronx River to the Yonkers border. It is the main thoroughfare. It has a direct connection to the Colonial-era Mile Square Road that ran from Yonkers (Mile Square) down to the old village green at Eastchester Creek. These 1925 photographs are the southeast corner of Mount Vernon Avenue and Bleeker Street (above) and the northeast corner of Mount Vernon Avenue and Bond Street (below).

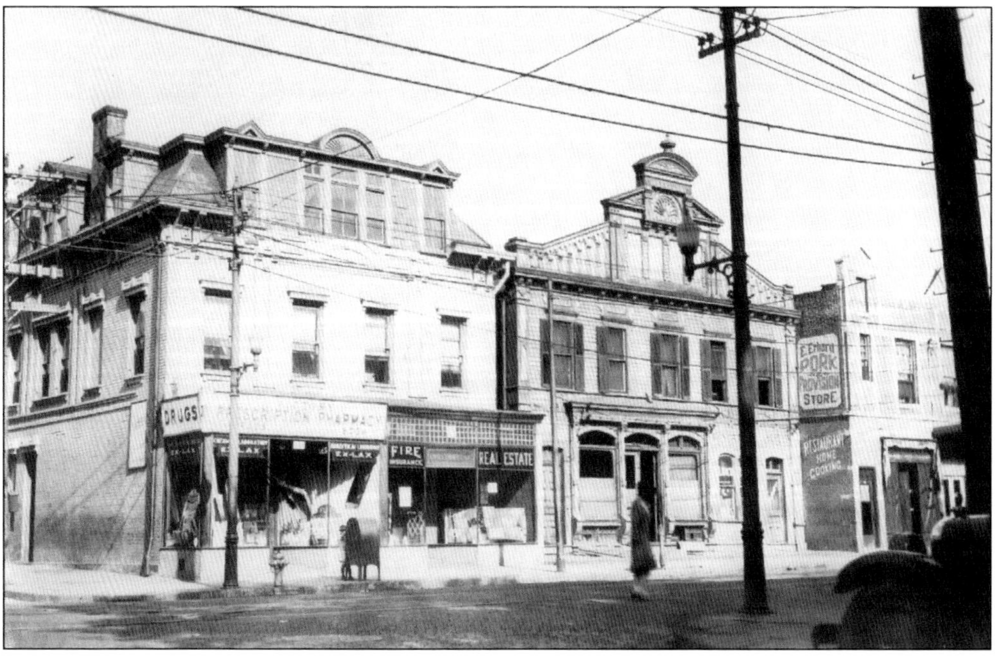

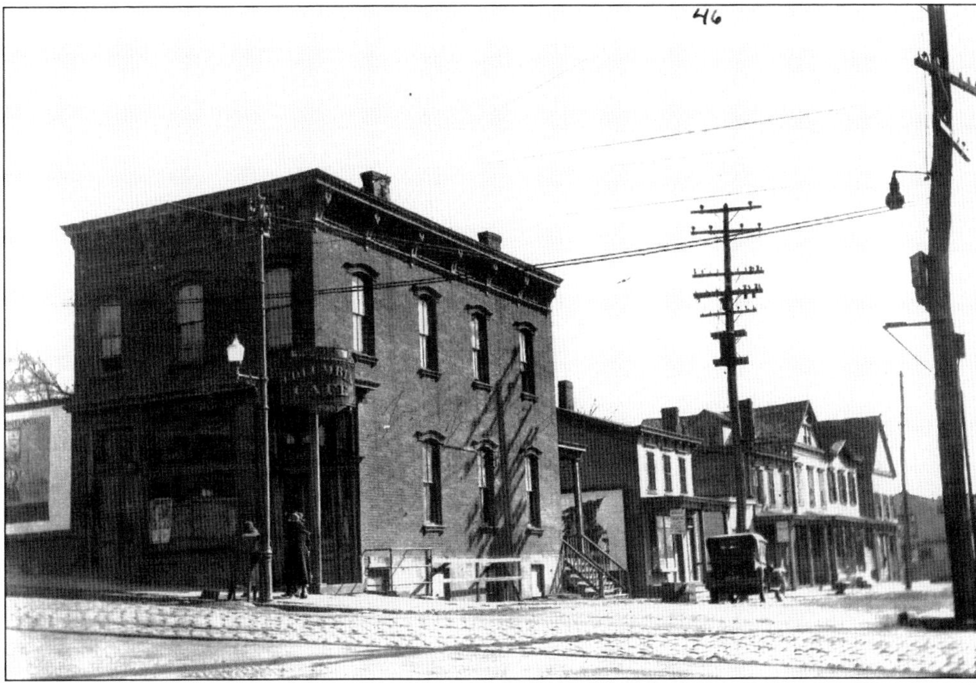

The picture above is the Columbia Café at the southeast corner of Railroad Avenue, currently known as McQuesten Parkway. The image below shows the northwest corner of Gramatan Avenue and North Street. At the top of the hill are the Mount Vernon Armory and an Italian American community that gave birth to the Italian Civic Association.

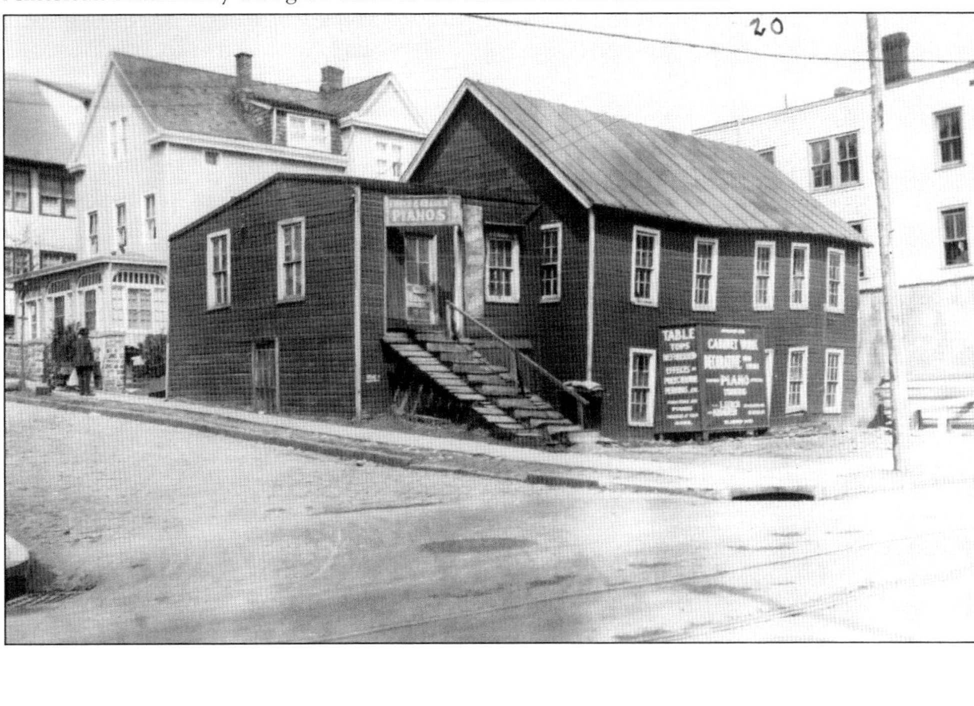

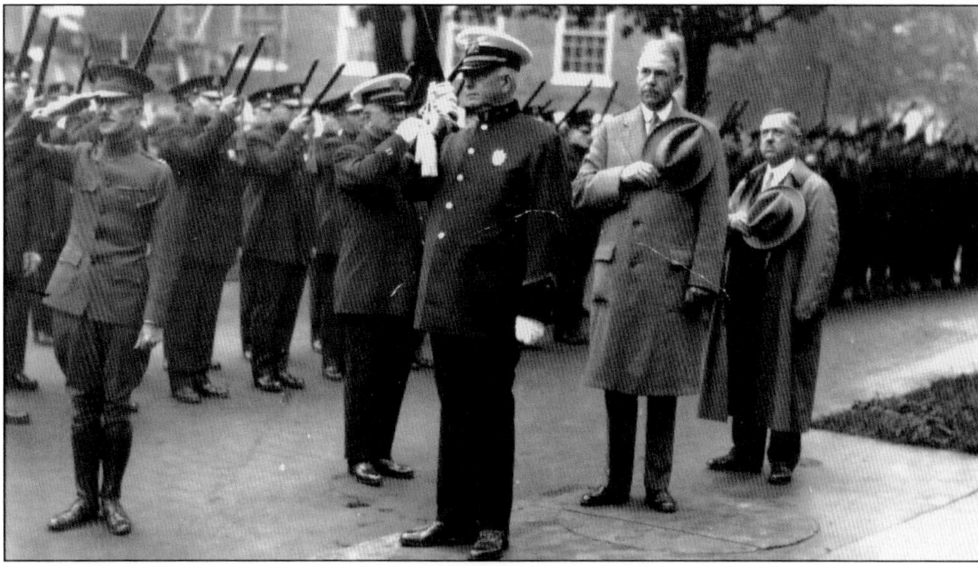

In the foreground is police commissioner George Atwell. To his right is police chief Michael Silverstein, and to his rear with their hats over their hearts are commissioner of public safety Mark Stiles and Mayor James Berg. The move from city hall located at the Lucas Building at the northeast corner of Fiske Place and Gramatan Avenue to the newly constructed building (1929) on Roosevelt Square was under the leadership of Berg.

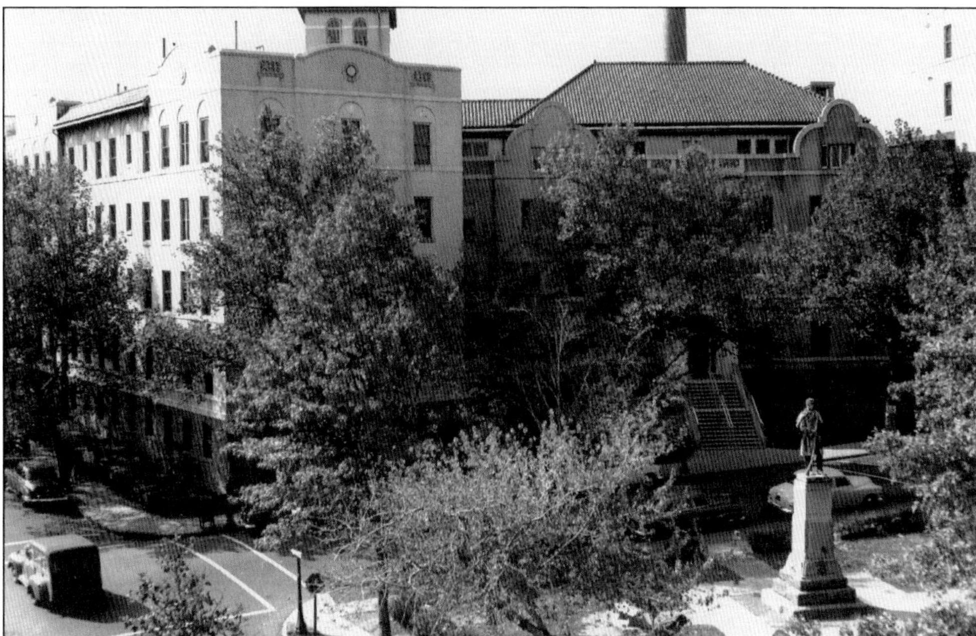

In the lower right-hand corner, facing Mount Vernon Hospital, is the city's first war memorial. Although the community was only 11 years old when the Civil War (1861) began, the village's young men were well represented in the Union army. John Van Santvoord formed an association to raise funds for a monument in memory of Mount Vernon's brave soldiers. Farnsworth Post conducted the dedication service on May 30, 1891. A few years later, a tablet was added, recognizing the role women played in the war.

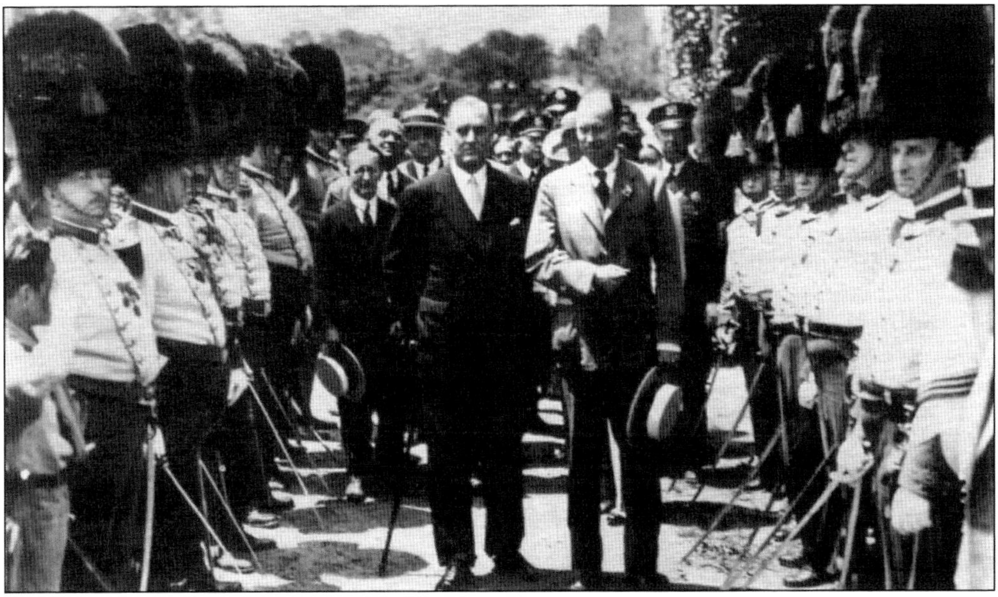

Franklin Delano Roosevelt and his mother, Sara Delano Roosevelt, had family connections to St. Paul's Church. James Roosevelt, an ancestor, lived in 19th-century Eastchester, owned a church pew, and served as a vestryman and later as the town clerk. Sara and a committee of eminent citizens undertook a 1931 fund-raising campaign to restore St. Paul's Church to its original charm and beauty. The restoration was completed in 1942. In the June 1931 picture above, then governor Franklin Delano Roosevelt worshipped at St. Paul's Church and then addressed a gathering of over 10,000 people assembled on the village green for the occasion of the first Descendant's Day. Sara had great influence on her son. She is pictured below hosting a costumed fund-raiser for the restoration of St. Paul's Church. (Courtesy of the St. Paul's Church National Historic Site.)

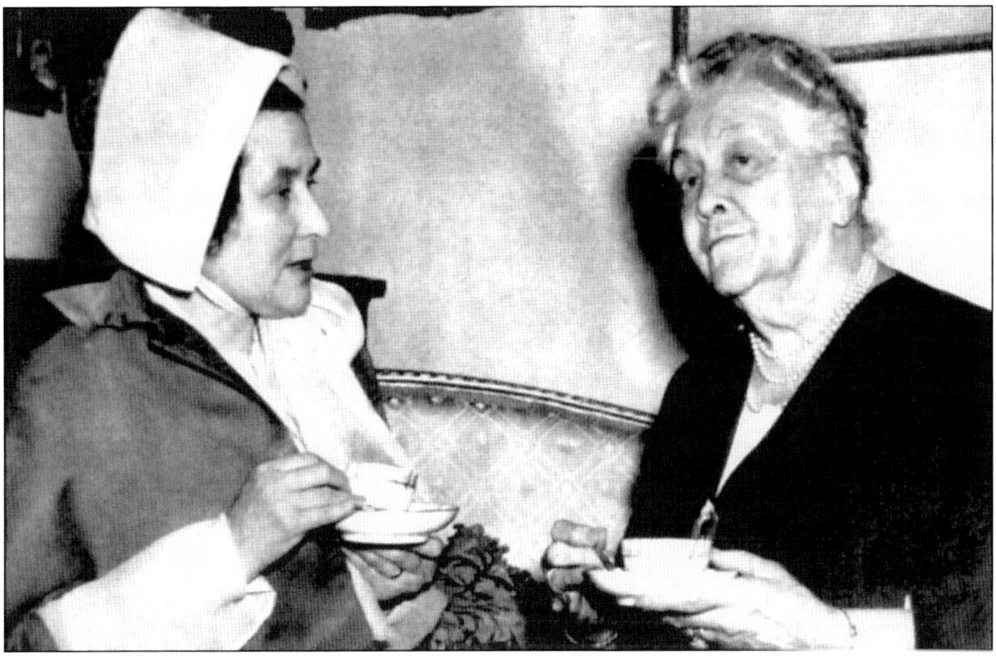

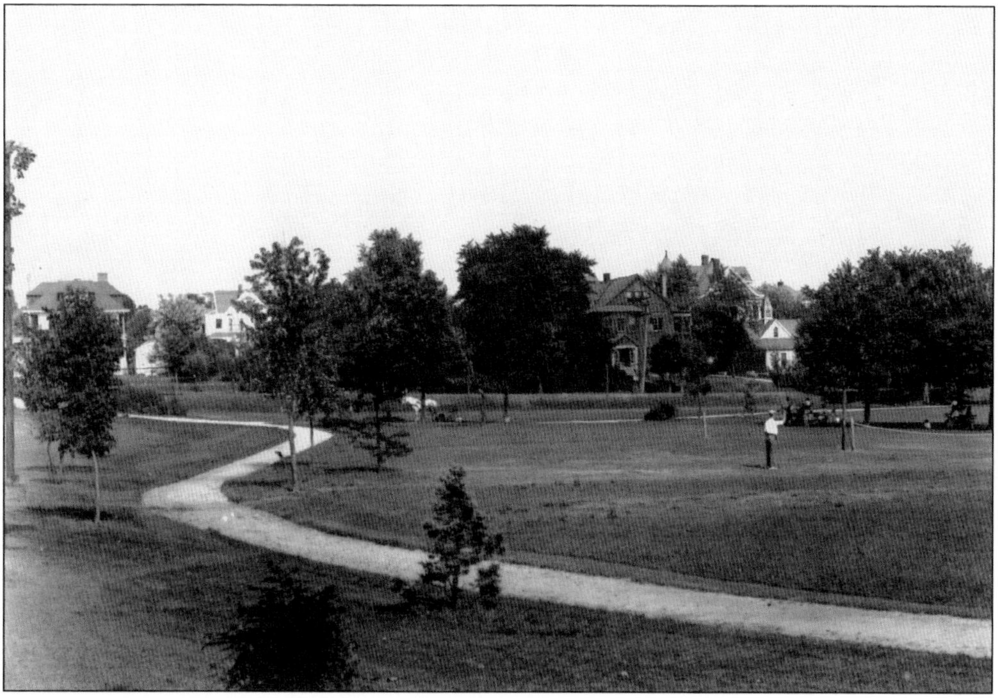

In 1901, Edward Hartley gave the city a gift of five acres of land bounded by East Lincoln Avenue, Crary Avenue, North Street, and Gramatan Avenue. It was stipulated that land was to be exclusively used as a public park. It carries his name. The picture above is a view of Hartley Park in 1903. The picture below from June 22, 1961, is the park at night, facing the circle.

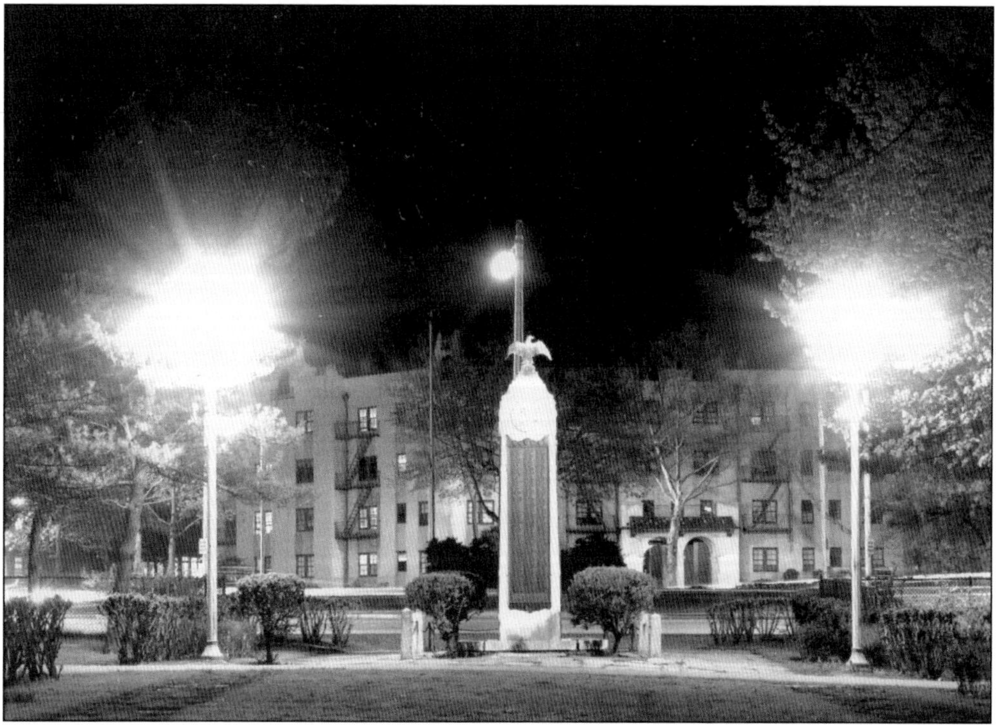

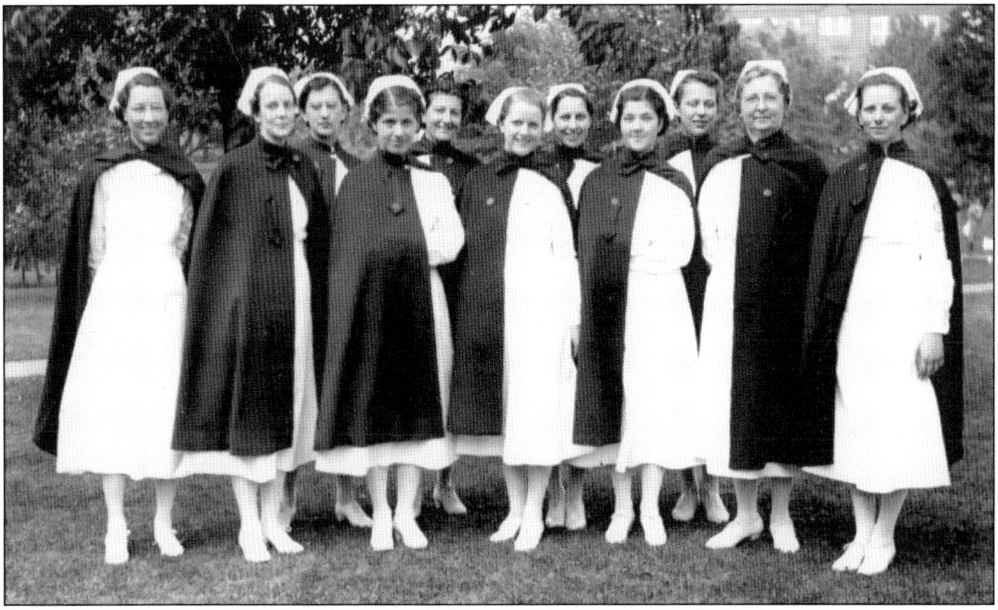

These Mount Vernon Hospital nurses posing at Hartley Park participated in the May 30, 1936, Memorial Day parade. From left to right are Virginia McClellan Moskowitz, former city historian, Ruth Osborne, Rose Antonachio, Rita Cariffe, Dorothy Petronio, Agnes Olam, unidentified, Frances Loveland, Dorothy Glaser, Jean Brown, and Polly Ashe.

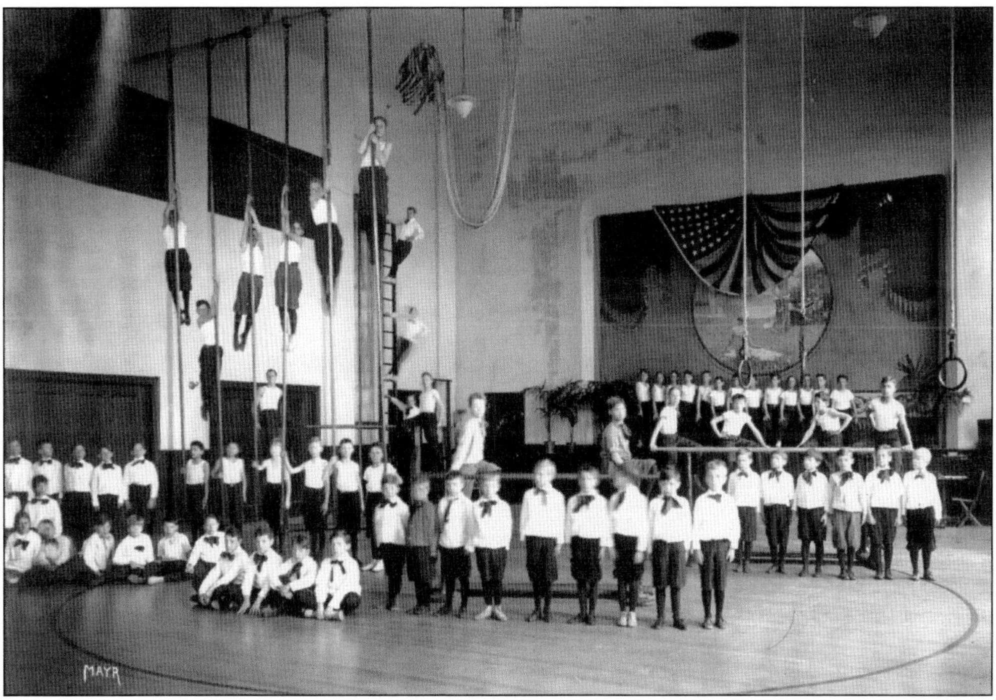

The West Mount Vernon German American community was the founder of Turn Verein (Turn Hall) on Stevens Avenue and the corner of North Tenth Avenue. It was enthusiastic about gymnastics. The photograph above was donated by Herbert Cordes to the public library in 1971. The Cordes family was a leading family at the beginning of the 20th century.

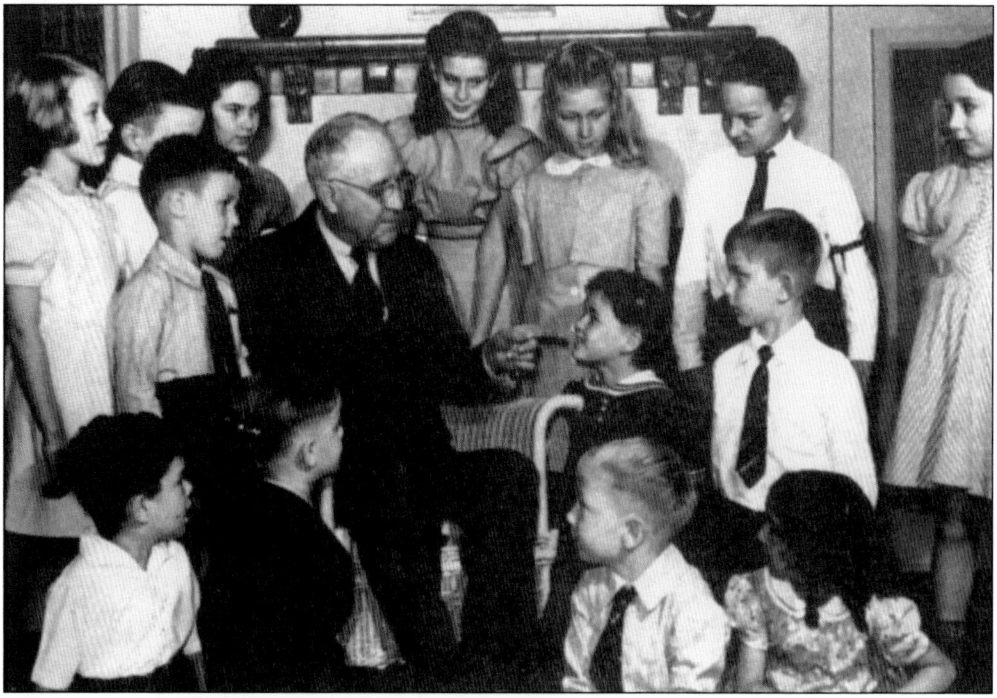

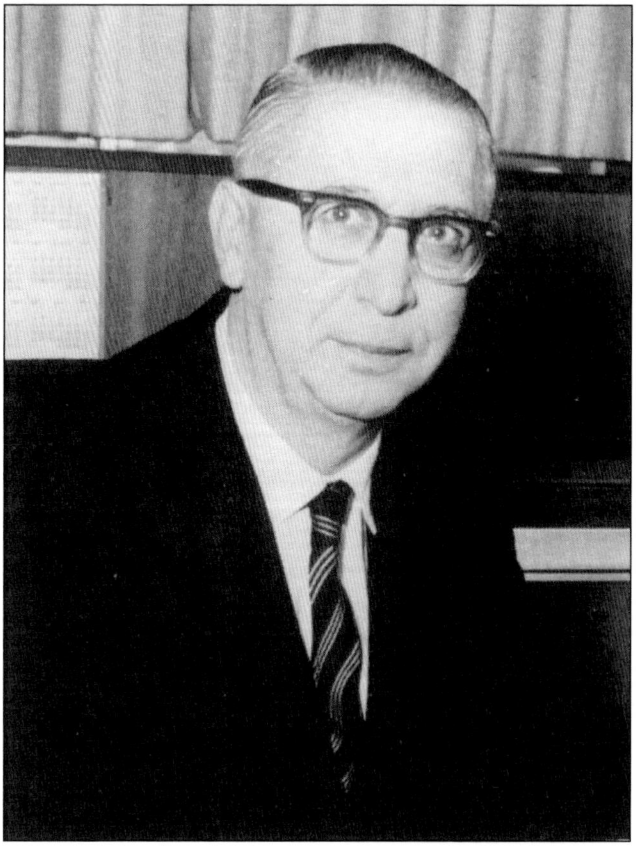

In the center of the photograph above is Dr. William H. Holmes, superintendent of schools from 1913 to 1940. He was a national educational leader. The reputation of Mount Vernon schools was objectively rated among the nation's most effective. Local millionaires, celebrities, and businessmen chose city schools over private institutions. At left is Dr. Alfred Franko, former city historian and superintendent of schools. He was a 1930s graduate from Duke and Columbia Universities and was forever grateful to Holmes for appointing him to become the first Italian American full-time educator in Mount Vernon schools. An elementary school is named after Holmes and a middle school after Franko.

The picture at right is of one of the greatest elementary social studies teachers in the history of the school district. Cecil H. Parker came to Mount Vernon in 1935 with a bachelor's degree from Boston University and a master's degree from New York University. There were only a few teachers with such an advanced degree. The city was not ready to integrate the teaching staff. She served as a substitute and night school instructor until 1942 when she was appointed as a full-time teacher at Nathan Hale Elementary School on South Sixth Avenue. Today the school is named in her honor. The picture below is of Charles Altschuler, hired in 1933 by Dr. William H. Holmes. He was the first teacher of Jewish descent. He was a very popular high school social studies teacher. A street is named in his honor. The A. B. Davis High School students are, from left to right, Dandee Lee, Debbie Hop, and Judith Roth. This image is from March 18, 1957.

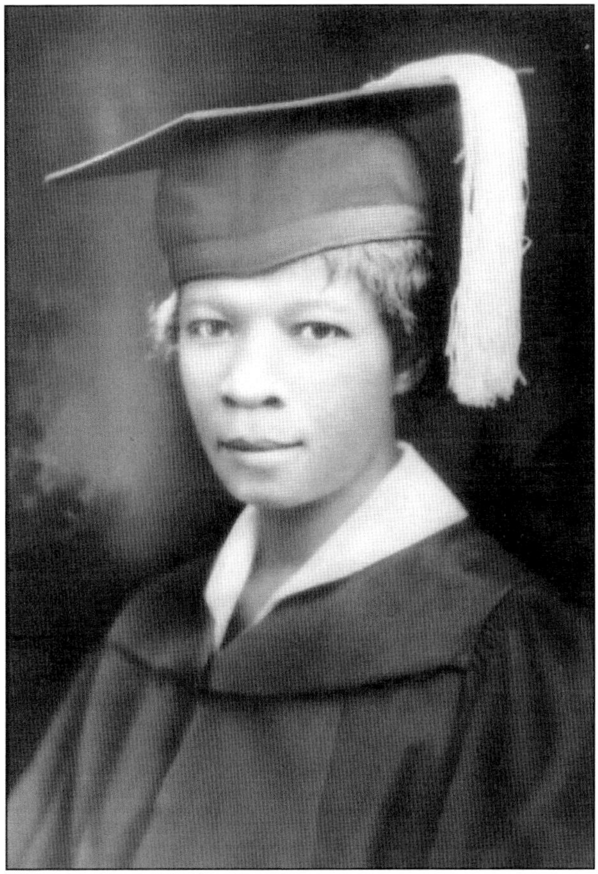

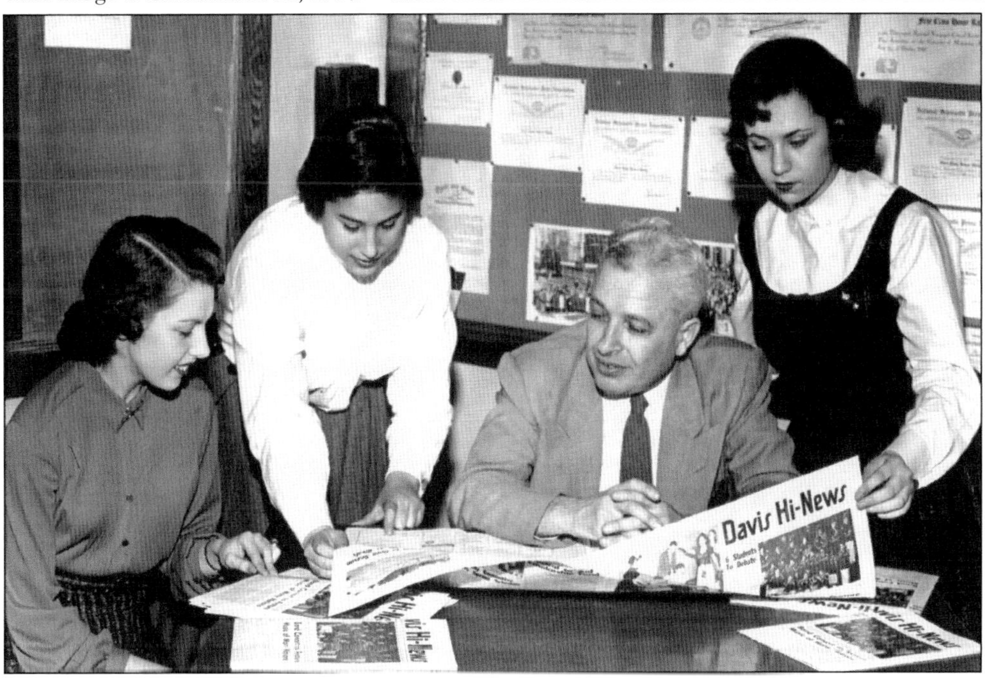

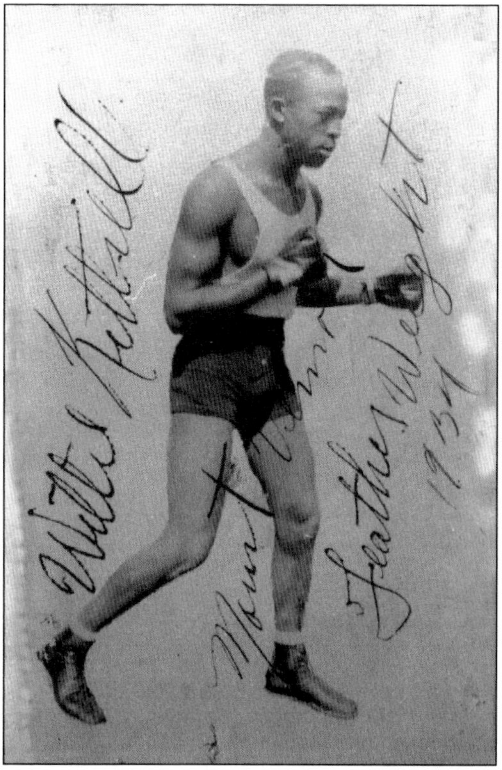

Between 1931 and 1934, Willie Kittrell had a brilliant professional boxing career. He was a world contender in the featherweight division and Mount Vernon's hope for a boxing world champion. He lost his first 2 fights and went on to score 23 victories. His powerful right hand landed 11 knockouts. He was considered one of the hardest hitters in the world. Kittrell was so tough that world champion Eligio "Kid Chocolate" Montalvo refused to fight him for $1,000.

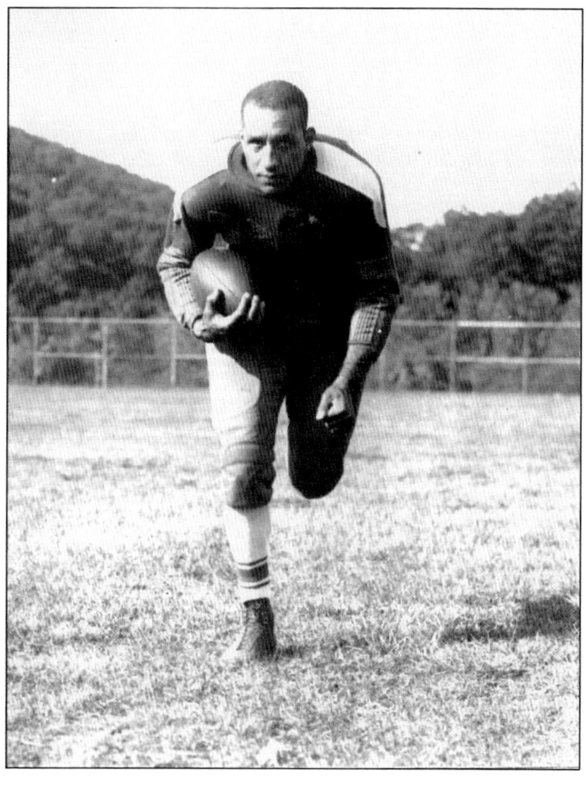

Edward Williams, a 1932 graduate of A. B. Davis High School had the distinction of being compared with the great collegiate athlete, scholar, actor, and singer Paul Robeson. Williams went to New York University and became a racial barrier–breaking athlete. In 1936, the segregated University of North Carolina played New York University. Williams was the starting fullback. This was the southern college's first integrated football game. Williams became a beloved educator and principal of Robert Fulton School, now named in his honor.

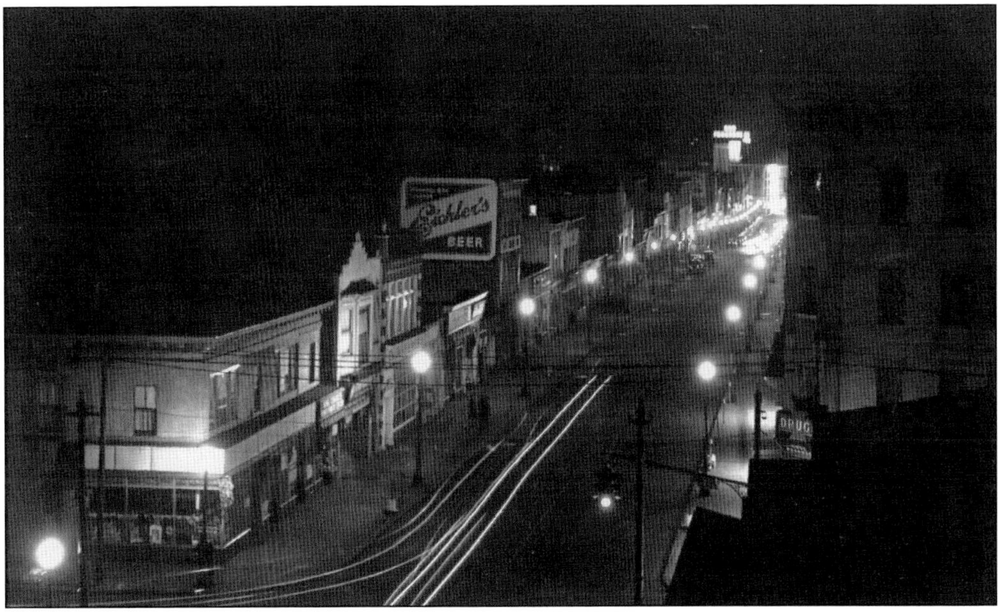

During World War II, there was a national security call for cities to turn off all nonessential lights at night. This is a March 9, 1942, blackout called by the government. It is a view looking from Third Street and Fourth Avenue north toward Gramatan Avenue.

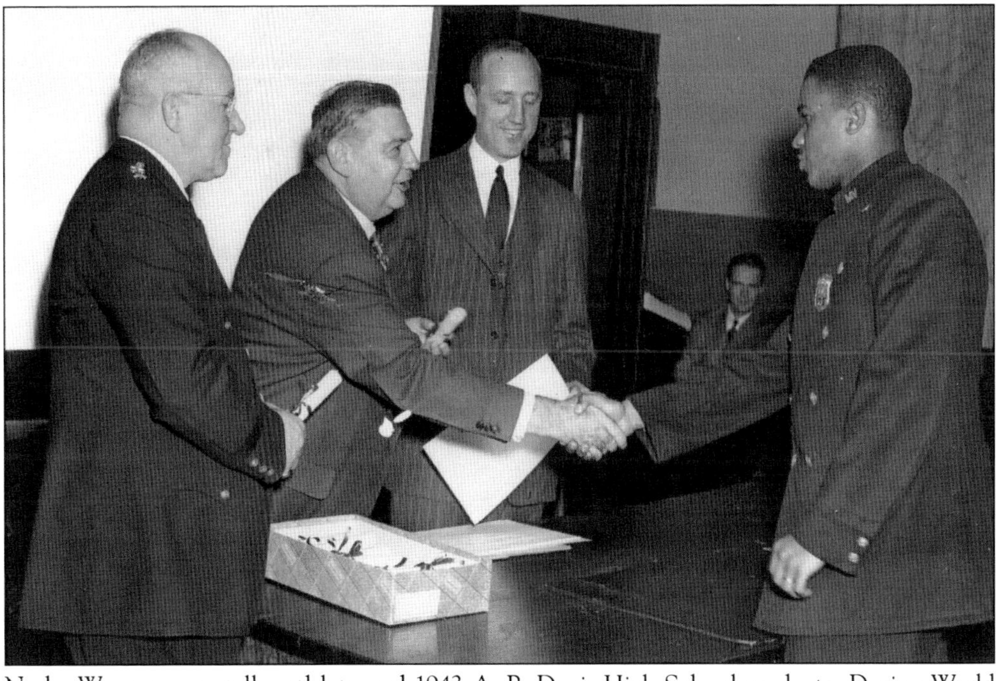

Nasby Wynn was a stellar athlete and 1943 A. B. Davis High School graduate. During World War II, he enlisted in the army and became a B-25 pilot in the 477th Bomber Squadron, obtaining the rank of flight officer. He logged in 800 hours in the air. In 1946, Wynn received an honorable discharge. On November 1, 1946, along with 23 other veterans, Mayor William Hussey appointed him as a police officer. Wynn became Mount Vernon's first African American patrolman. He later obtained the rank of sergeant and commander. He retired in 1980.

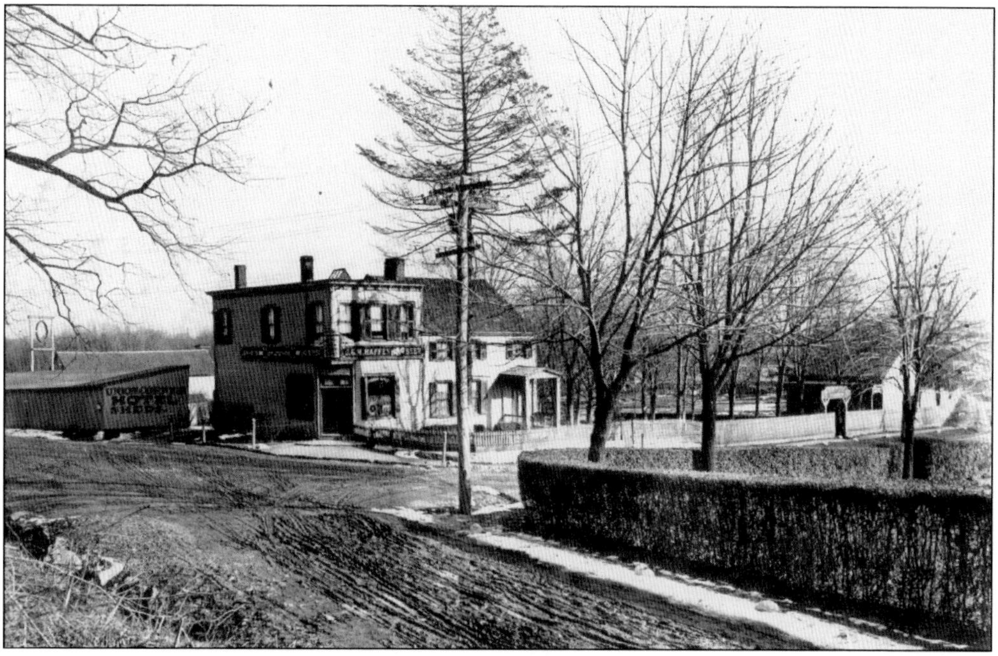

The 1910 photograph above is of Union Corners, the intersection of New Rochelle and California Roads. It was a muddy dirt road with rural surroundings. Although in the 1930s mansions were built along California Road, as the 1948 image below shows the intersection was paved but the area remained relatively undeveloped. This gateway to Tuckahoe and Bronxville was definitely not the busy northeast commercial hub it is today. The construction of the current high school and the extension of the Cross County Parkway forever changed this exclusive sector of the city. (Above, courtesy of the Walter A. Miles collection; below, courtesy of the Westchester Camera Club collection.)

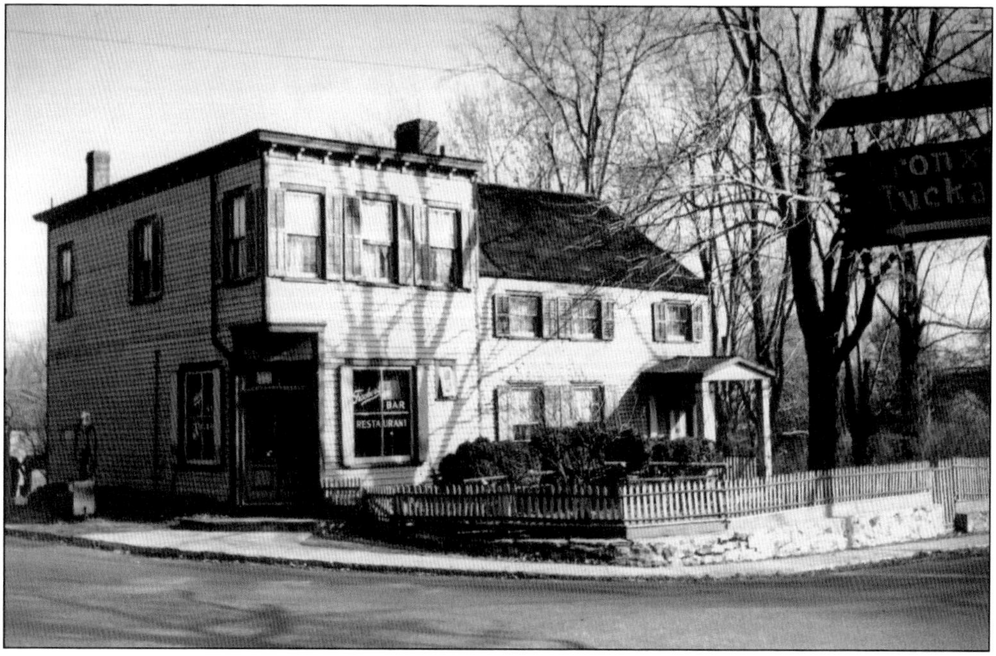

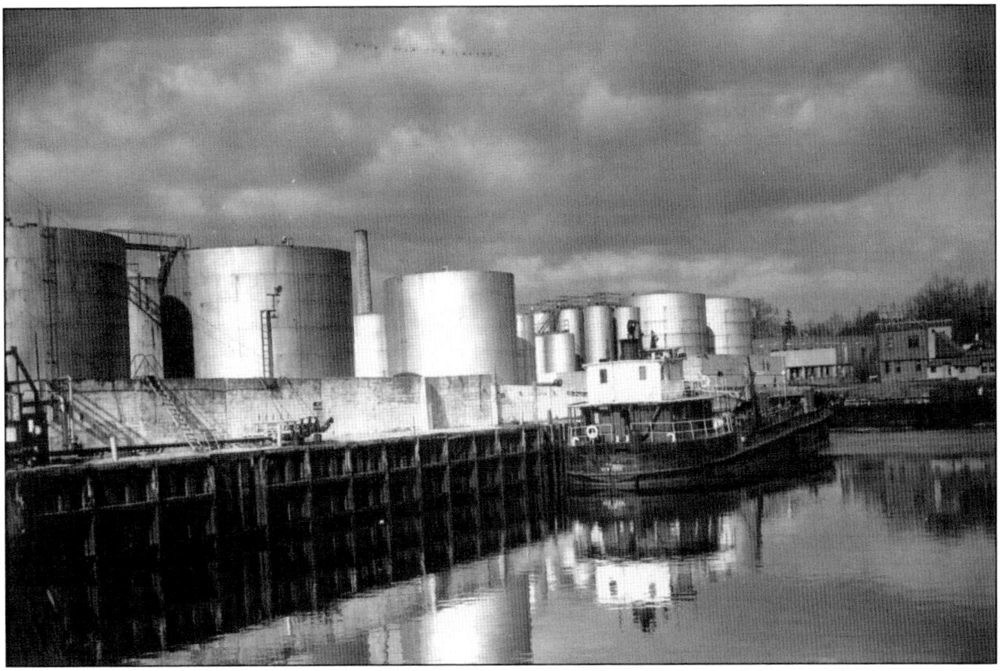

Many often forget that Mount Vernon is a port city with a town dock. As early as the 1850s, Eastchester Creek was considered a site for industrial development. When oil became the home heating and automobile fuel of choice, plans were developed to widen and dredge the creek to make it a deepwater port to handle barges loaded with oil. By the 1930s, "Oil City" was supplying fuel to most of the county and much of the Northeast. Just as most of the industries along Eastchester Creek have closed, for the past 40 years Oil City has also been in steady decline.

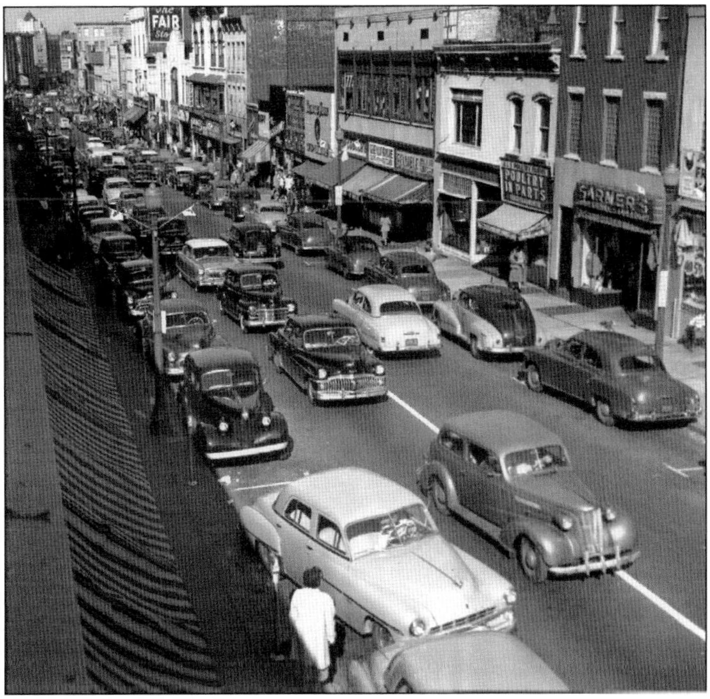

Today it is difficult to imagine Fourth Avenue as a two-way street. This view is looking north toward Gramatan Avenue from a roof on South Fourth Avenue between First and Second Streets. This image is from 1953.

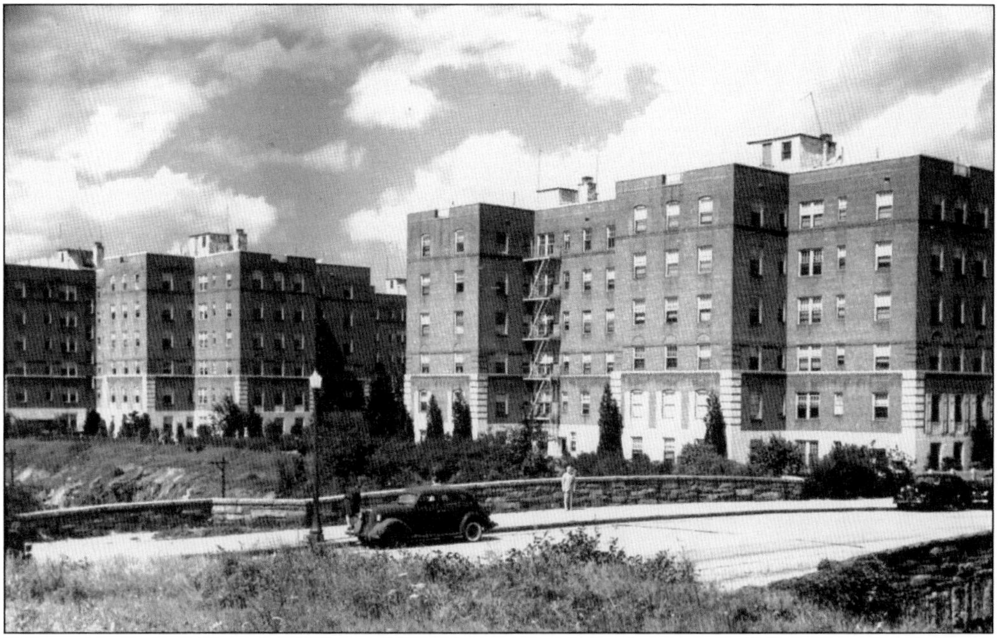

In the 1920s and 1930s, Mount Vernon began to build apartment buildings for its growing middle class. The construction of the Bronx River Parkway, the nation's first roadway exclusively for automobiles, encouraged developers to build apartments near the emerging parkway system. The apartments above were built on the site of the former New York Christian Home for Intemperate Men located west of Gramatan Avenue opposite Birch Street. This image is from 1947.

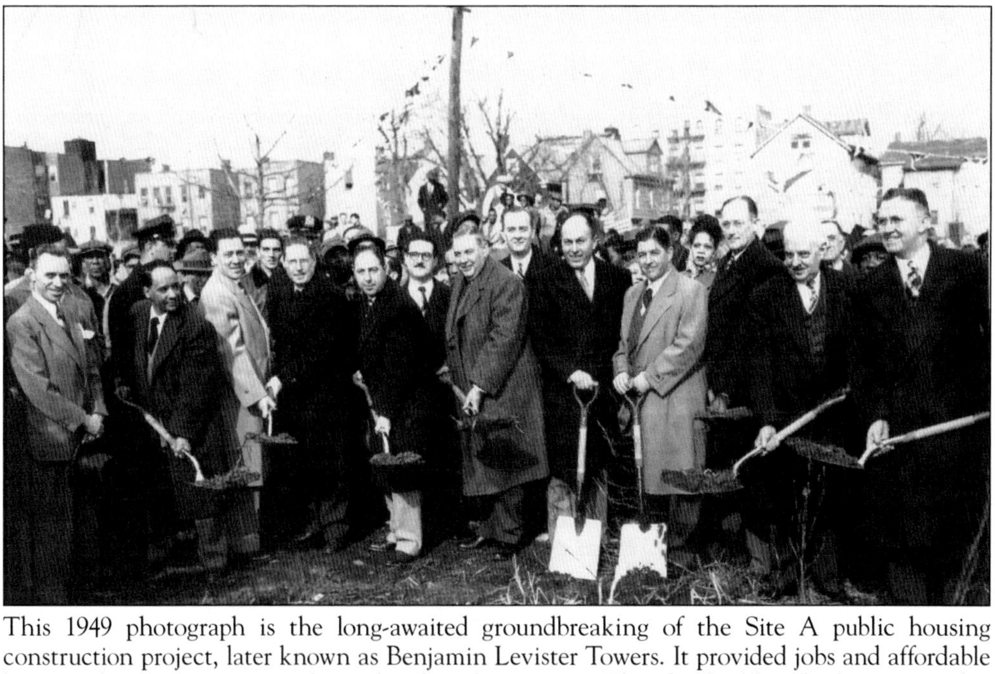

This 1949 photograph is the long-awaited groundbreaking of the Site A public housing construction project, later known as Benjamin Levister Towers. It provided jobs and affordable housing for war veterans and people of modest means. This five-building high-rise complex changed the city. Mayor William Hussey is in the center and to the far left, with the shovel, is the late Dr. William Randolph of the housing authority.

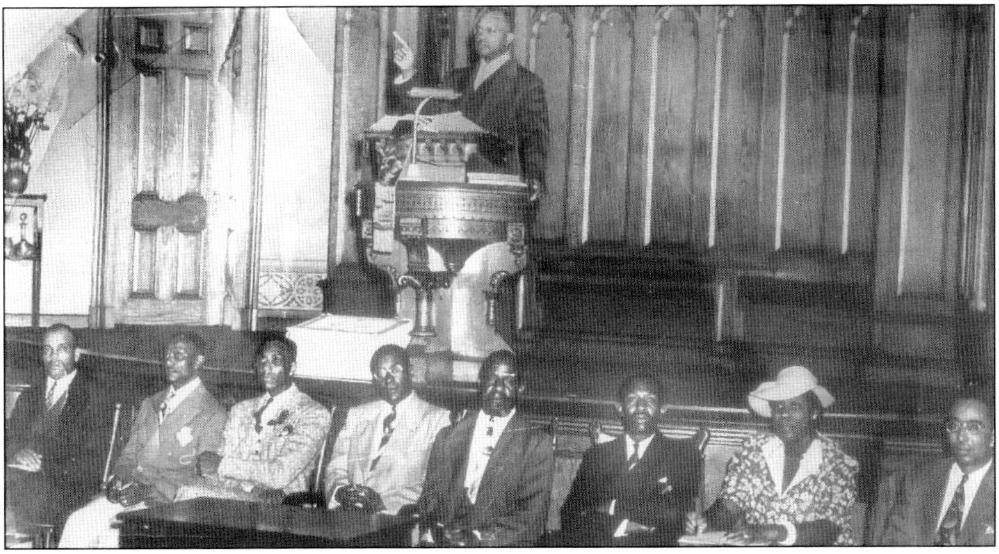

The picture above is the interior of Grace Baptist Church in the 1940s. The woman in the hat and flowered dress is Eleanor Thomas, an influential woman and political operative in the Republican Party. She and these other gentlemen were coparishioners with Benjamin Levister, the father of the public housing movement in Mount Vernon. Levister was a Depression-era community organizer and led the struggle to desegregate elite restaurants and integrate Westchester County beaches. Outraged by city slum conditions, his Housing Advisory Committee organized an interracial movement, lobbied, and held rallies until the city established the Mount Vernon Housing Authority and built low-income housing. He died before the completion of the construction. In the image below, Julia Levister, his wife, reads the commemorative plate for the Site A housing project. The complex, consisting of five 10-story buildings, was named in honor of Benjamin Levister. On the far right is Mayor Joseph P. Vaccarella. This photograph was taken 1954.

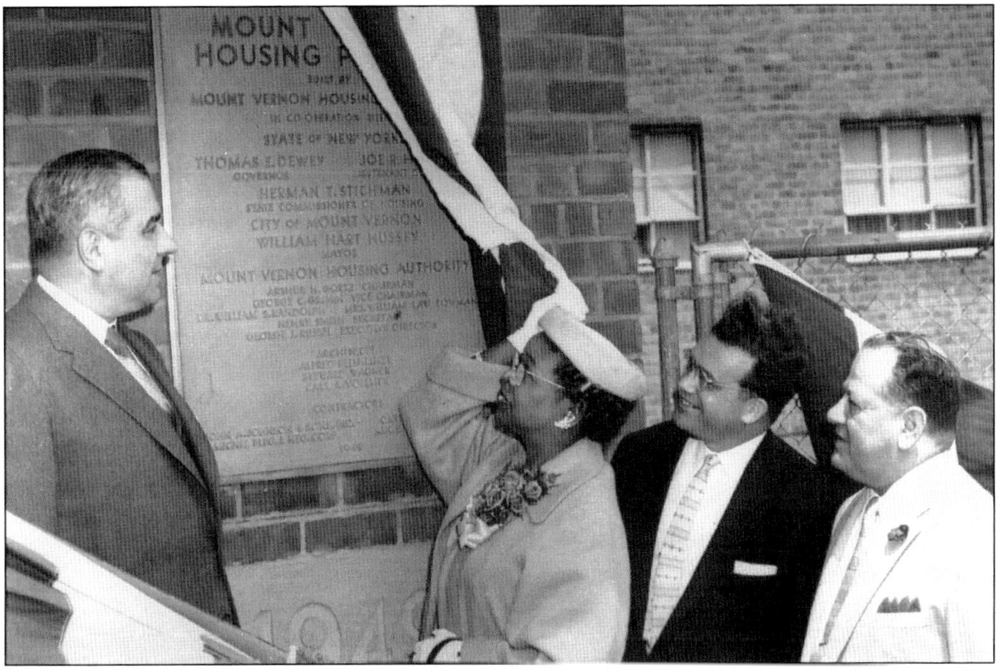

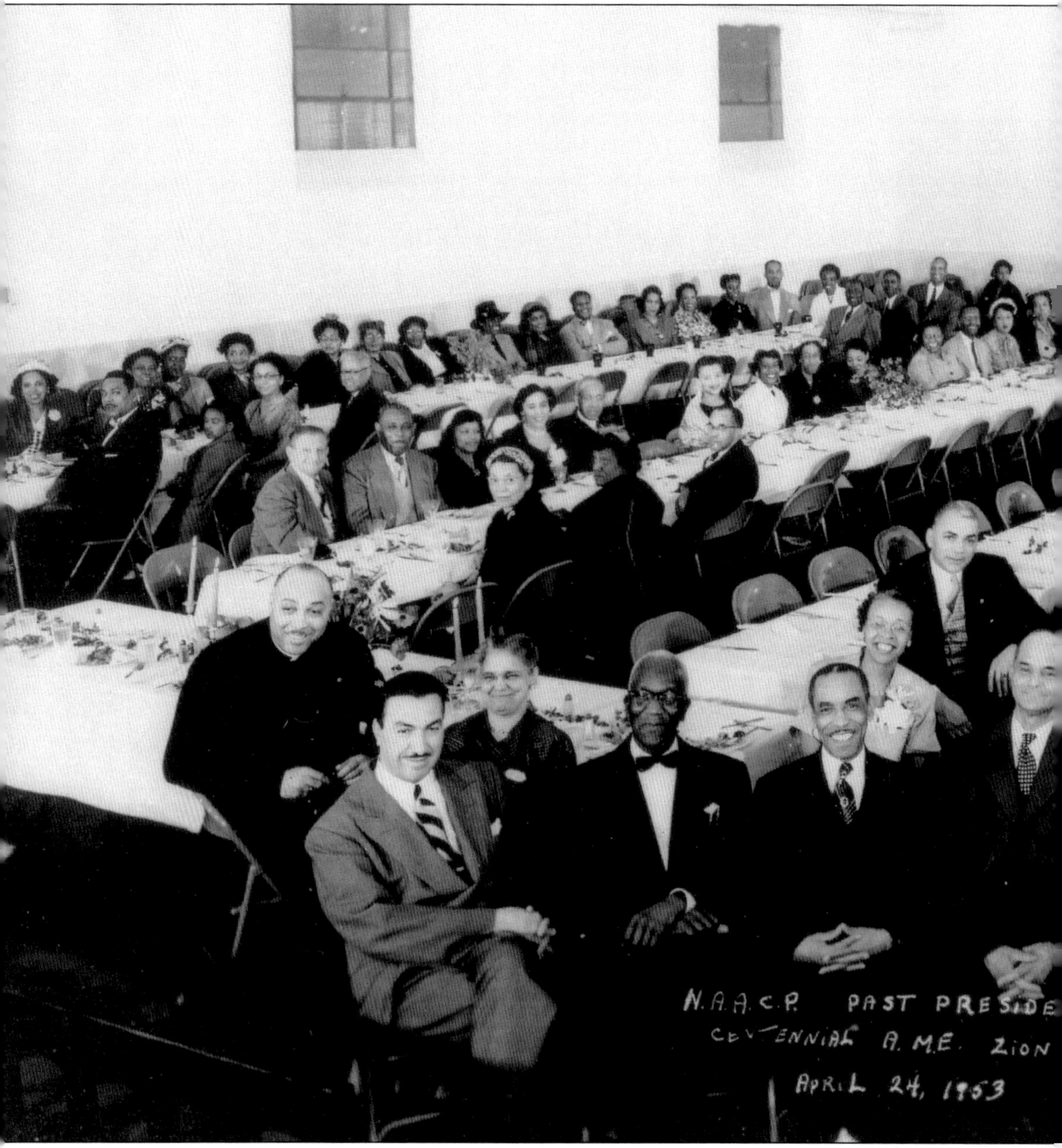

By the early 1950s, African Americans were preparing for a direct confrontation with segregation. The past was changing, and racial barriers were being broken each year. A driving force in the movement for integration was the NAACP. The photograph above is of the Past Presidents Banquet of the Mount Vernon NAACP held on April 24, 1953, at the newly constructed Greater Centennial African Methodist Episcopal Zion Church. Among those in the front row are Pastor

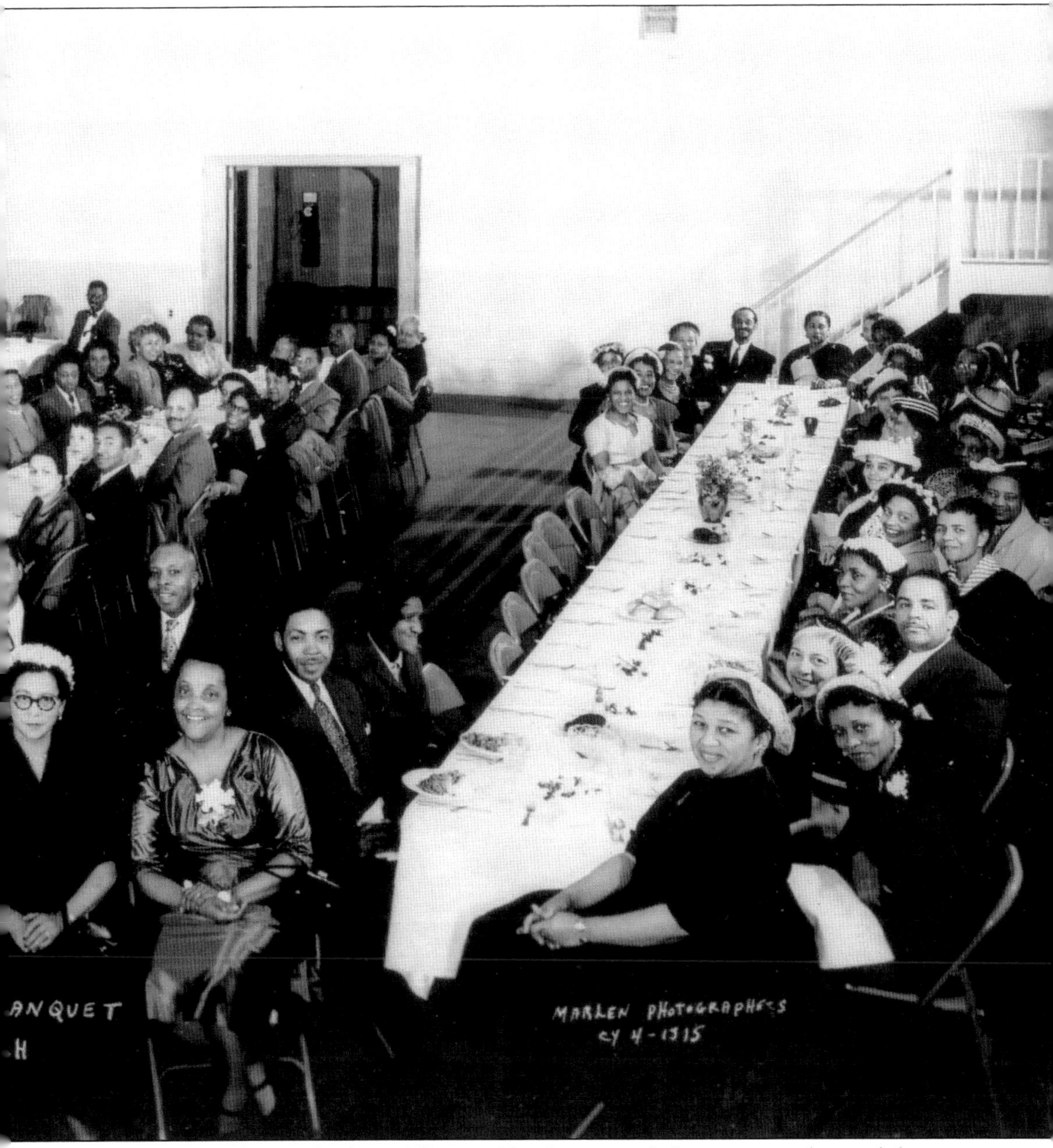

Clinton Wilcox, Thomas Bridges, Allierson Henderson, and the guest speaker and former city resident Harlem congressman Rev. Adam Clayton Powell. Greater Centennial African Methodist Episcopal Zion Church is located at the corner of Eighth Avenue and Fourth Street. Wilcox came to Mount Vernon from Montgomery, Alabama. During the 1954 Montgomery Bus Boycott, he actively supported the integration movement.

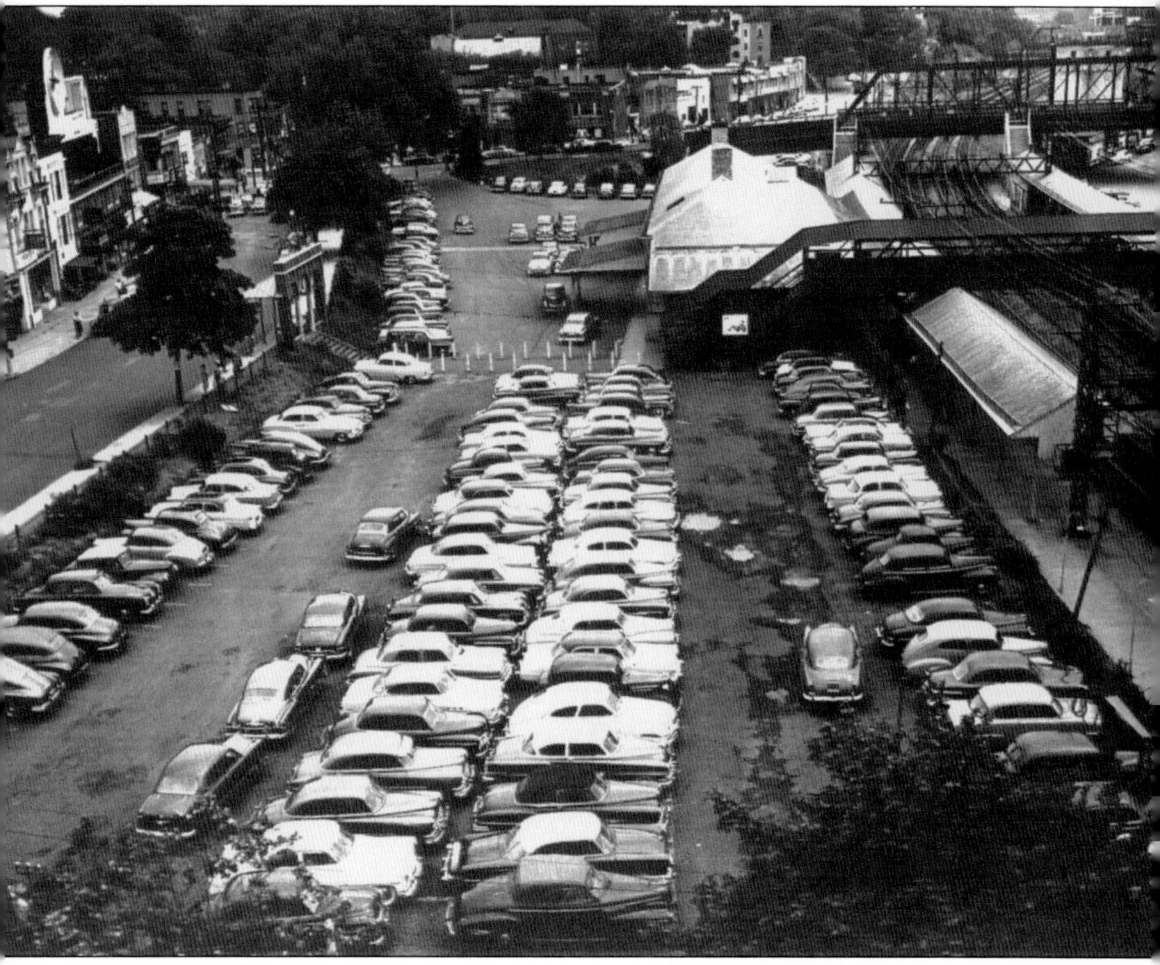

By the mid-20th century, the same forces that initiated the founding of the city 100 years earlier were at work shaping its future. Mount Vernon's proximity to New York City and the post–World War II steady influx of new residents seeking affordable suburban home ownership led to the city becoming one of the most densely populated cities in the nation. Available rail transportation and expanded parkway construction remained deciding factors to purchase or rent in the city. This view of Mount Vernon East shows the growing phenomenon of park and ride. Grand Central Station was only 22 minutes away.

Four

A Changing Community, a New Direction 1954–2008

By 1953, the population was nearly 75,000, the second largest in Westchester County, making Mount Vernon one of the nation's most densely populated cities. Most descendants of founding families moved and abandoned ancestral houses, shops, and churches. They left a void as well as new opportunities. The city hosted Centurama, its centennial celebration. The highlight was the dramatic political success of Italian Americans. Through efforts of the Italian Civic Association (1917), doors were opened to education and the middle class. Eileen Petrillo, the Centennial Queen, was a proud descendant of an enterprising 1890s family. Joseph P. Vaccarella was mayor, Joseph Reitano was president of the common council, Frank Nardozzi had served with distinction on the school board, and P. Raymond Sirignano was a judge. Subsequent Italian Americans became mayors, council persons, school officials, and civic leaders.

The second half of the century witnessed the emergence of African American, Portuguese, and Hispanic American communities. New professionals and working people with middle-class aspirations purchased the older but substantial south- and east-side houses. African American churches and advocacy groups measured racial progress by a series of firsts such as Cecil H. Parker (teacher), Nasby Wynn (policeman), Edward Williams (fireman), Harold Wood (county board of supervisors), Dr. William Randolph (city council), Dr. Clarence Pair (Mount Vernon Hospital), Harold Hamilton (corporation counsel), Dr. Alfred Brandon (police surgeon), Allierson Henderson (school board), Dr. Clinton I. Young Sr. (school principal), Geraldine Hedgewood (teachers' union), and Clinton I. Young Jr. (school board president).

During the 1970s, people from the Caribbean came, and the city was soon a majority of minorities. On January 25, 1984, Ronald Blackwood became the first elected African American mayor in Mount Vernon and New York State. He was the ideal politician to try to heal a divided city. He was from Jamaica and a former Republican in a Democratic city. Today African Americans control the public schools, city government, and county and state political offices. Mayors Ernest Davis and Clinton I. Young Jr. are both African Americans, and the school board and superintendent of schools are predominately African American.

In the past 156 years, Mount Vernon held open arms to successive ethnic groups pursuing the American dream. In time, they fully participated in shaping the city. John Stevens's goal of home ownership continues. There are new waves of first-time buyers looking for affordable Mount Vernon houses. They know that the quantity and quality of Mount Vernon homes cannot be matched anywhere within 22 minutes of Grand Central Station.

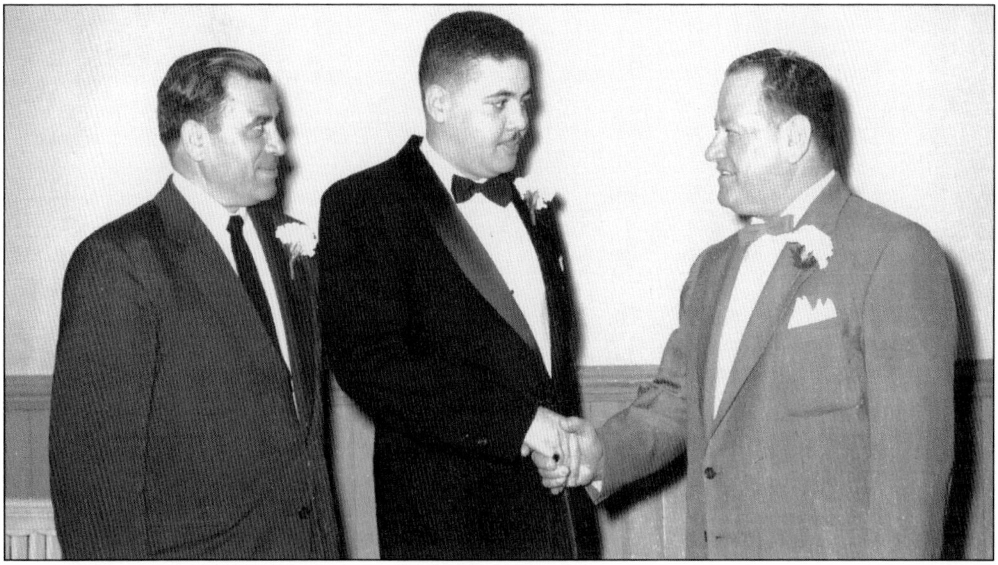

Mount Vernon residents were supportive of the emerging civil rights movement and made local efforts at what was called interracial cooperation. From left to right are city judge P. Raymond Sirignano, Pastor Shelton Doles of the Grace Baptist Church, and Mayor Joseph P. Vaccarella. This image is from June 12, 1954.

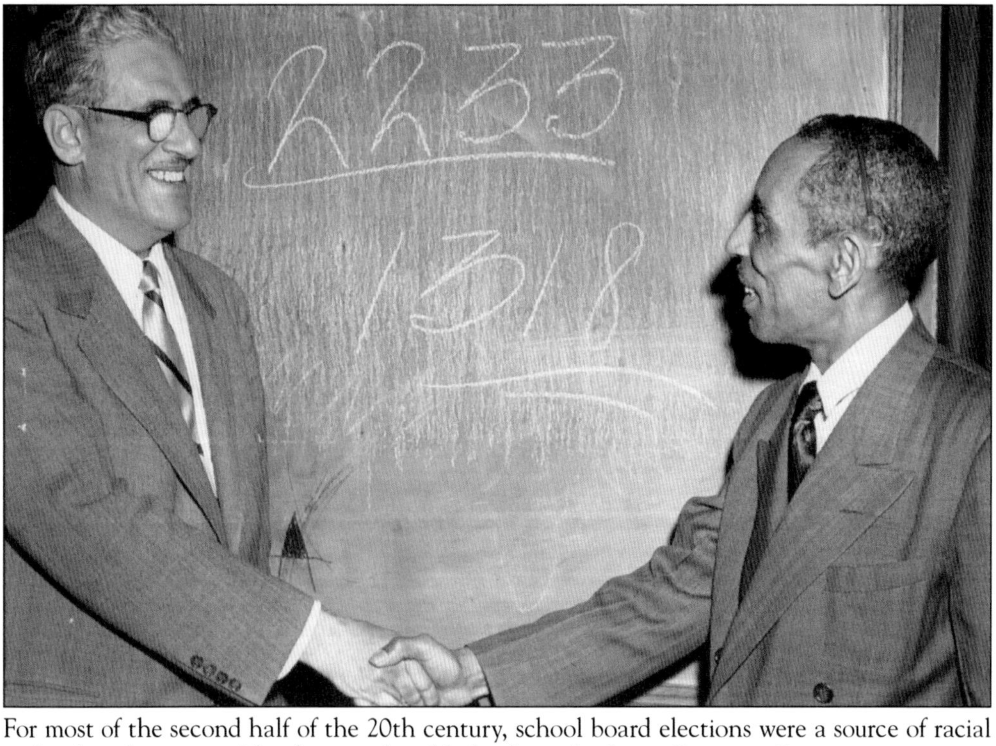

For most of the second half of the 20th century, school board elections were a source of racial and political tension. This historic handshake from Anthony Scarpino Sr. represents a new day and congratulations to Allierson Henderson, the first African American elected to the Mount Vernon School Board. This image is from May 4, 1954. Henderson died in office on September 4, 1954.

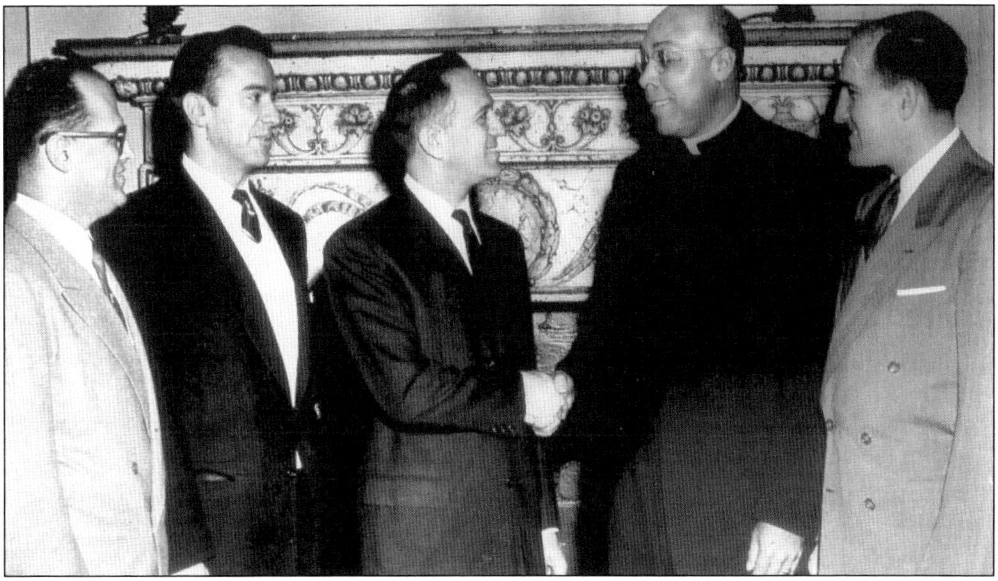

Rev. Clinton Wilcox of Greater Centennial African Methodist Episcopal Zion Church was a leading proponent of interracial cooperation. Under his leadership, the southern and city struggles for integration and equal opportunity were important to his church ministry.

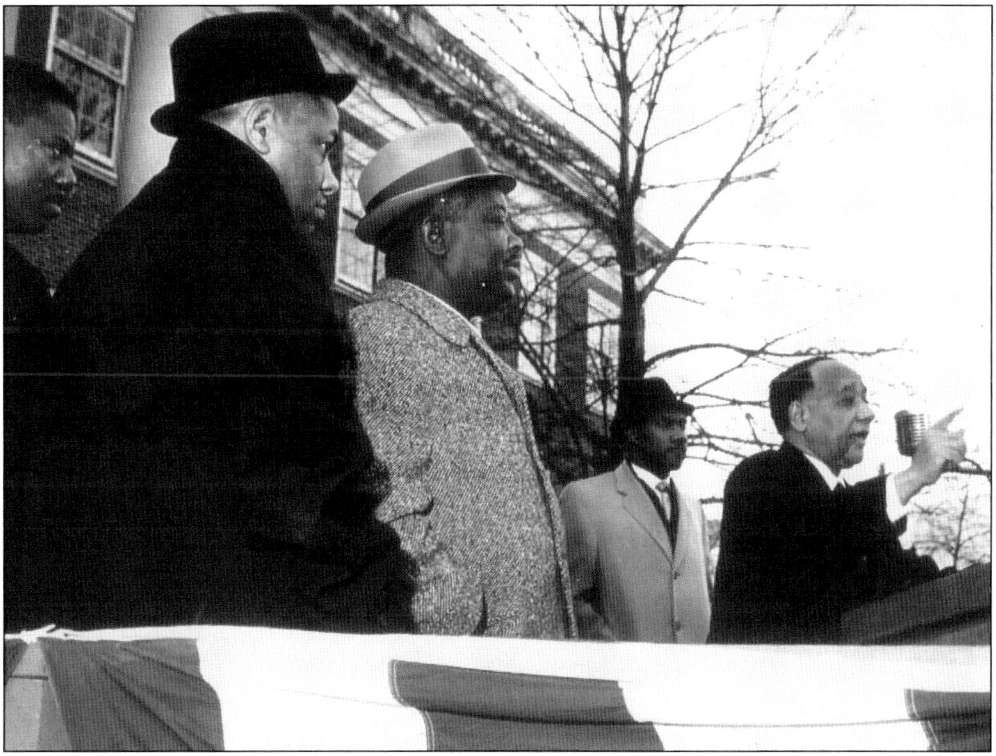

Seen here is Dr. William Randolph speaking at a protest rally in front of city hall as, from left to right, Lloyd King of the NAACP; Rev. Richard Dixon, pastor of Macedonia Baptist Church; Benjamin Anderson, journalist and publisher of the *Westchester Observer*; and Rev. Samuel Austin, pastor of Grace Baptist Church watch. This photograph was taken in 1966.

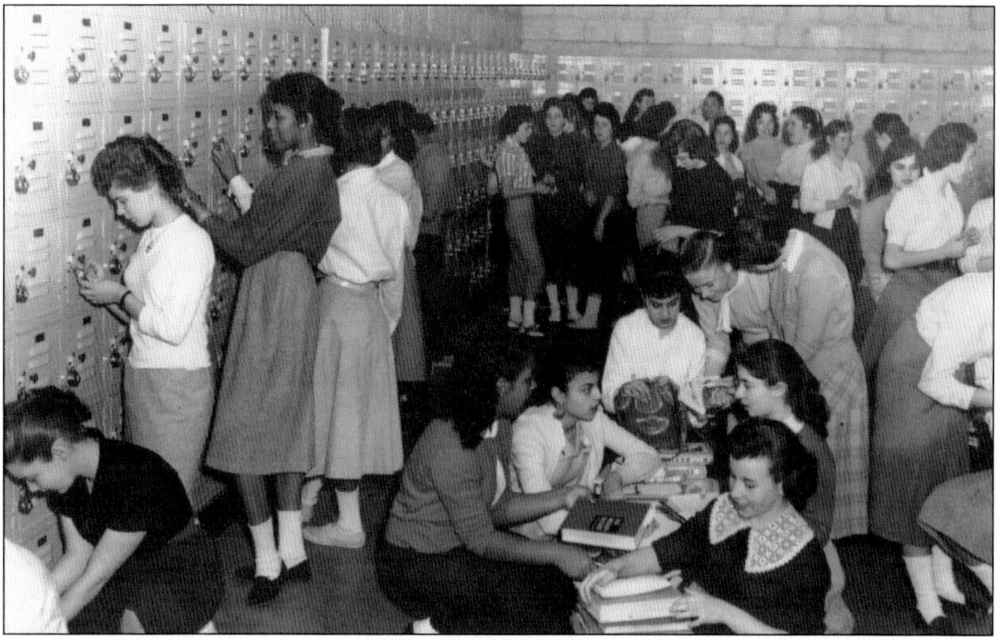

This photograph was used as evidence of the need for a new comprehensive high school, combining the academic and vocational and technical curricula of both Edison and A. B. Davis High Schools. This overcrowded hall at A. B. Davis High School was photographed to support the arguments for a new high school. The long skirts and bobby socks are quite a contrast to students today. This photograph was taken in 1954.

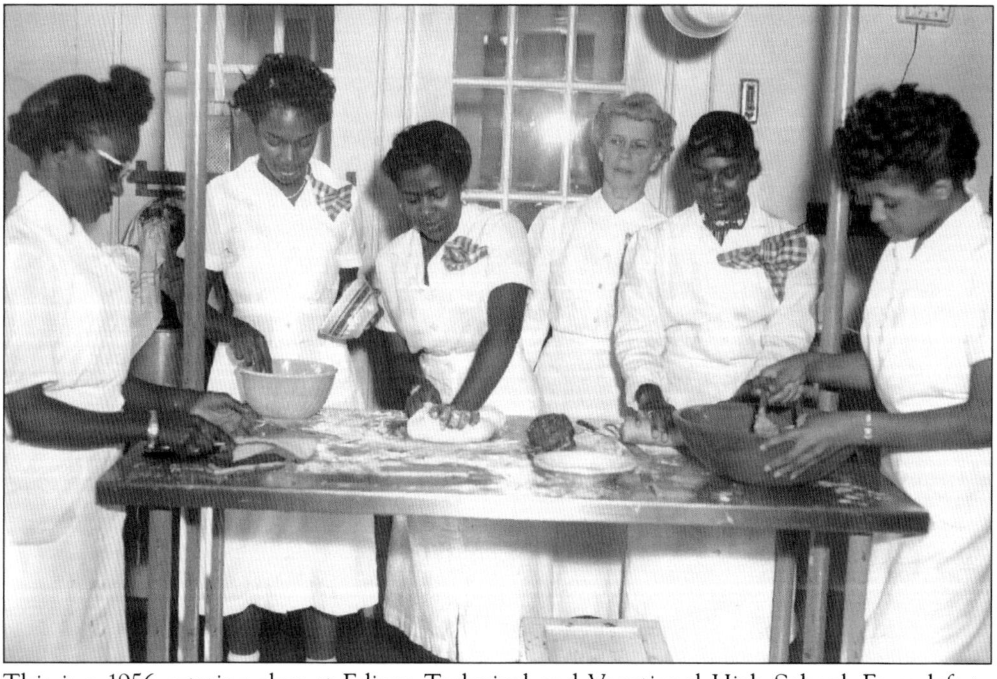

This is a 1956 catering class at Edison Technical and Vocational High School. From left to right are Leola Gaines, Barbara Saunders, Ruth Middleton, Julius Kuhnert, Yvonne Bunch, and Helen McLauglin.

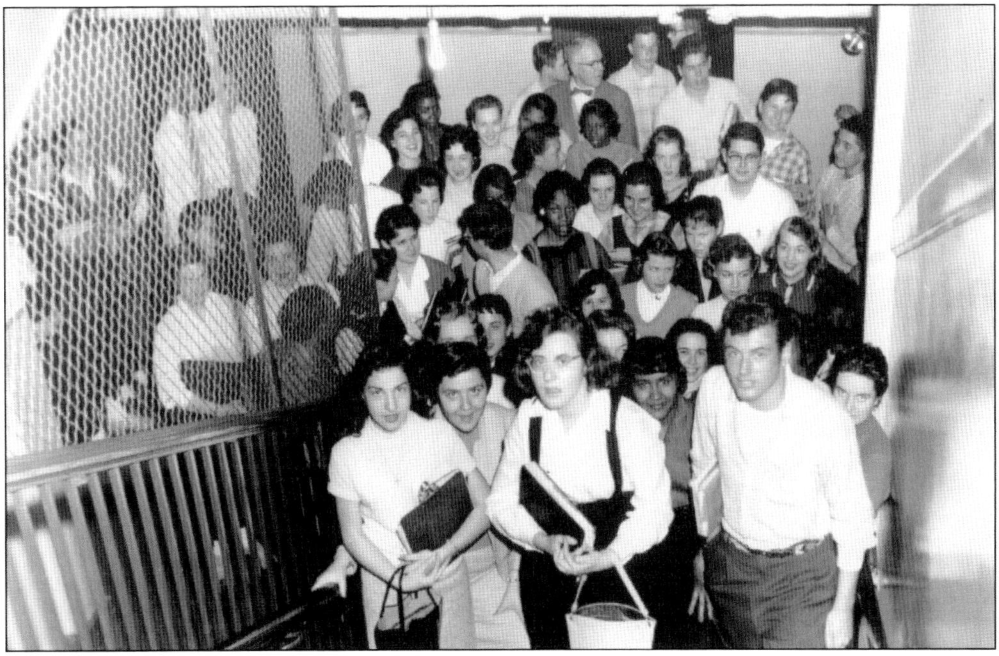

The 1954 photograph above was taken of a crowded Edison Technical and Vocational High School stairwell to show conditions in favor of building a new high school. The modern air-conditioned, state-of-the-art Mount Vernon High School was built and completed on California Road in 1963.

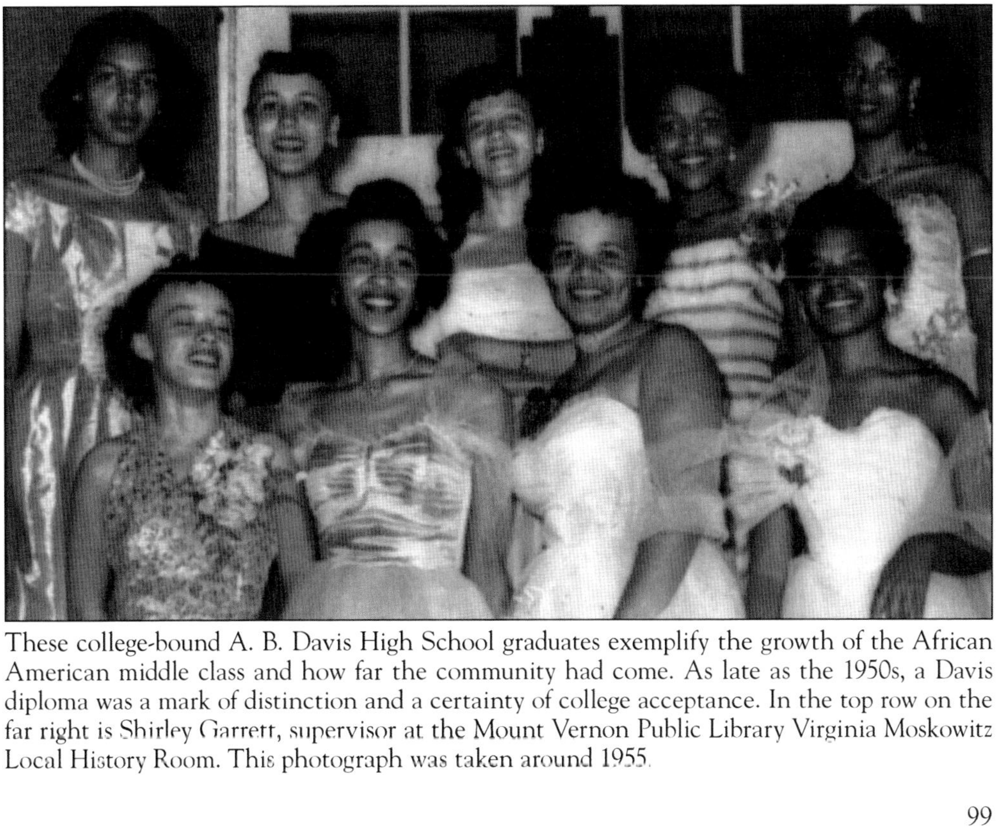

These college-bound A. B. Davis High School graduates exemplify the growth of the African American middle class and how far the community had come. As late as the 1950s, a Davis diploma was a mark of distinction and a certainty of college acceptance. In the top row on the far right is Shirley Garrett, supervisor at the Mount Vernon Public Library Virginia Moskowitz Local History Room. This photograph was taken around 1955.

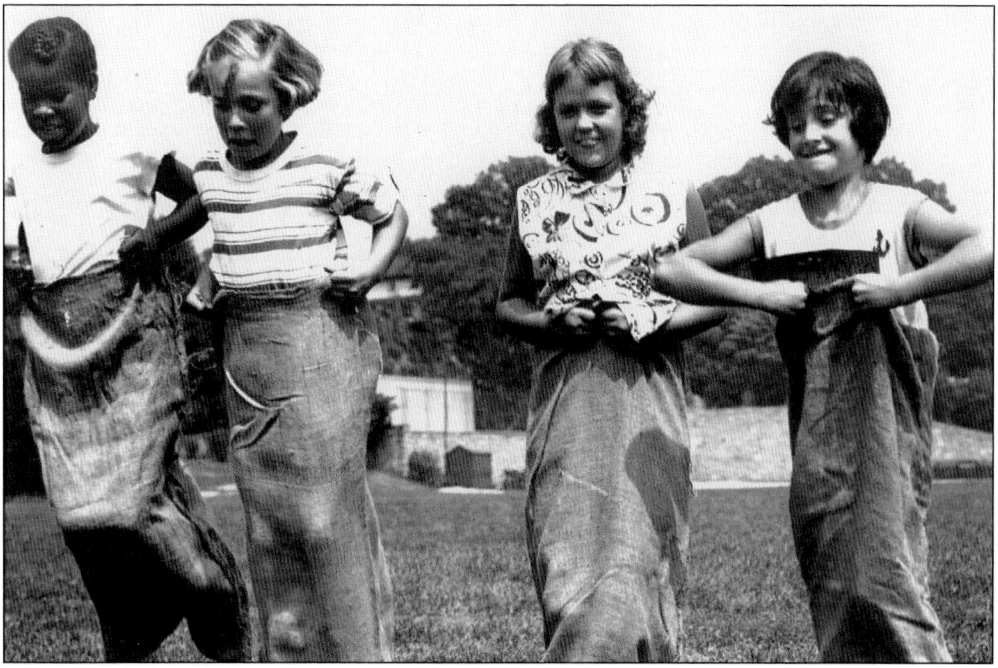

It did not take expensive equipment to keep children busy in the summer. Checkers, jacks, jump rope, dodgeball, and even an old-fashioned sack race (seen above) at Memorial Field was considered great fun. The photograph below is from a summer arts-and-crafts event at the Holmes School playground. Second from the left is Susan Finklestein.

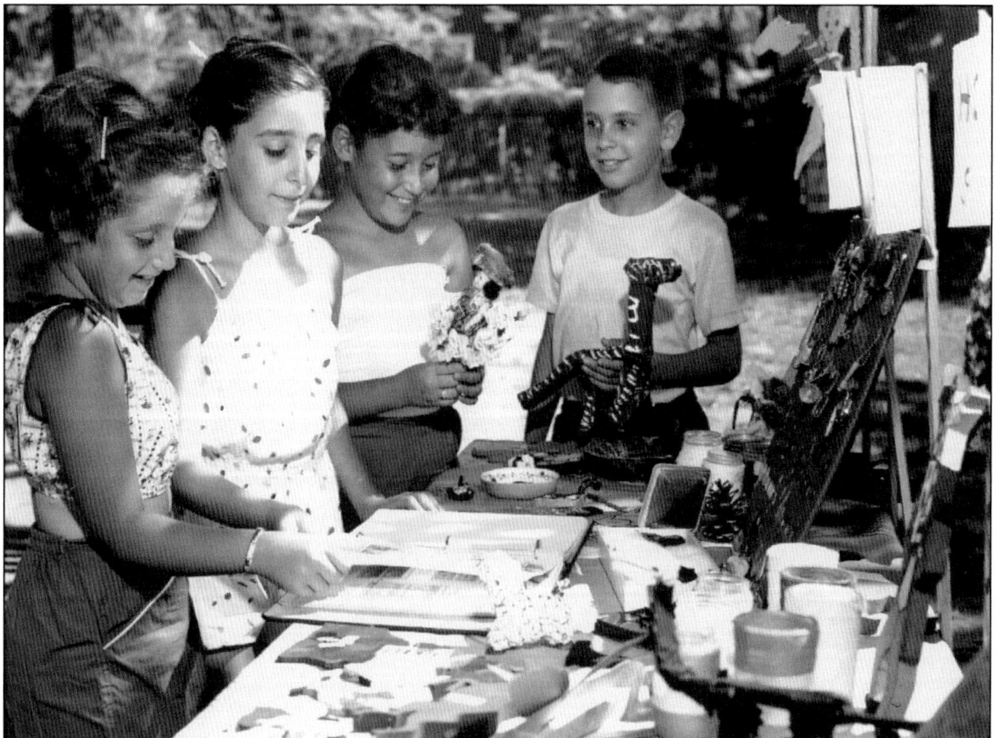

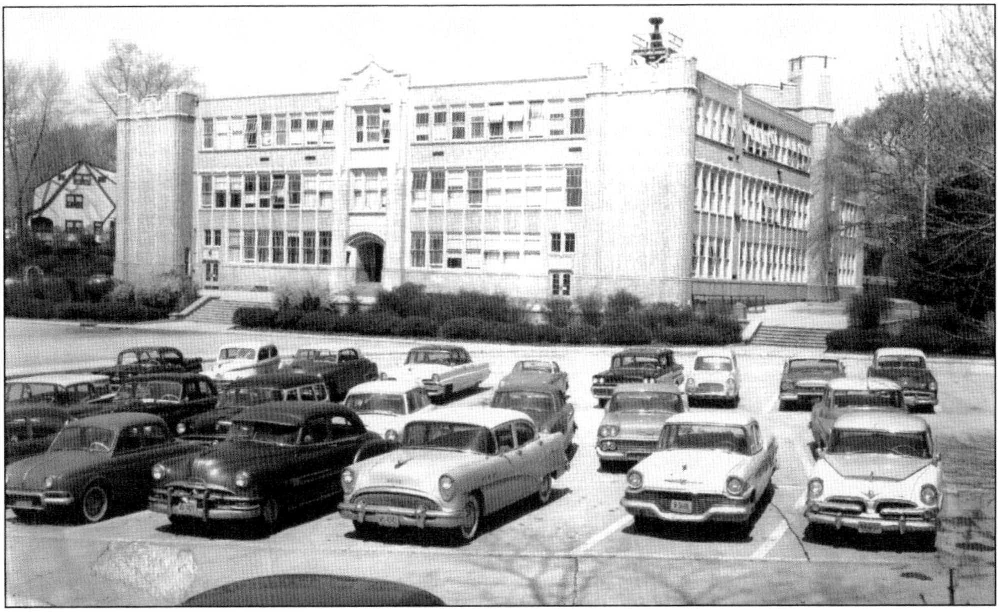

The photograph above is the William Wilson School. This building was torn down and replaced with the current Traphagen School. This image is from around 1959. At the center of citywide summer youth services were its school playground recreation programs. Many residents can still remember their summer "playground teachers." They were usually college students home for the summer. The photograph below shows the Traphagen School playground. This photograph was taken around 1958.

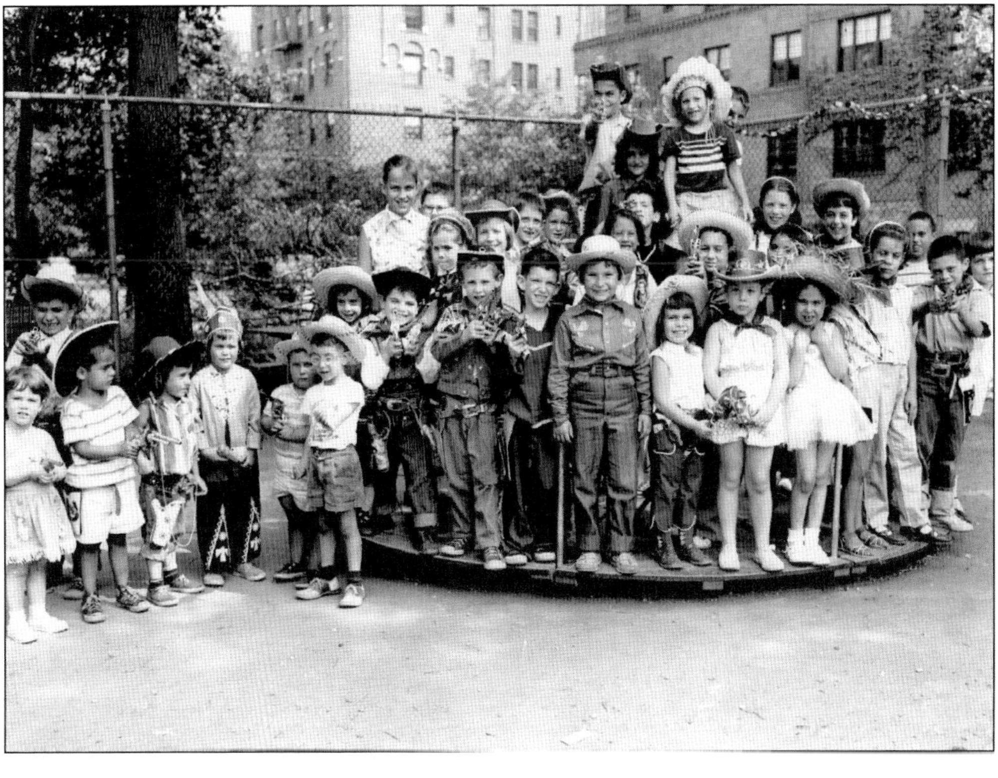

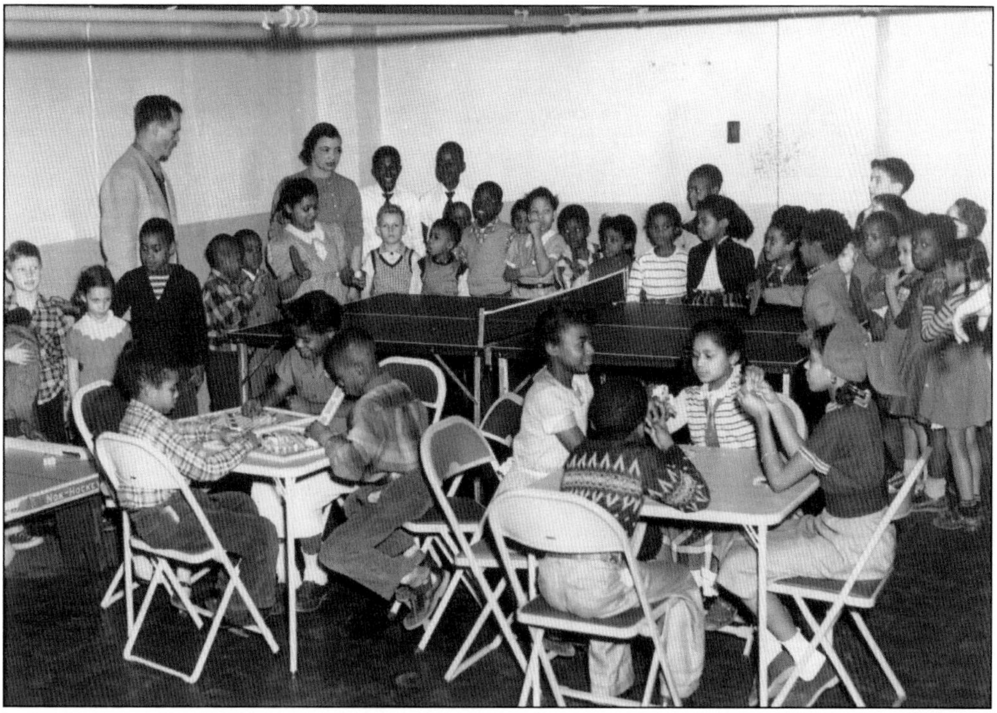

Dorothy Lee and Andy Karl are recreational leaders supervising the opening of the Site A (Benjamin Levister Towers) social room at 244 South Seventh Avenue. Jerry Sarno took this February 1, 1954, photograph.

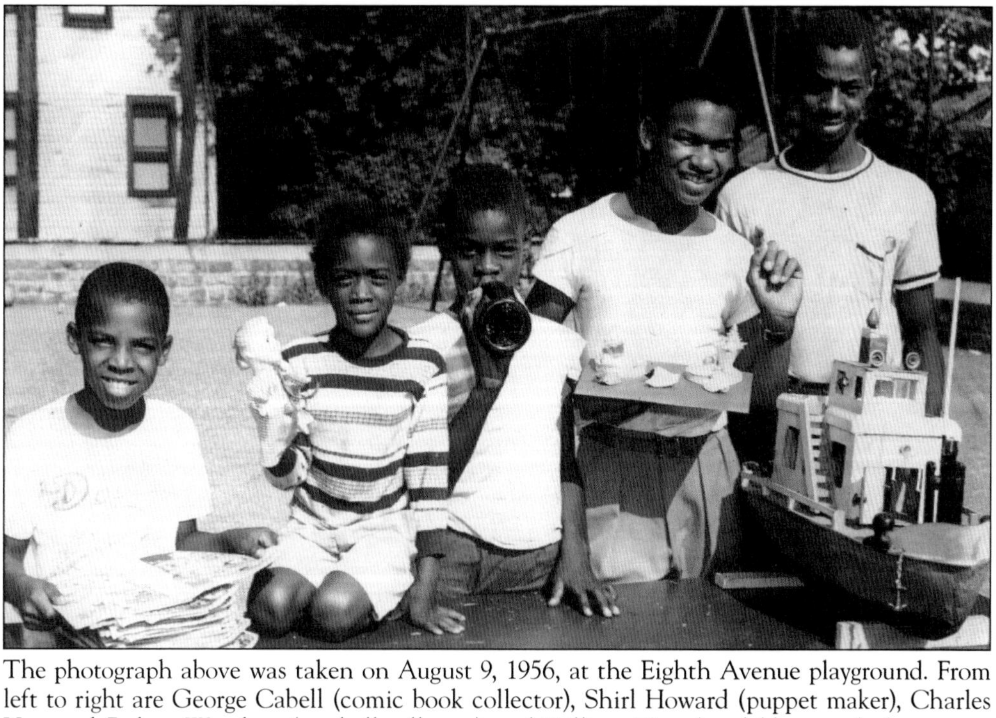

The photograph above was taken on August 9, 1956, at the Eighth Avenue playground. From left to right are George Cabell (comic book collector), Shirl Howard (puppet maker), Charles Hayward, Robert Woodson (seashell collector), and William West (model boat maker).

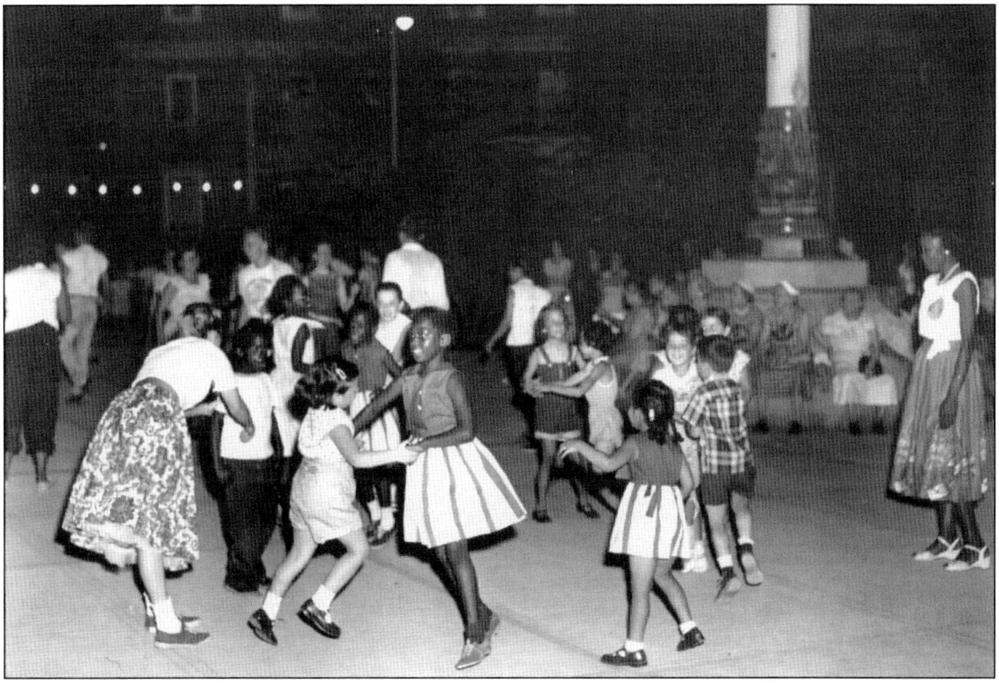

In the summers, city hall plaza became an open-air square dancing floor. On the far right is recreation department worker Mattie Smalls. The photograph is dated July 15, 1958.

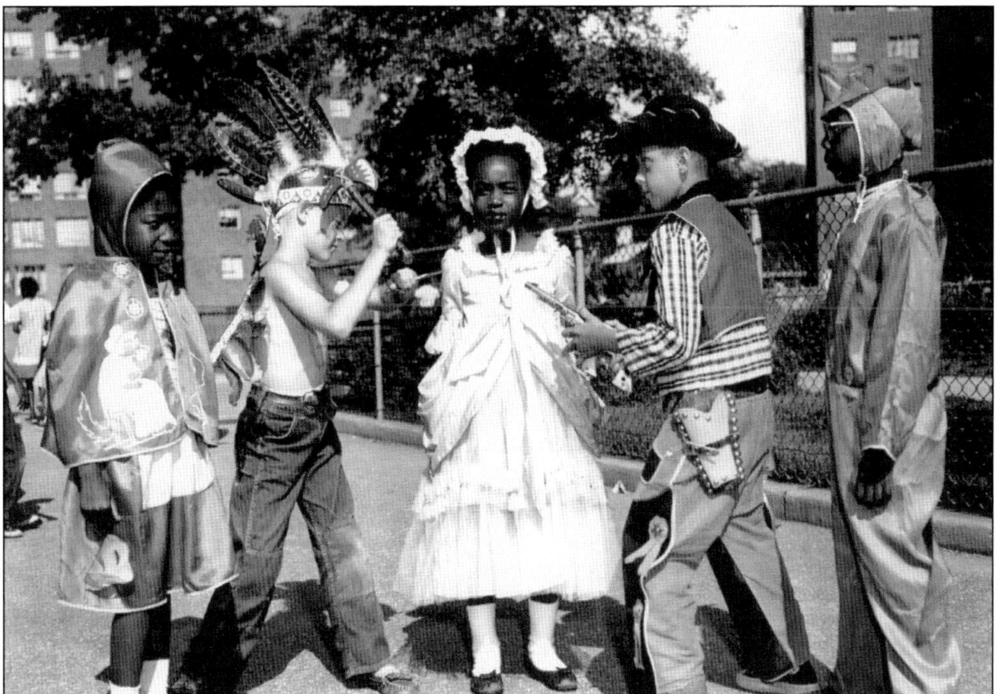

From left to right, Pamelia Gibbs, Kenneth Mcconnely, Patricia Grant, Larry Brown, and Frank Williamson participate in a vaudeville show at the Ninth Avenue (between Third and Fourth Streets) playground. Al Carlino took this August 2, 1956, photograph.

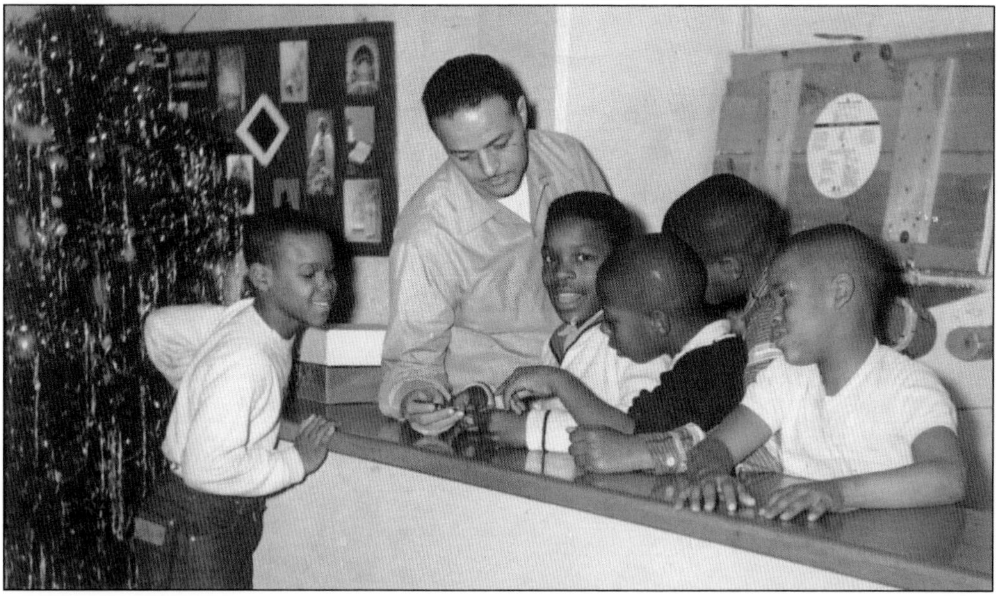

One of the features of the newly constructed Benjamin Levister Towers at 240 South Seventh Avenue was the youth services facility called the social room. Pictured above is Ruben Tyree, a recreation department worker, with children from the building. Tyree lived in the building on 241 South Ninth Avenue.

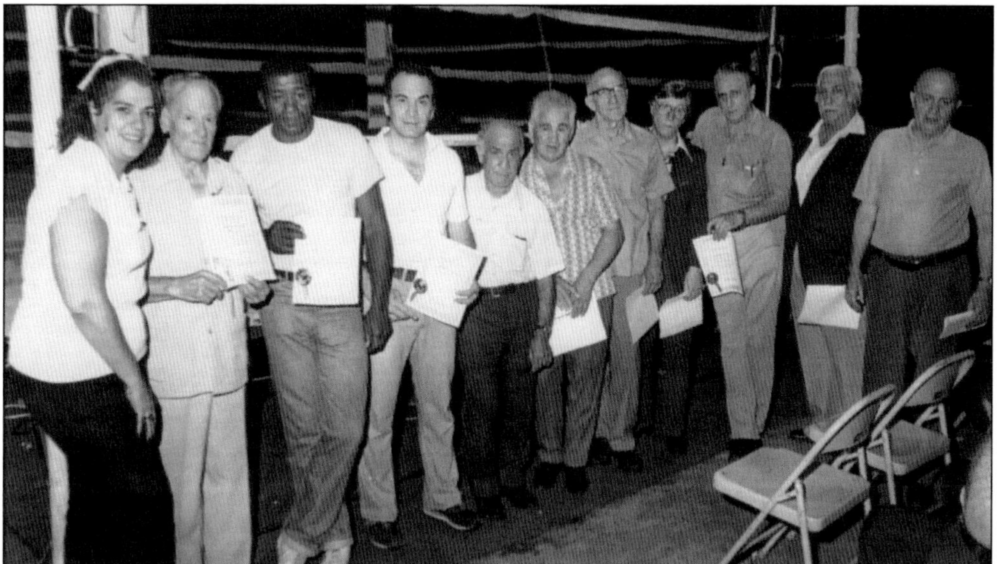

Heavyweight champion Floyd Patterson has always been considered a native son. Members of his family have lived out their lives here. He was an American two-time heavyweight boxing champion. At 21, Patterson became the youngest man to win the world heavyweight championship and then the first to regain it. He had a record of 55 wins, 8 losses, and 1 draw, with 40 wins by knockout. The city held a parade for him upon winning the championship from Ingemar Johansson of Sweden. Mayor Joseph P. Vaccarella was a former boxer and Patterson fan. Above are Barbara Manzo, assistant commissioner of recreation, and Patterson at the Mount Vernon Armory.

In 1958, Macedonia Baptist Church engaged Rev. Richard Dixon, a young clergyman from Pontiac, Michigan, to become its pastor. He came to Mount Vernon with new ideas and a fresh approach to serving a community. Dixon and his wife were able to bring the legendary Marian Anderson to perform in the city. This picture is of Ernestine Dixon (left) and Marian Anderson on February 26, 1960.

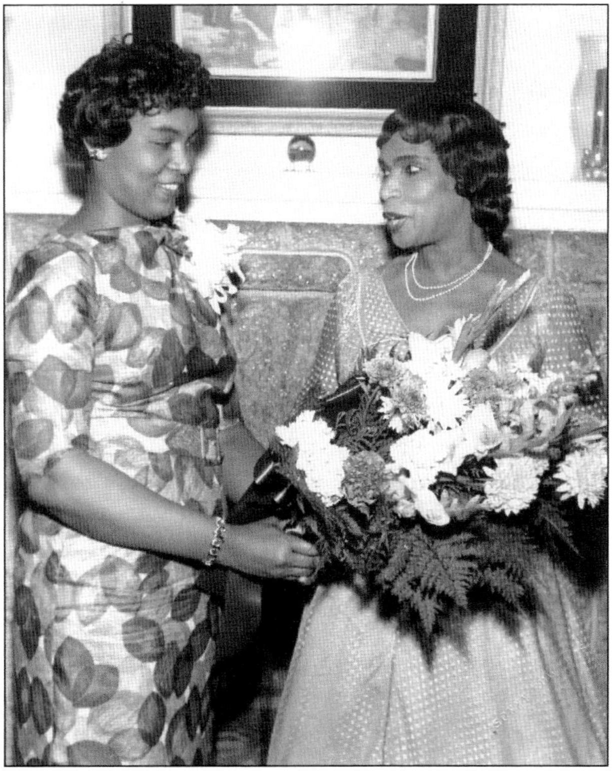

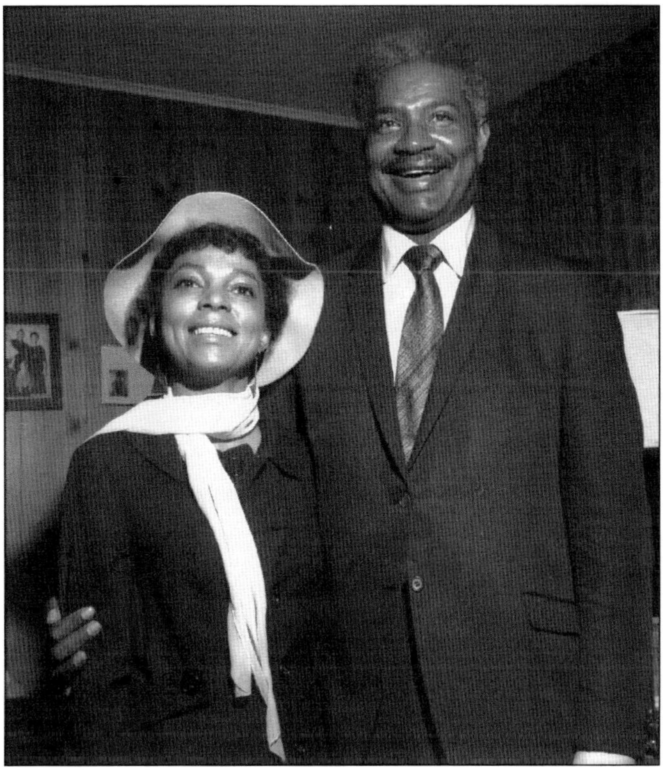

While acting in a Broadway production, Ossie Davis and Ruby Dee met in 1946. The couple was married in 1948. They went on as collaborators and individual stars in theater, television, film, and audio recordings and as authors. In the 1950s, they moved to Mount Vernon and were faithful members of Grace Baptist Church. They were close friends with both Martin Luther King Jr. and Malcolm X. In the image at left, they were photographed in Pastor Samuel Austin's church office. It is from around 1966. (Courtesy of the Rufus Merritt/Alif Archives.)

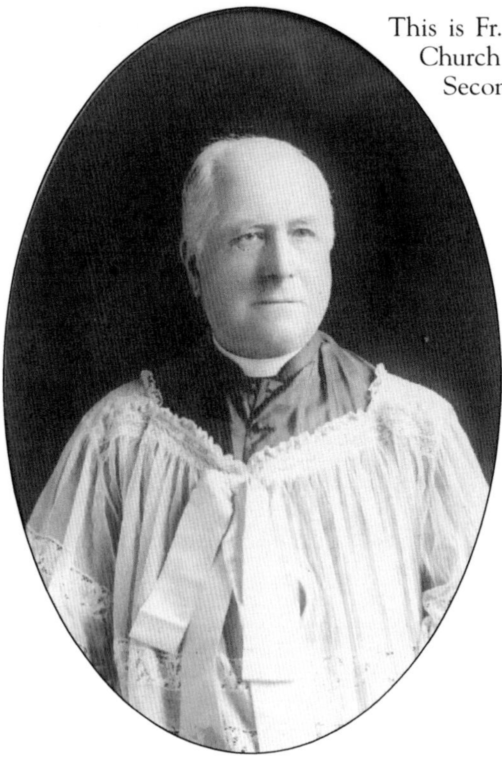

This is Fr. E. J. Flynn, priest of Sacred Heart Catholic Church at the southeast corner of Fifth Avenue and Second Street, founded in 1856.

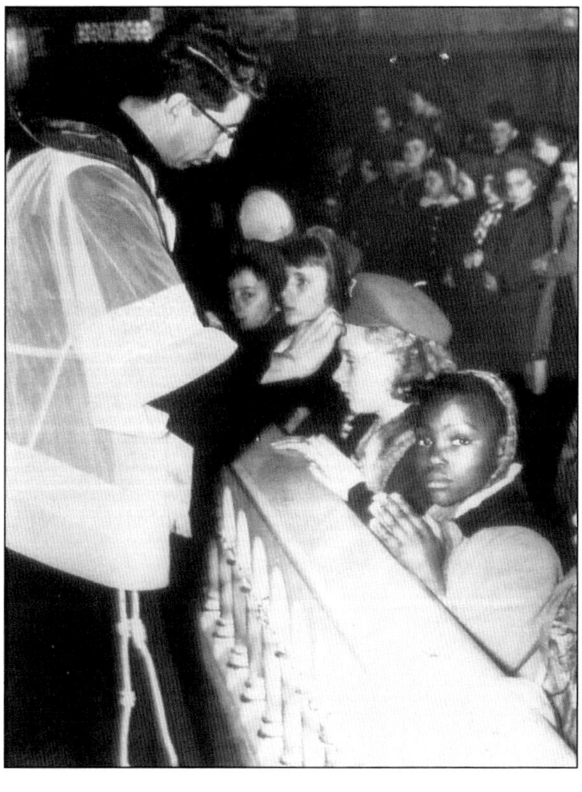

Seen here is Father Bernardi, dispensing ashes to schoolchildren at Our Lady of Mount Carmel Church located at First Street and Tenth Avenue. The image is from March 3, 1954.

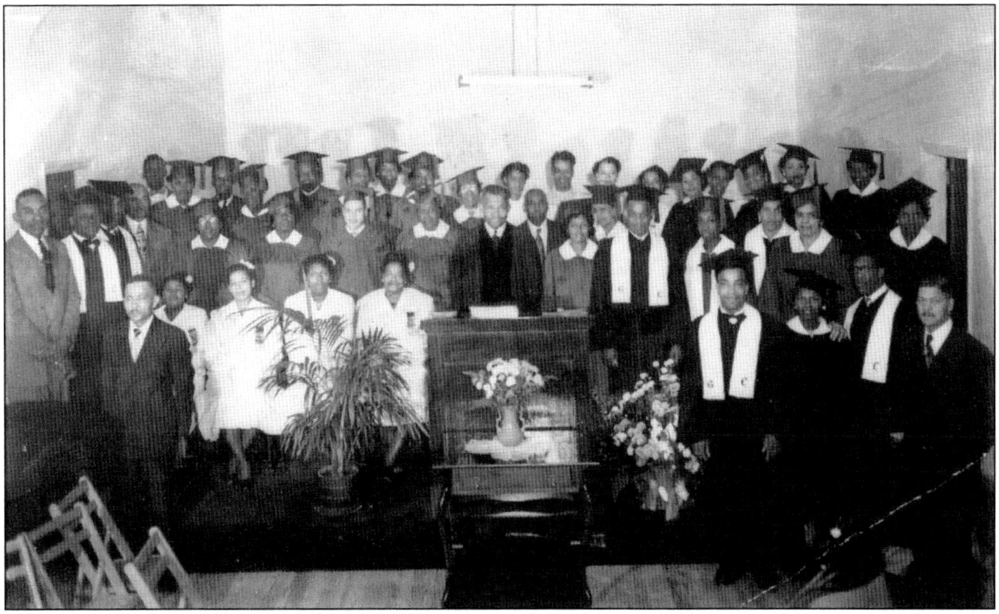

After World War II, many African Americans left their southern roots, came to the city, and joined the First Church of God in Christ (founded in 1929) at 410 South Ninth Avenue. Rev. Ernest W. Allen (standing at the pulpit) pastored the small Pentecostal church for 46 years. In 1950, a new church was built. Today the church is known as Allen Memorial Church of God in Christ Family Life Center on Crary Avenue, one of the largest church facilities in the city. This photograph is from 1953. (Courtesy of the Alif Archives.)

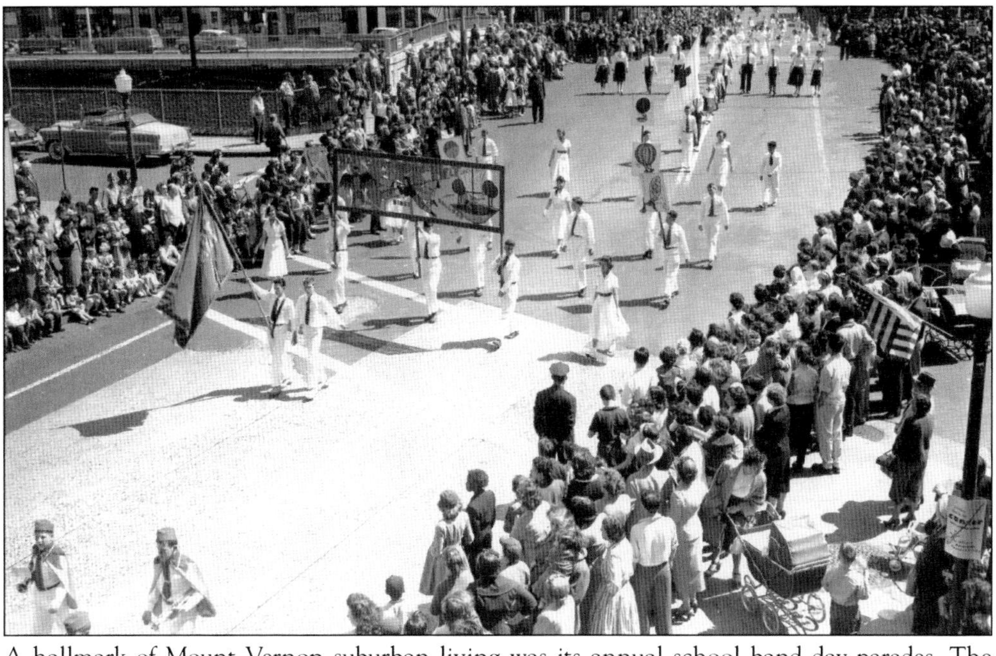

A hallmark of Mount Vernon suburban living was its annual school band day parades. The photograph above was taken from the Proctor's building looking south across the railroad tracks down South Fourth Avenue. It was not unusual to have 25,000 people along the parade route from Lincoln Avenue to Third Street. This photograph is from the 1960s.

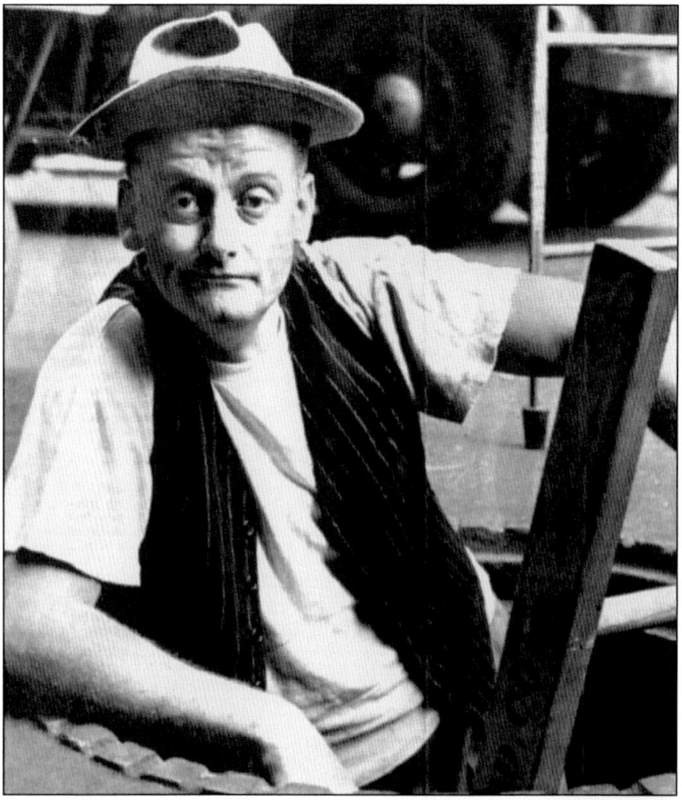

Arthur William Matthew Carney, also known as Art Carney, was a 1937 graduate of A. B. Davis High School. He is best known for his five Emmy Awards for his television role as Norton, Jackie Gleason's sidekick in *The Honeymooners.* He also won a Golden Globe and an Academy Award for best actor in the 1974 motion picture *Tonto.* He grew up on Rich Avenue along with another Academy Award winner and movie mogul, Arthur B. Krim, chairman of United Artists Corporation and founder and chairman of Orion Pictures.

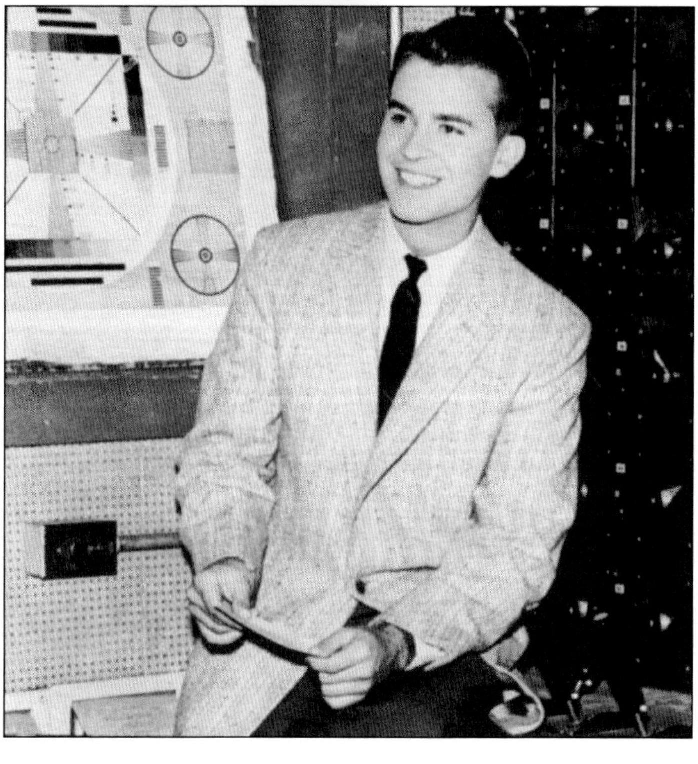

Dick Clark, "America's Oldest Teenager," was born and raised in Mount Vernon. He spent 18 years of his life at 2 Park Lane, apartment 2D. He said that he had an "ideal and terrific childhood." He is a 1947 graduate of A. B. Davis High School. His show *American Bandstand* influenced generations of Americans.

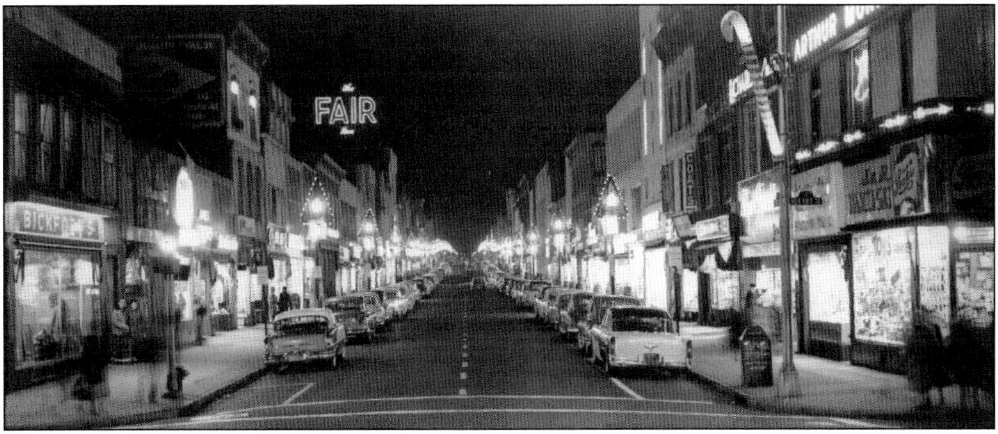

For Mount Vernon residents Fourth Avenue is known as "the Avenue." This 1961 view is from First Street looking south toward Second and Third Streets. This is the heart of the city. From its 1853 village origins, it was not only the residential but also the commercial center of the community. In the upper far right corner there is a neon sign for Arthur Murray's Dance Studio. *American Bandstand*'s Dick Clark had fond memories of taking lessons there. These two 1960s photographs of the Avenue remind residents of many magical shopping days.

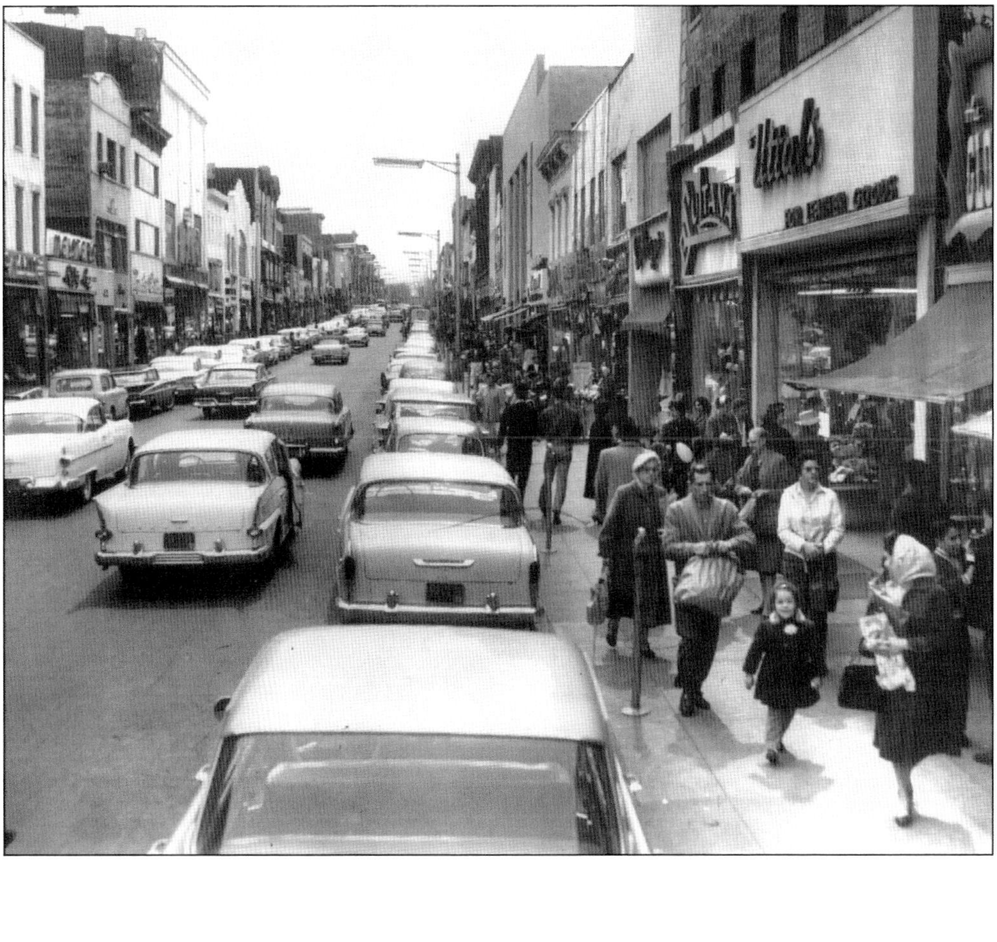

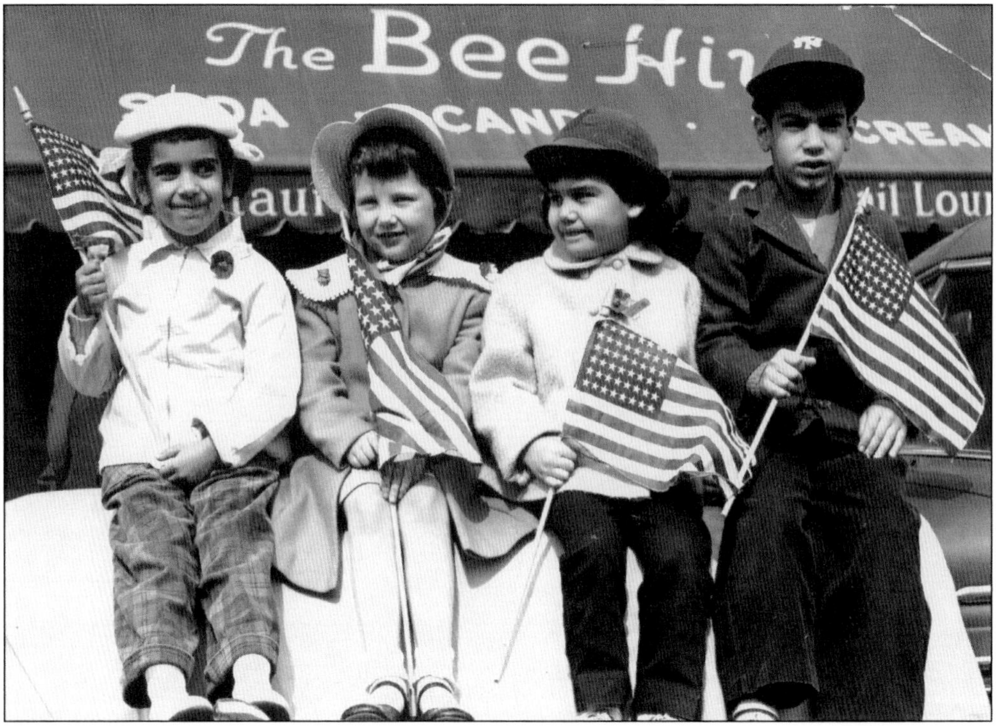

A prime seat at this May 30, 1956, parade was in front of the Bee Hive restaurant. These lucky youngsters are, from left to right, Kathy Praino, Margie Walsh, and Barbara and Philip Praino. The photograph below is a back-to-school carnival sponsored by the Mount Vernon Chamber of Commerce. In the background is the memorable Bee Hive restaurant. The picture is dated September 1958.

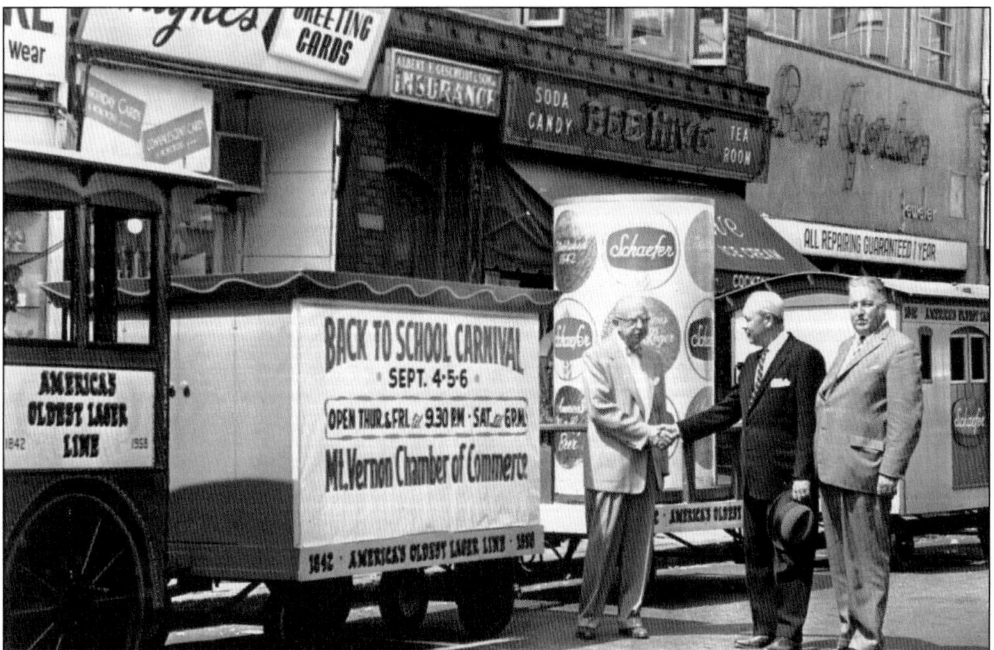

By the 1980s, several city icons became eyesores and were taken down. The gigantic Borden's milk bottle on top of the old Willow Brook Dairy on Washington Street represented the days of bottled home milk delivery. It also served as a water tower containing 26,000 gallons of water. The "round house" was at the southeast corner of Ninth Avenue and Fifth Street. For decades, it was the place to purchase propane gas and later became a scrap paper, rags, and metal warehouse. It was torn down to build the Centennial Homes, a low-rise housing complex.

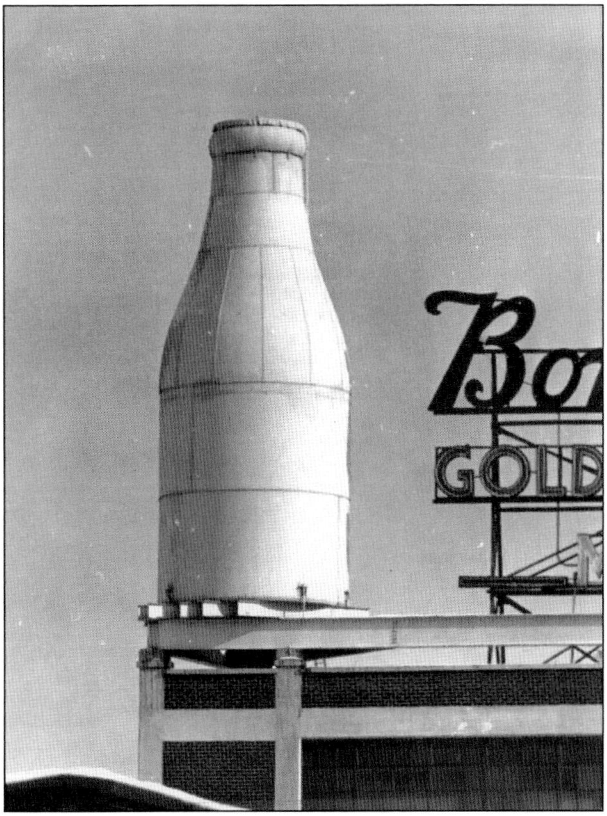

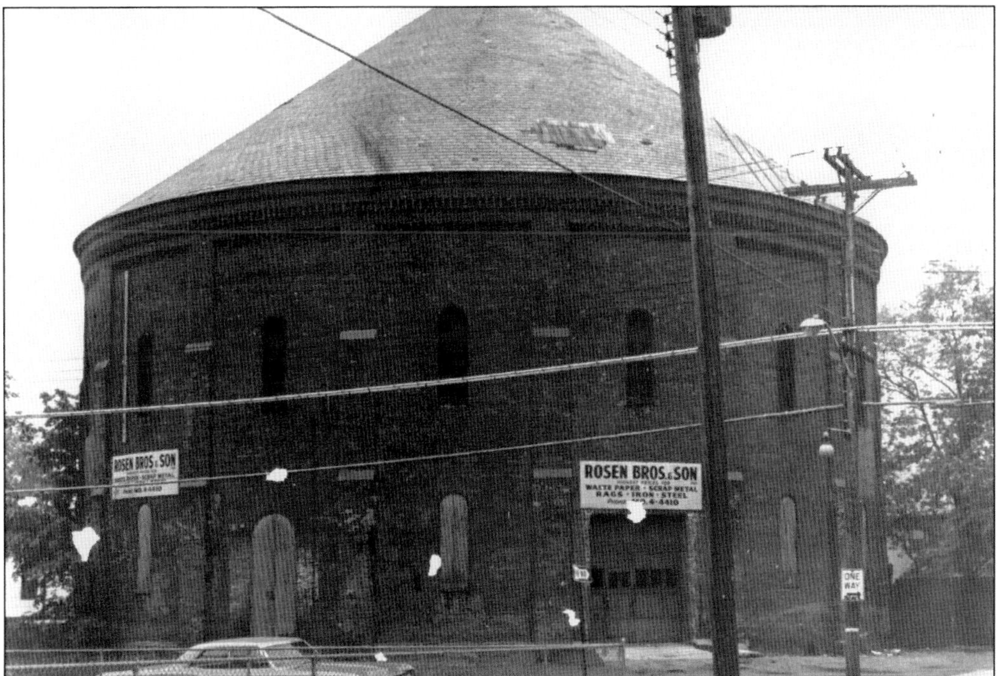

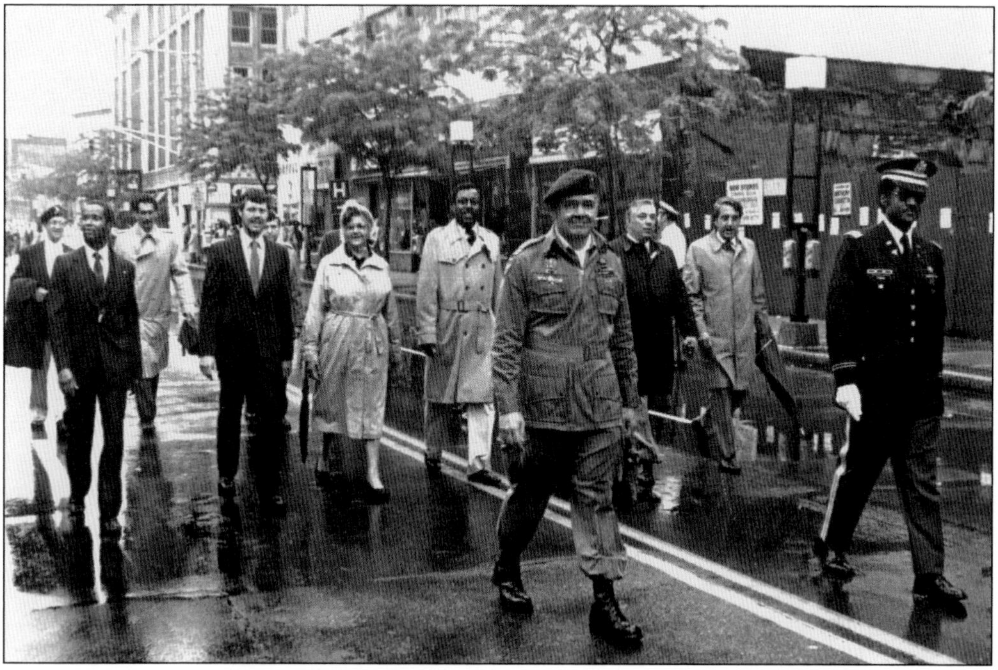

Mayor Thomas E. Sharpe was born in Mount Vernon and orphaned and was raised by the Powers family. His stepfather ran the Sharpe Funeral Home. In 1963, he married Viola D'Ettore. They had three children. When August Petrillo died in office, Sharpe was elected mayor in a 1976 special election. Under his leadership, the Democratic Party won successive victories. By 1983, Democrats held every elective office in Mount Vernon. The picture above is a Memorial Day parade led by Sharpe and former city councilman James Finch. Ronald Blackwood, Ronald Wiersma, Carmella Iaboni, James Jubilee, and Peter Pucillo follow them. Below is the groundbreaking for the Rev. Richard Dixon Senior Citizens Homes at the northwest corner of Fifth Avenue and Third Street. After suffering a stroke, Sharpe died in office on October 27, 1984.

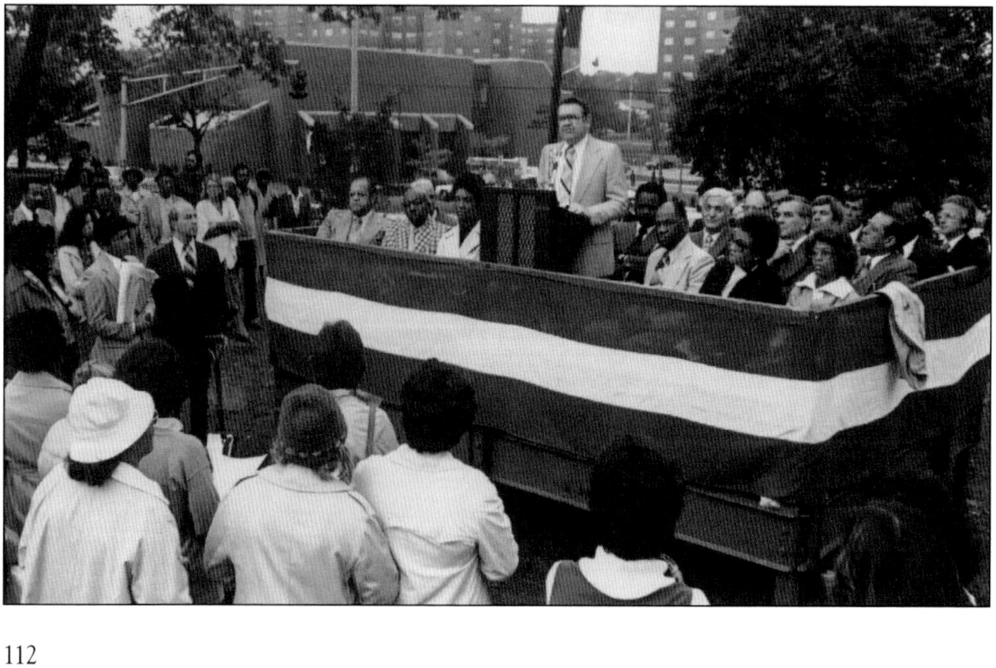

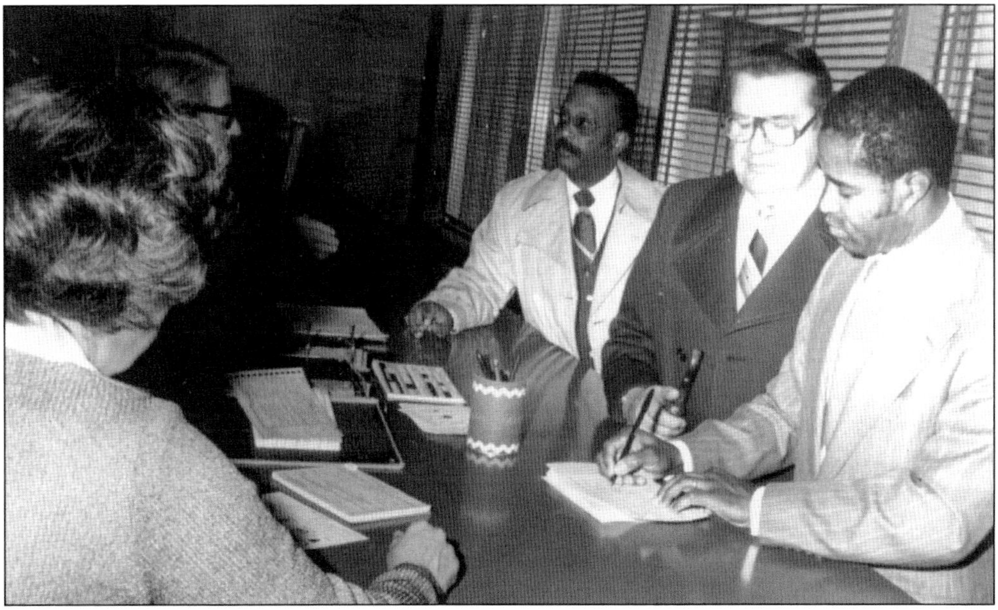

Due to the August 26, 1976, death of Republican mayor August Petrillo, Ronald Blackwood, a Republican and city council president, became acting mayor. Although he was a popular politician, the Republican Party failed to nominate him as its candidate for mayor. Most observers believed he would have won. This "racial slight" changed local politics to the present day. Sharpe, a Democrat, won the election. In the photograph above, Sharpe and Democratic Party chairman David Ford register Blackwood in their party. Sharpe died while in office. Blackwood won the Democratic nomination and on January 25, 1985, became New York State's first African American elected mayor. The photograph below is his election night victory salute at Democratic headquarters. (Below, courtesy of the Alif Archives.)

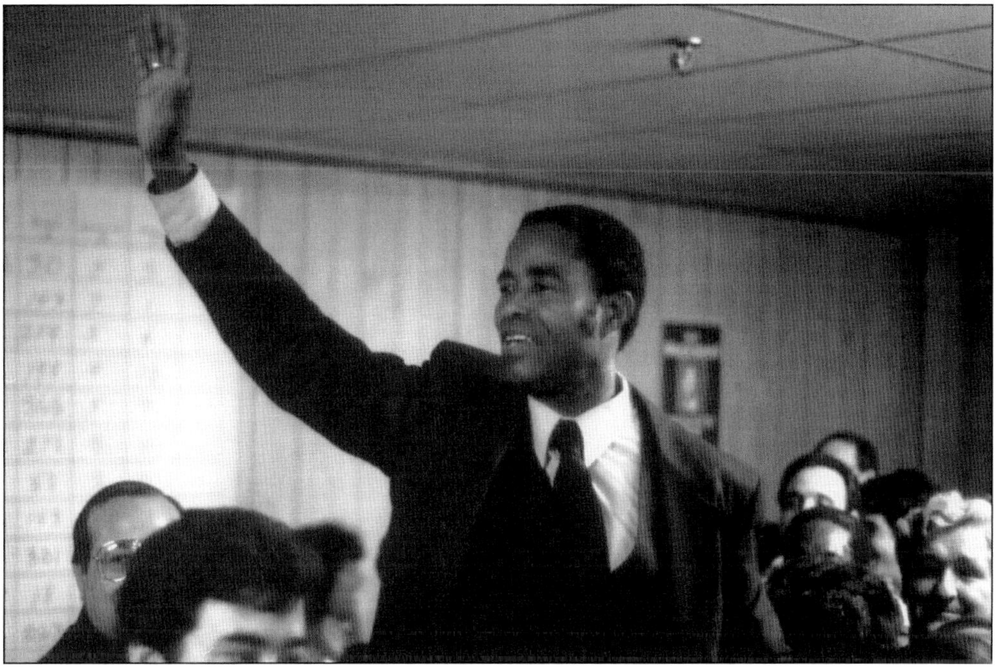

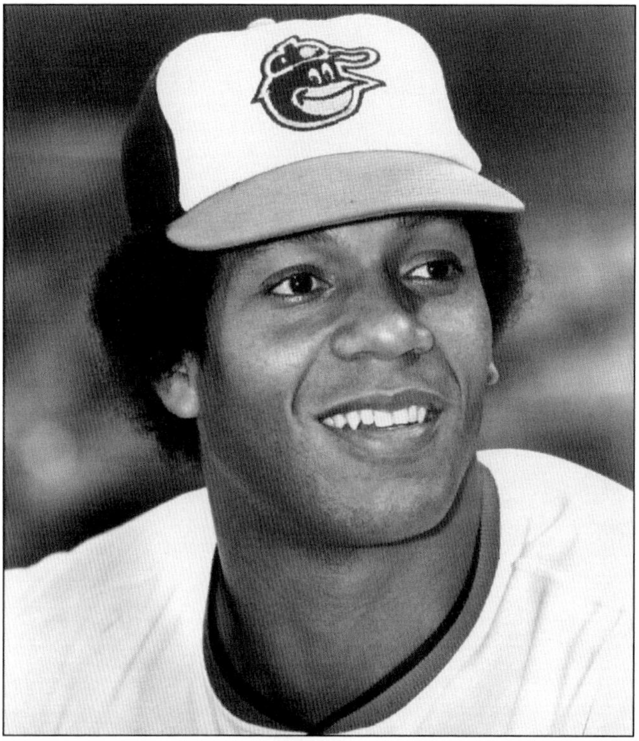

Kenneth Wayne Singleton is a retired Major League Baseball outfielder and designated hitter and currently a sports announcer. He is a varsity letterman in baseball and basketball and a 1965 Mount Vernon High School graduate. He was drafted in 1967 by the New York Mets, then traded to the Baltimore Orioles. In Baltimore, he played the best baseball of his career, winning two pennants and the 1983 World Series. Singleton grew up in a house once owned by the family of former Brooklyn Dodger Ralph Branca.

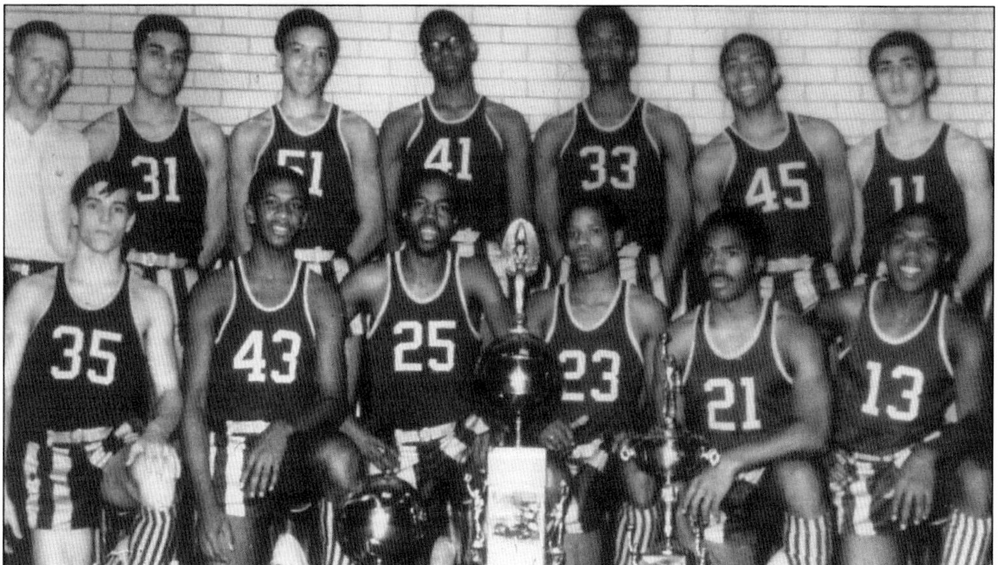

Mount Vernon is known for its ability to produce NBA players. Gus and Ray Williams, Rodney and Scooter McCray, Ben Gordon, Lowes Moore, Earl Tatum, Rudy Hacket, Rudy Bennett, and Curtis Moore are among the most notable. Before the NBA opened up to the city's athletes, there was the trailblazing 1967 high school championship team. Seen above are, from left to right, (first row) Brian Bochow, Kenneth Covington, William Sullivan, Phillip McQuay, Enrique Warner, and Michael Spruill; (second row) coach Vincent Olsen, Anthony Fiorentino, Robert Lee, Ulysses "Bill" Pleas, Galen Smalls, Richard Garner, and Benjamin Fiorentino.

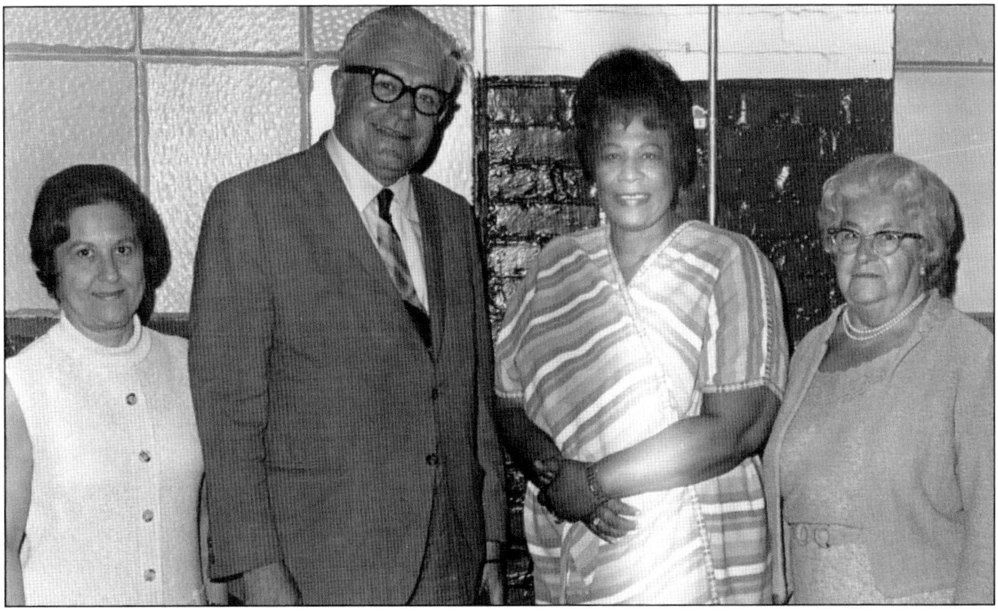

The 1938 construction of the Joseph H. Wood Auditorium at Washington School created a cultural gem in Mount Vernon. Many of the nation's great artists performed in this magnificent theater. Above is a photograph of Mayor August Petrillo and the great jazz vocalist Ella Fitzgerald. Frank Shiffman of Apollo Theater fame was a city resident and sponsored concerts by Louis Armstrong and others.

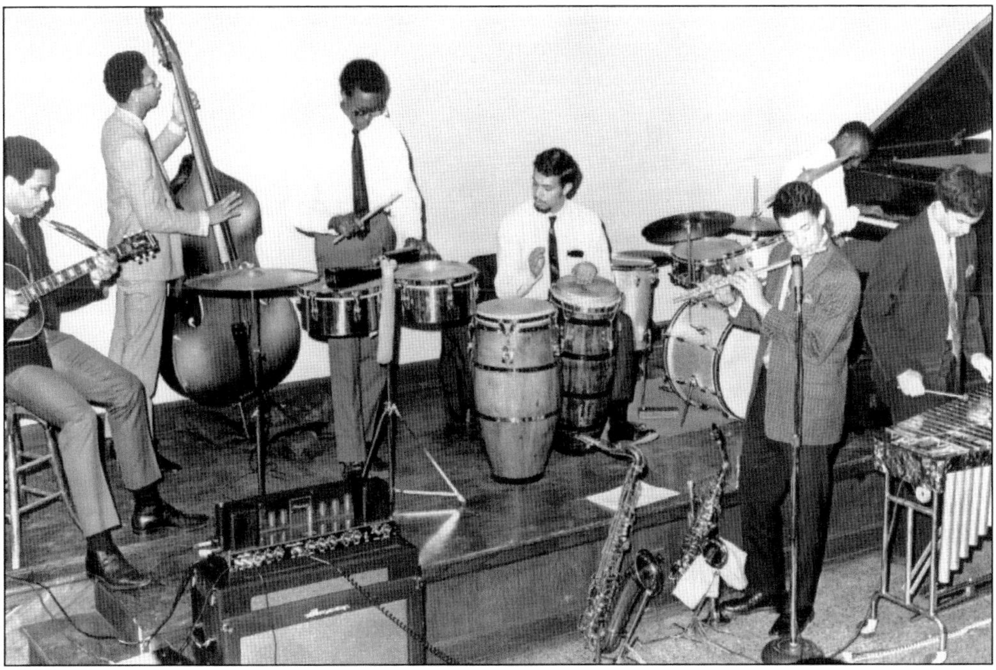

In 1968, this Mount Vernon High School jazz band was a testimony to a vibrant music program involving a variety of instruments. These talented musicians are Keith Johnson, guitar; Fred Hunter, bass; Thomas James, piano; Phillip Knight, drums; and Richard and James Purcell, flute and xylophone.

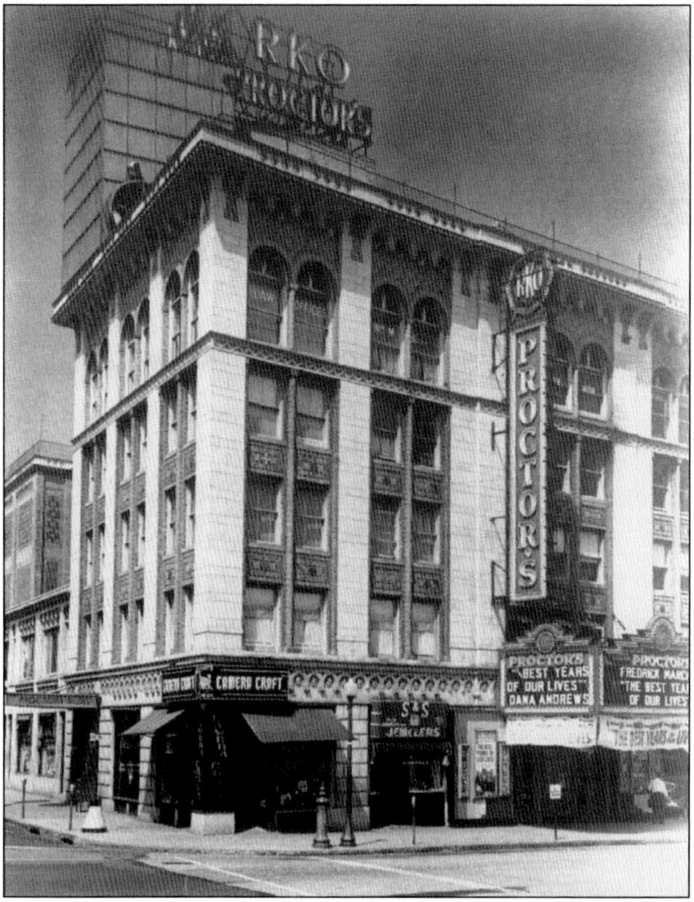

Mount Vernon had six theaters, the RKO Proctor's, Biltmore, Embassy, Mount Vernon, Parkway, and Plaza. The RKO Proctor's Theatre (left) was at 6 Gramatan Avenue. It opened on November 24, 1913, with a vaudeville show. It was part of a five-story office building with stores on the street level. By the 1920s, the RKO Proctor's Theatre added movies to the programs. At the start of the talkies, vaudeville was dropped when all Proctor's theaters became part of the RKO circuit. The Biltmore Theatre (below) was at 30 South Fifth Avenue near the corner of First Street.

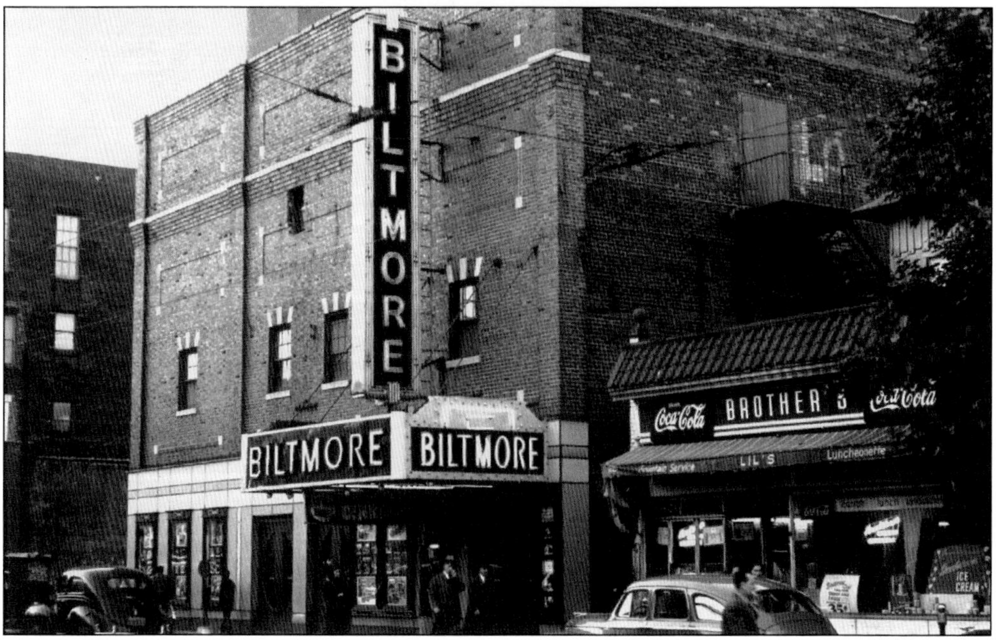

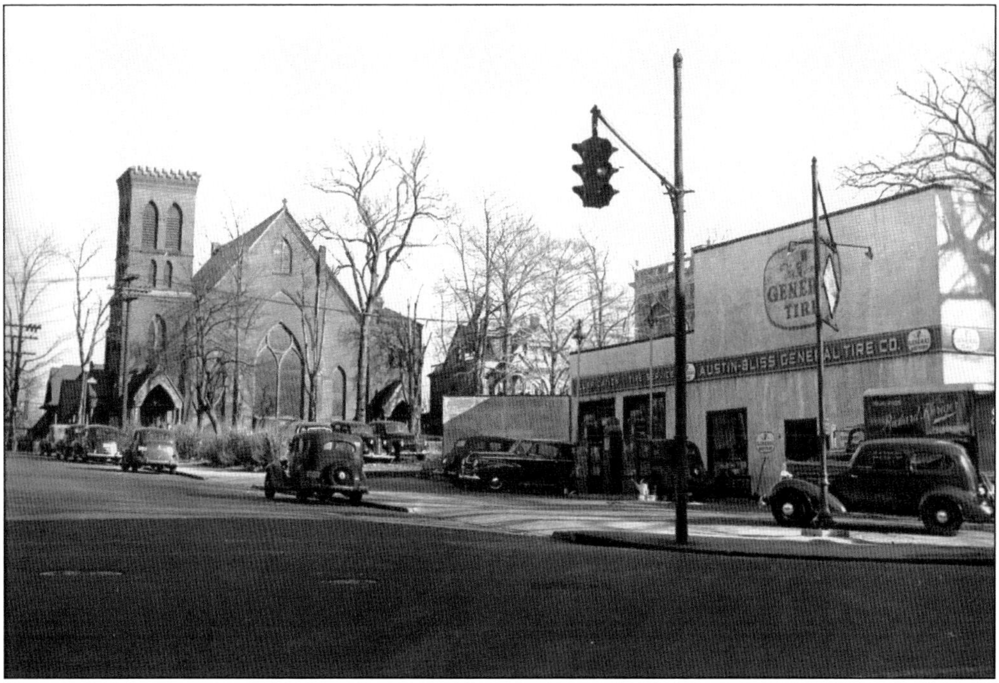

Most residents will not remember this picture of the southeast corner of Second Street and Third Avenue. It was torn down to make room for the rear of a supermarket. The entire community between Third and Second Streets on Third Avenue was removed. The church on the corner is now Unity Baptist. This photograph is from 1948.

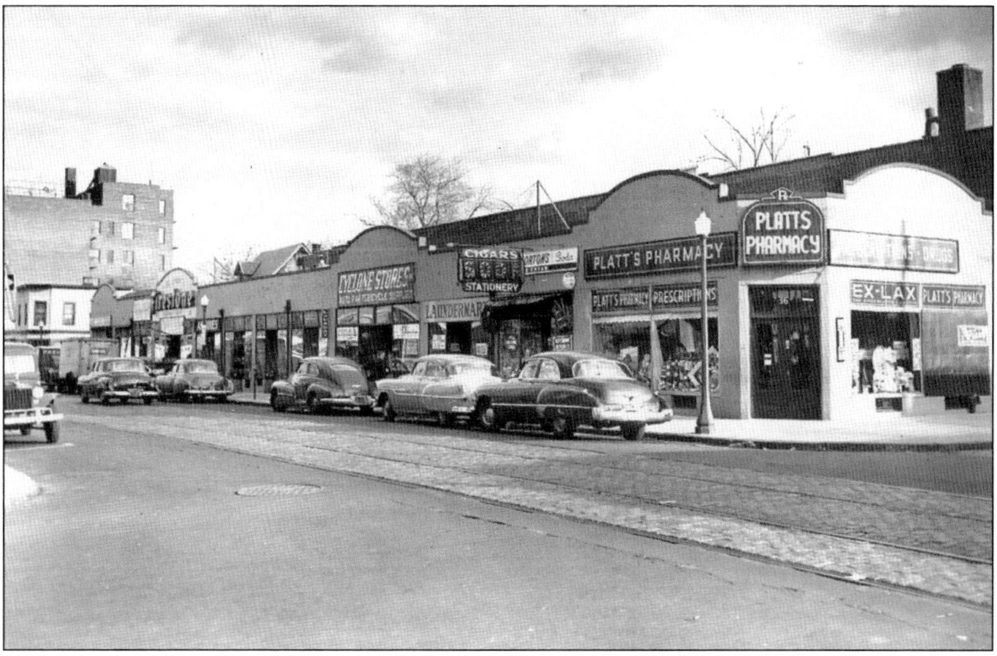

This 1949 view of the southeast corner of Second Avenue and Third Street reveals the defunct trolley tracks leading to Pelham. The drugstore has been gone for nearly two decades. However, unlike other old photographs, this corner, although renovated, still feels familiar.

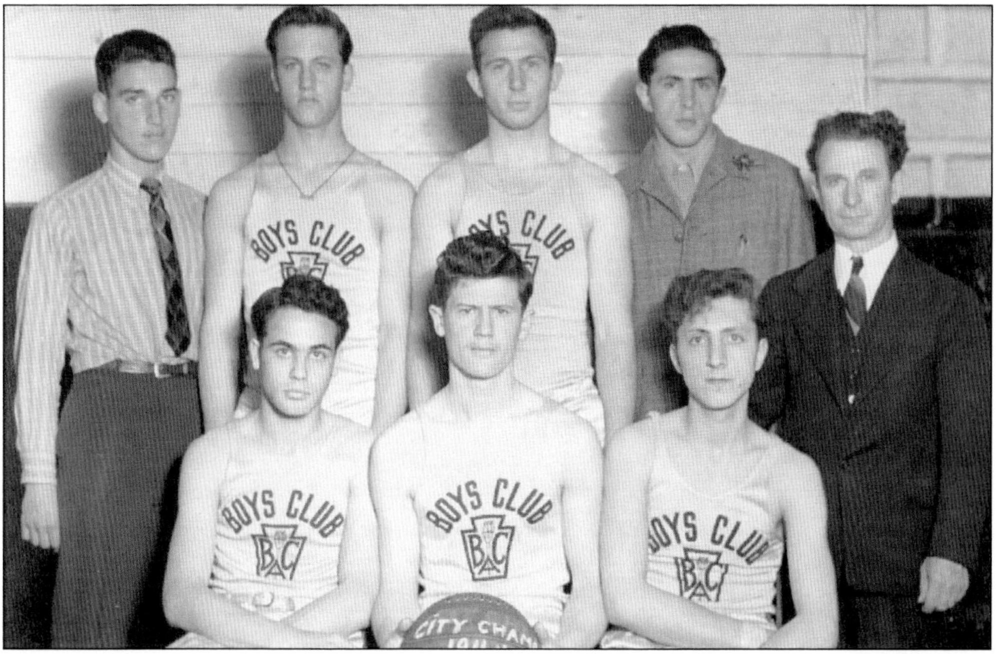

Above on the far right is Frank Celestino, director of the Mount Vernon Boys Club. His skill and leadership touched hundreds of young men. He inspired William (Billy) Thomas, who took on the traditional Boys Club programs and made them available to new generations of young people. There has been national publicity given to Thomas and Denzel Washington, former Boys Club member and Academy Award winner. In the photograph below are coach Ralph Gelardo, James Thomas, Andrew Carmen, James Coleman, Sterling Henderson, John Sherill, and James Barksdale. (Courtesy of the William Thomas collection.)

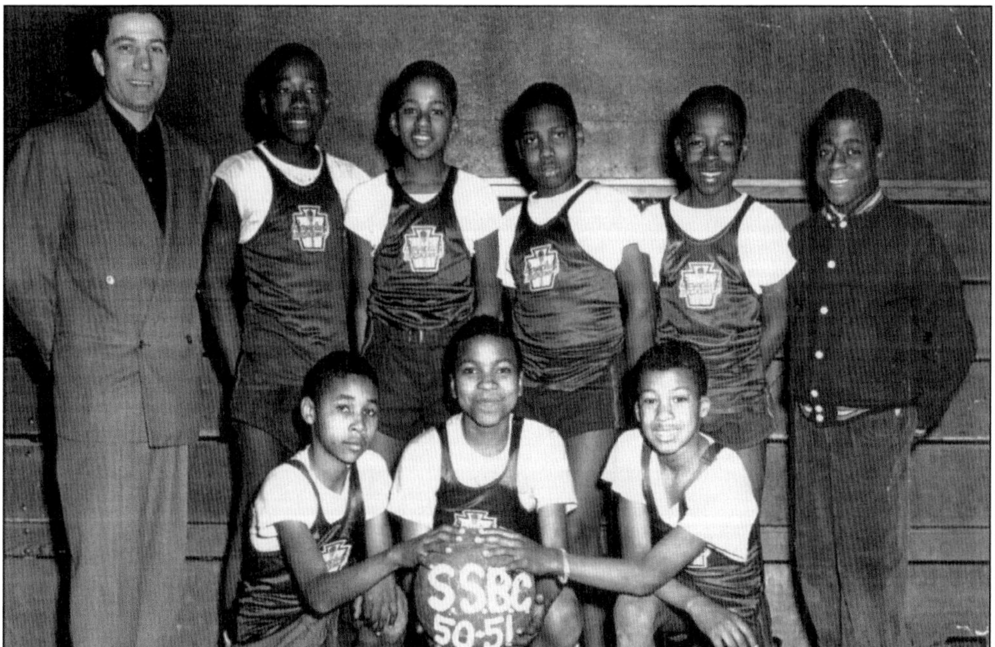

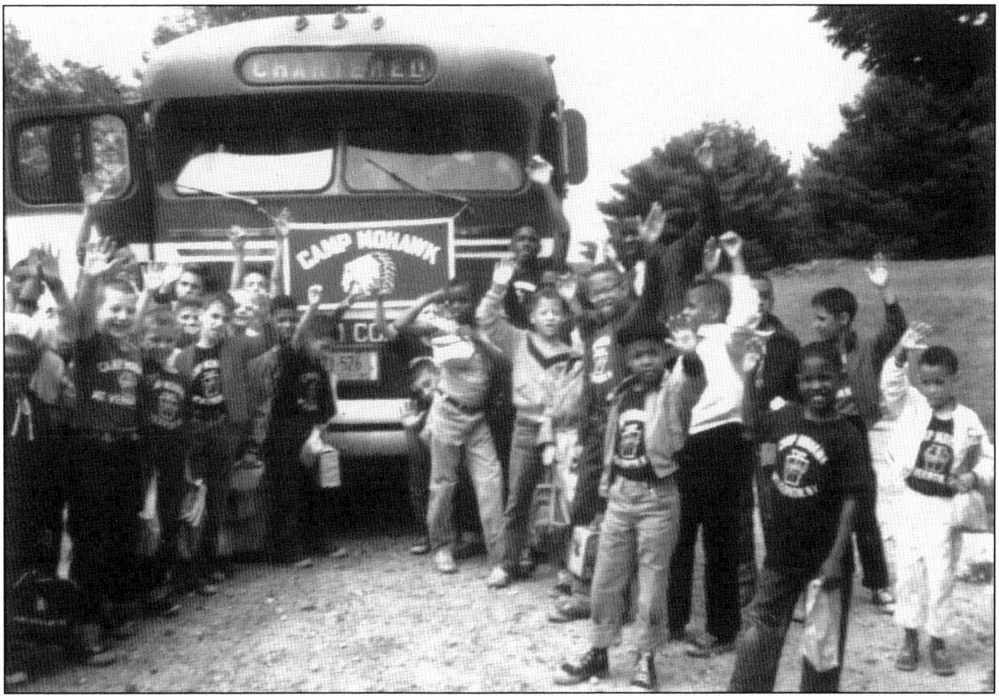

These two pictures feature the Boys Club's 1960s Camp Mohawk and City Official for a Day programs. On the right of the foreground in the photograph above is a youthful camper, Denzel Washington, film star and Academy Award winner. In the image below is Chief Harry Travers, and beside him is Washington, police chief for the day. Washington is the national spokesman for the Boys and Girls Clubs of America. (Courtesy of the William Thomas collection.)

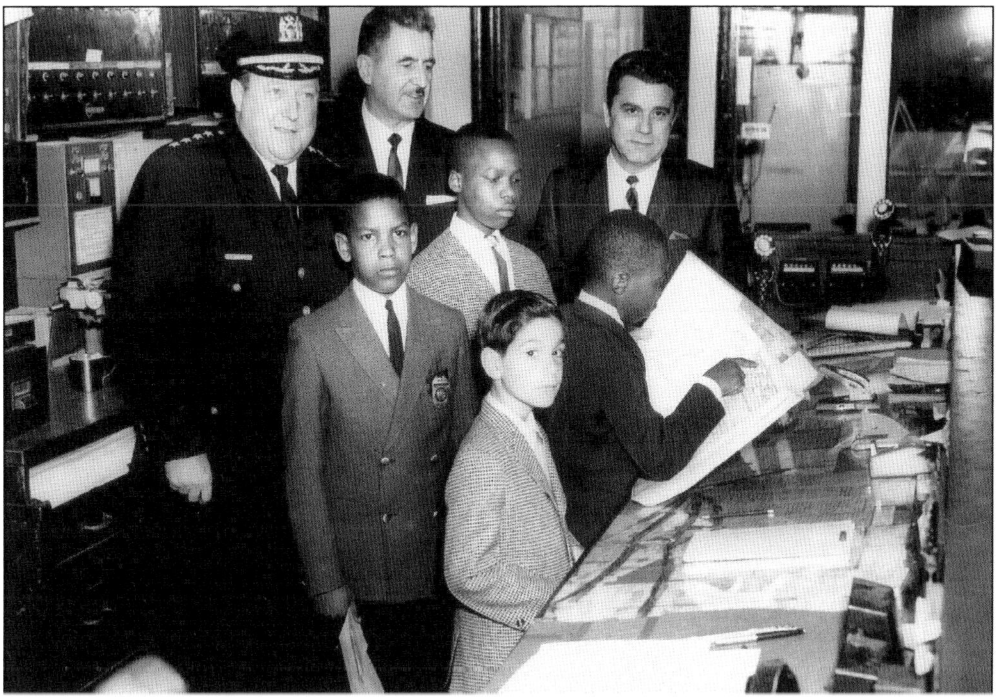

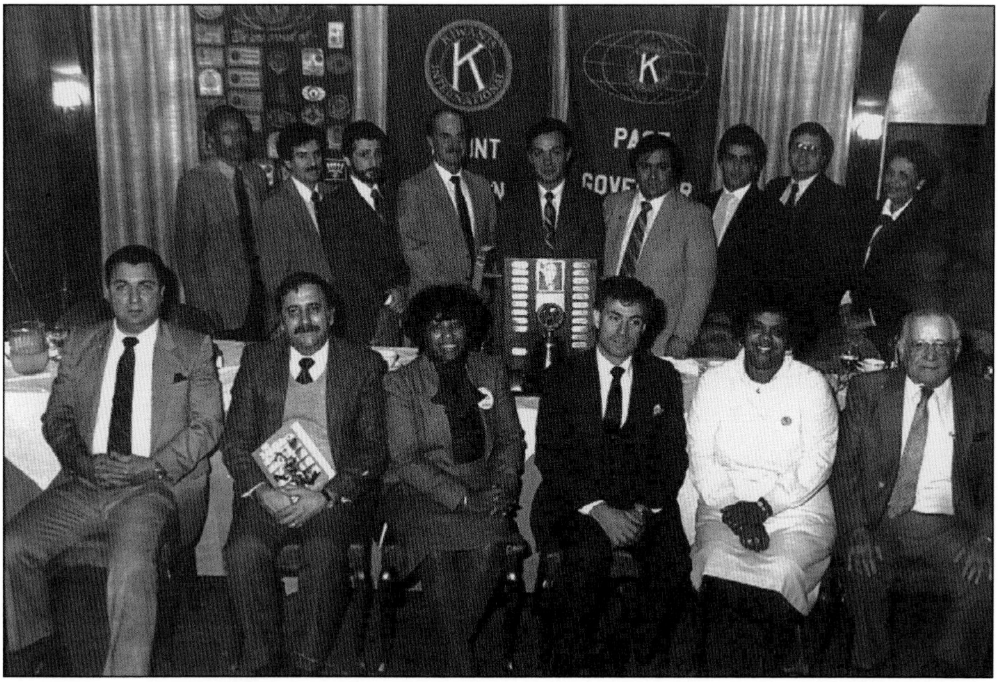

The picture above shows the leaders of the Mount Vernon schools during the 1990s. Among them are Alphonso Grimes, Richard Cappozola, William Pratella, superintendent George Albano, Louis Cioffi, Mario Sclafani, Joan Morrison, Peter Ragalia, Mary Spells, Thomas Pesce, and Nellie Thornton.

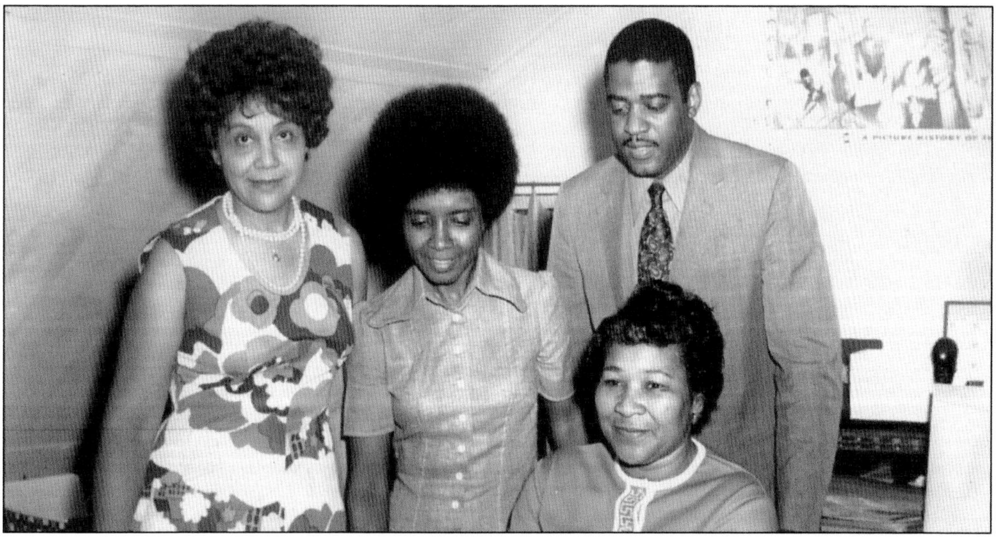

These are founding members of the Afro-American Workshop (AAW). Seated is Ruth Warner, the founder and director. The AAW provided community-based African American history instruction and research. It funded the popular exhibition and publication *A Time To Remember, the History of the African American Community of Mount Vernon, New York*. Warner was the driving force in the renaming of Nathan Hale School to Cecil H. Parker Elementary School in honor of the city's first African American educator. Standing are Marjorie Day (far left) and Elmer Coley. (Courtesy of Alif Archives.)

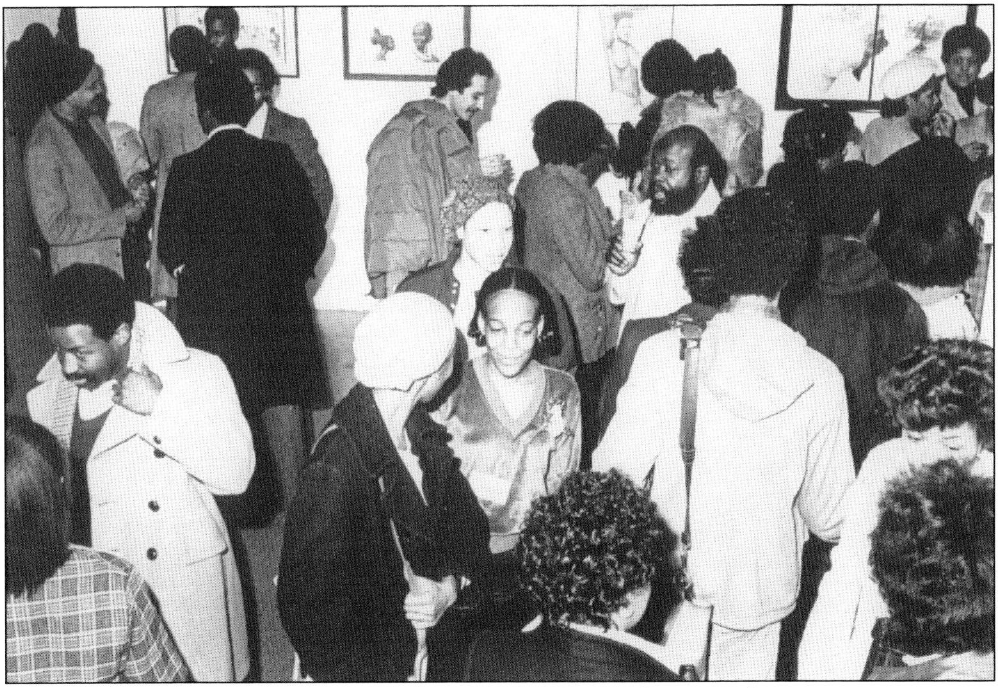

In 1977, the AC-BAW Center for the Arts at 128 South Fourth Avenue began as a movement to link the arts and downtown commercial development. In 1978, the organization rented and later purchased an abandoned furniture warehouse on the Fourth Avenue and employed high school dropouts to convert the facility into a professional gallery and cultural center. Over the past three decades, it has produced critically acclaimed art exhibitions and programs. The gallery remains an important cultural resource. Above is a picture of the inaugural exhibition on December 30, 1979. (Courtesy of the Alif Archives.)

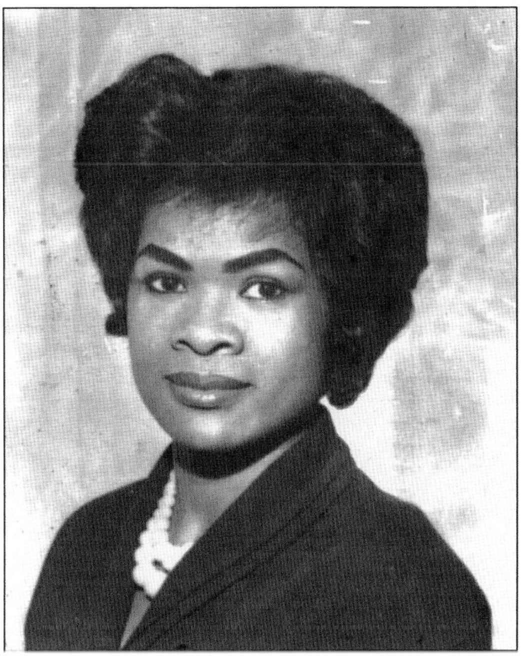

In the 1950s, Tina Sattin (right) was one of several Broadway actors who moved to Mount Vernon. In 1976, she founded the Mount Vernon Fine Arts Cultural Center. Ozzie Davis and Ruby Dee were here. Sidney Poitier soon followed and moved to Beekman Avenue. There was also a young man not yet 10 years old living on the same block; his name was Denzel Washington. It was in Sattin's theater program that Washington was introduced to acting. What both Poitier and Washington shared was not just the same block nor future Academy Awards but Tina Sattin.

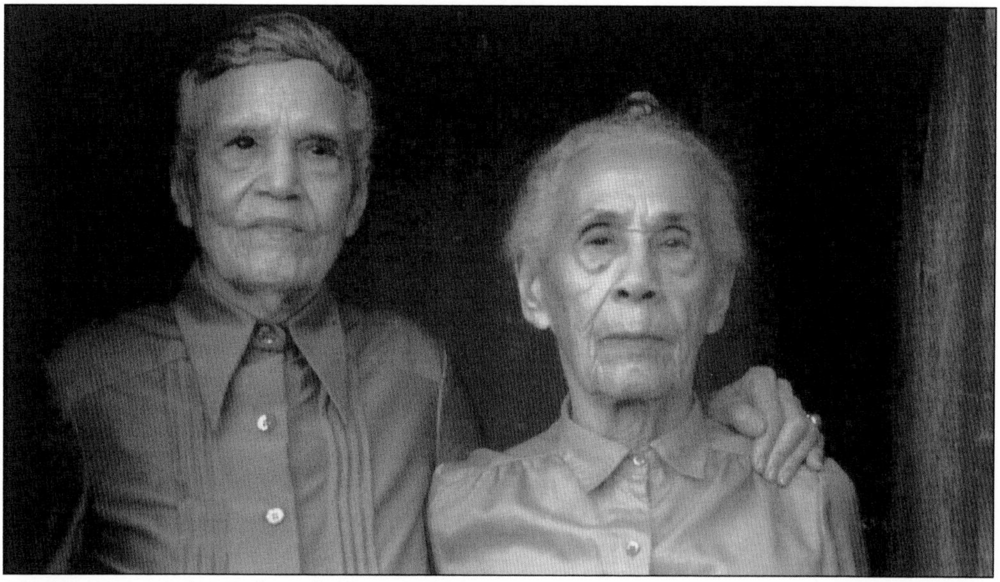

Sarah Louise "Sadie" Delany (left) and Annie Elizabeth "Bessie" Delany were authors and civil rights pioneers. In 1992, they collaborated on *Having Our Say: The Delany Sisters' First 100 Years*, which dealt with the trials faced during their century of life. It was a best seller and became a Broadway play and in 1999 a television movie starring Diahann Carroll and Ruby Dee. The sisters lived in Mount Vernon for a large portion of their adult lives. This photograph is from around 1993. (Courtesy of the Alif Archives.)

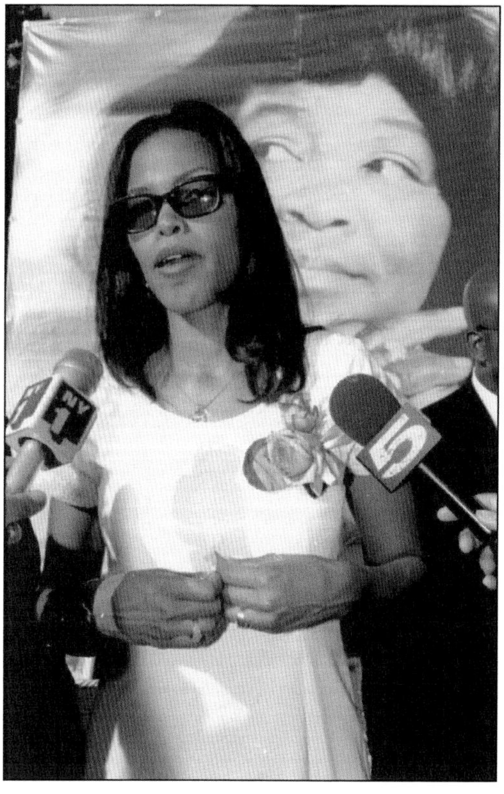

Dr. Betty Shabazz and Malcolm X's six daughters, Attallah, Qubilah, Ilyasah (left), Gamilah, and twins Malaak and Malikah, grew up in a house on East Fifth Street. According to Ilyasah's autobiography, *Growing Up X*, after her father's death, her mother (background image) worked hard to ensure that they were well provided for. She writes that her mother got help from close friends to acquire a "large, beautiful home" in Mount Vernon. Shabazz was beloved for her sense of optimism. One of her favorite phrases was "find the good and praise it!"

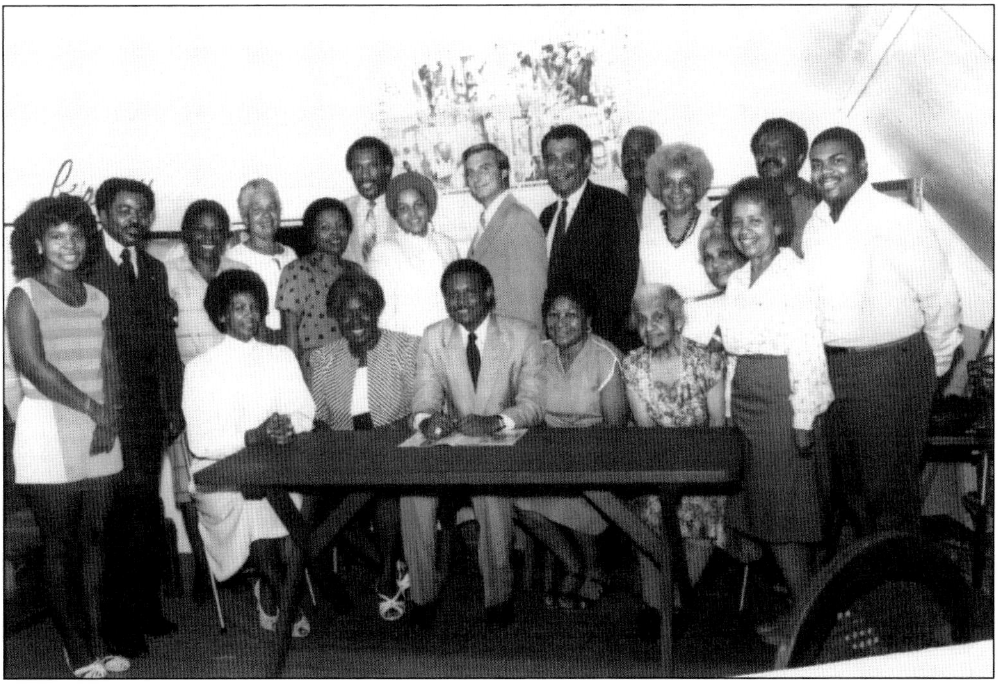

This picture of the journal committee for the renaming of Nathan Hale School to the Cecil H. Parker Elementary School includes, among others, Eunice Austin, Serapha Halevi, Derrick Byrd, Ronald Mack, Lloyd Wallace, Clinton I. Young Jr. (school trustee), Ruth Warner, and Olyve Jeter Haynes, the wife of Dr. George Edmund Haynes, founder (1910) of the National Urban League.

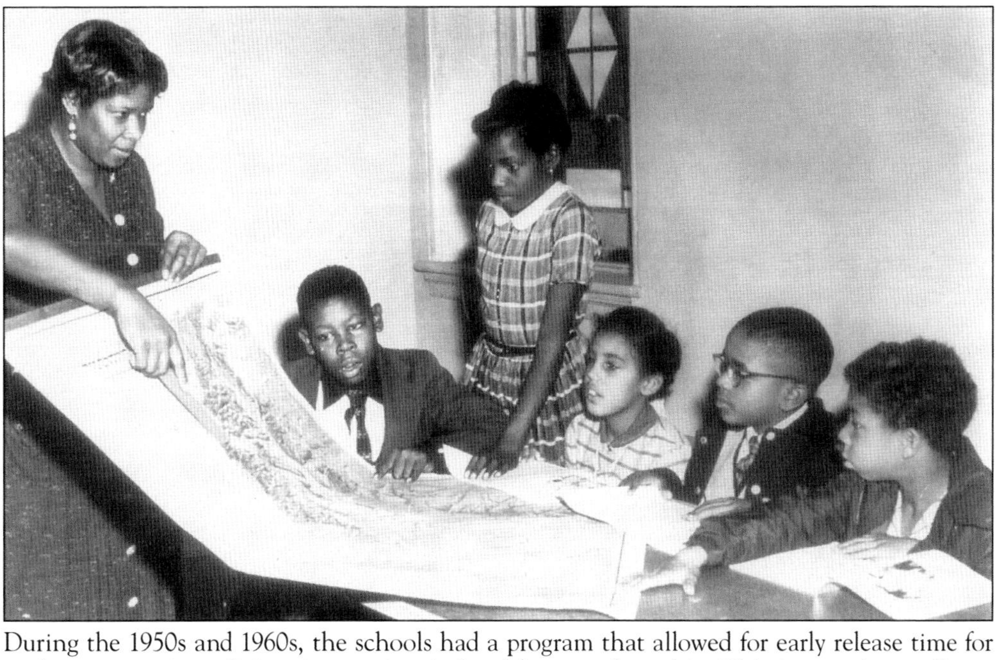

During the 1950s and 1960s, the schools had a program that allowed for early release time for students to receive religious instruction in local houses of worship. This is a session at Grace Baptist Church. Among the students are Valon Miller and Cheryl McCoy. This photograph was taken in 1958.

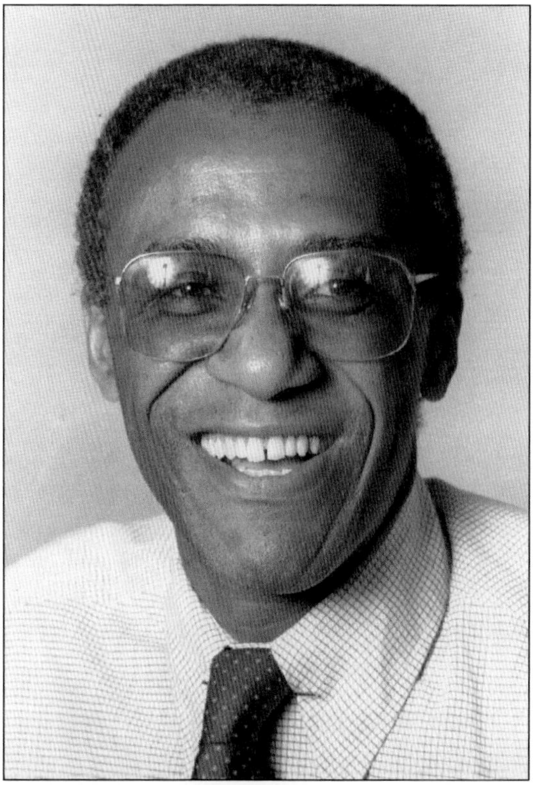

Mayor Ernie Davis, an architect, managed an aging city, a shrinking tax base, and the task of redesigning the face of the city's oldest residential and commercial enclaves and major thoroughfares. His bold plans included a hotel and sports complex covering the center city railroad tracks. In recent years, Mount Vernon has undergone a transition from mediocre businesses to a city with robust residential construction and commercial life. His administration changed the economic life of East Sandford Boulevard. Between 2000 and 2006, Mount Vernon's economy grew 20.5 percent, making it one of the fastest-growing cities in the metropolitan area. Davis created a regional artistic presence for the city. The Third Street festival grew from his promotion of Mount Vernon being a cradle for hip-hop and rap. The Summer Breeze Concerts brought talented musicians and vocalists to perform. Below are Davis and jazz trumpeter Wynton Marsalis after a Roosevelt Square concert.

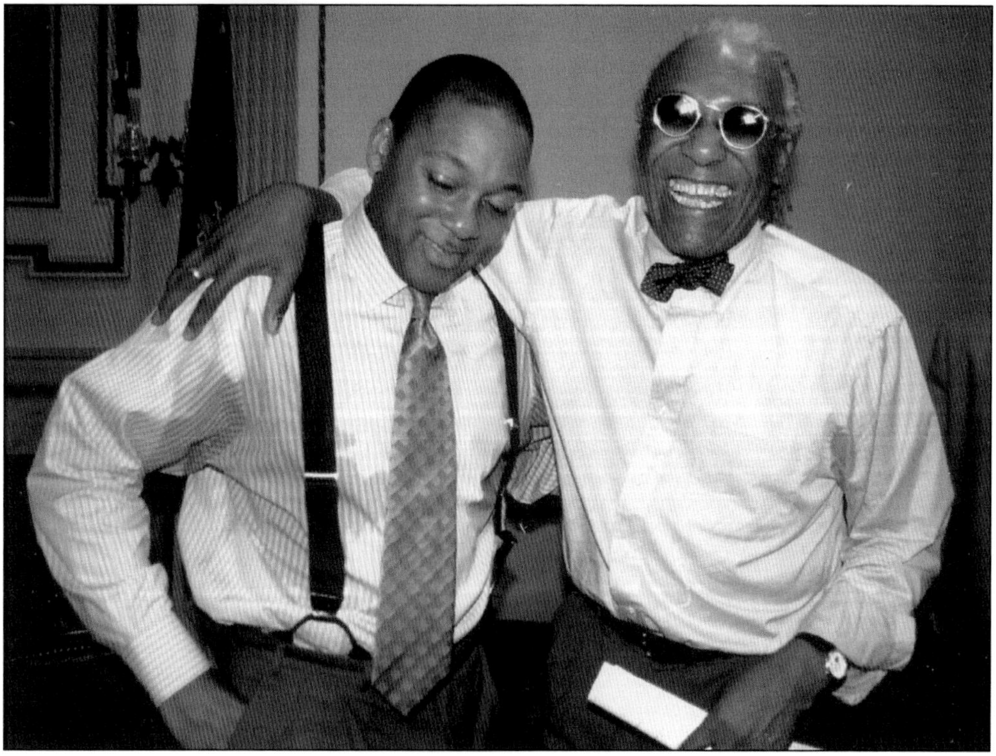

Clinton I. Young Jr. was elected mayor in 2007. He has begun an aggressive planning and redevelopment campaign. He believes that it is important to work with what the city has—talented people, good infrastructure, and an extraordinary location. His model of leadership involves combining the power of urban diversity with the middle-class values of its founding families. A vibrant economy, citywide peace and safety, great schools, effective religious and cultural lifestyles, and the efficient delivery of essential services are his priorities. Achieving them will require public dialogue and consensus, investment, and most of all patience.

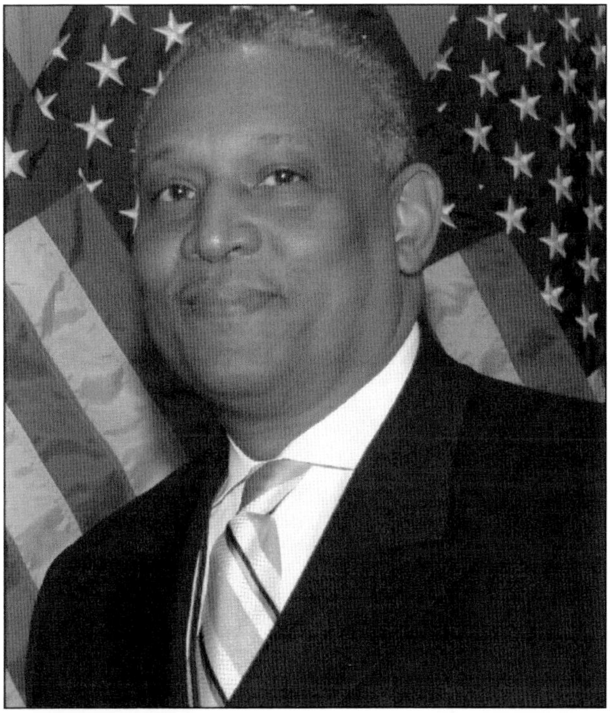

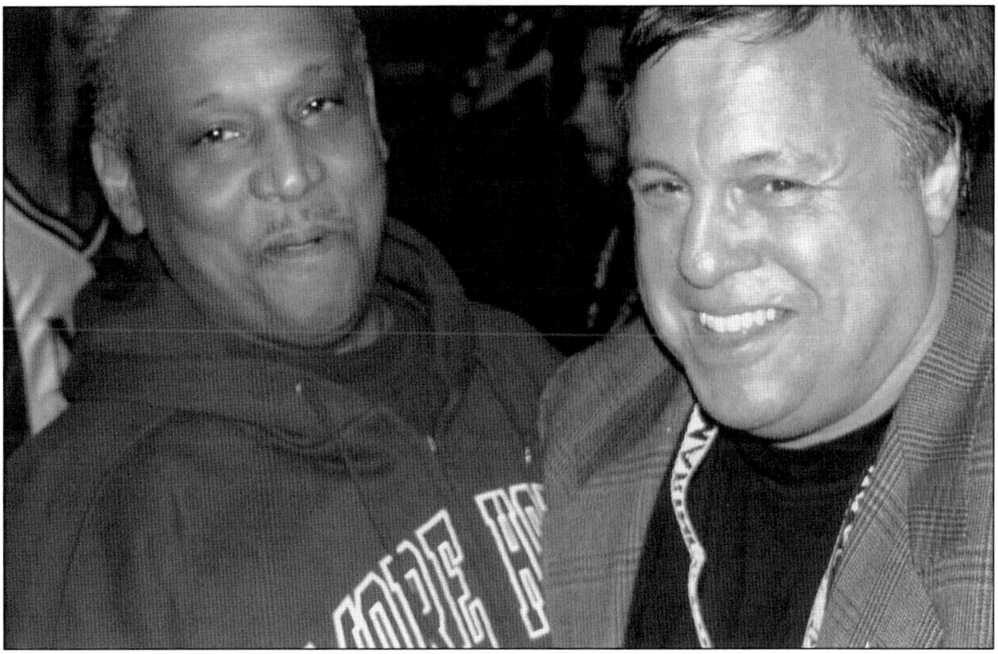

Young worked hard to raise funds for arts agencies and the school district's sports programs. He has successfully solicited entertainment and sports celebrities while making direct appeals to the residents to support young artists and student athletes. Before becoming mayor, Young was a major supporter of school athletics. Above is county legislator Young and Robert Cimmino, high school basketball coach, in Glenn Falls at the 2003 state basketball championship. Mount Vernon was No. 1 in the state.

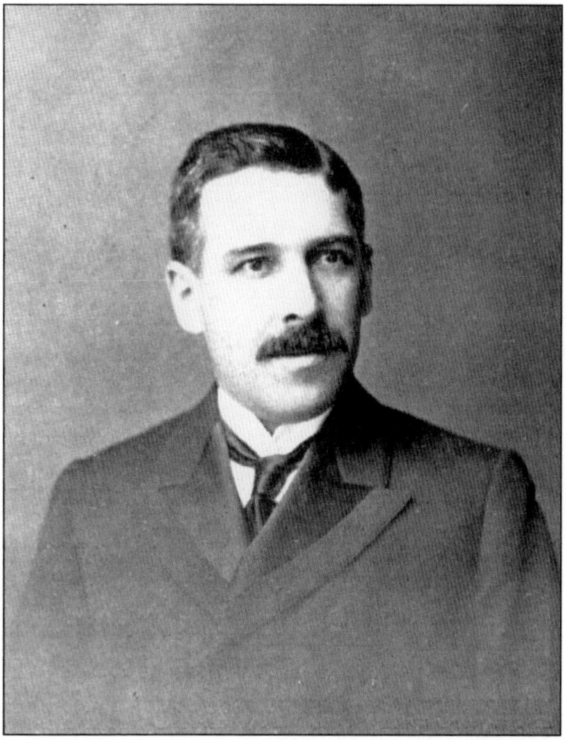

For the past two decades, the city has been known across the nation as "Money Earnin' Mount Vernon." The title comes from a 1989 rap lyric by Dwight Meyers of Heavy D and the Boyz. In fact, the Hollywood movie *Dead Presidents* (implying the former presidents on paper currency) was filmed primarily in the city. Artists such as Doug E. Fresh, Shawn "P. Diddy" Combs, and a host of others lived in Mount Vernon as aspiring artists. A century earlier (1889), Clarence S. McClellan (left) founded the First National Bank. By 1939, it had over 17,500 depositors and over $12 million. The photograph below is a facsimile of a legitimate $10 bill issued by the bank in 1929. McClellan's signature is beneath the seal on the right-hand side. Virginia McClellan Moskowitz, the beloved former city historian, is his niece. These notes are now collectibles. (Below, Donna May-Jackson collection.)

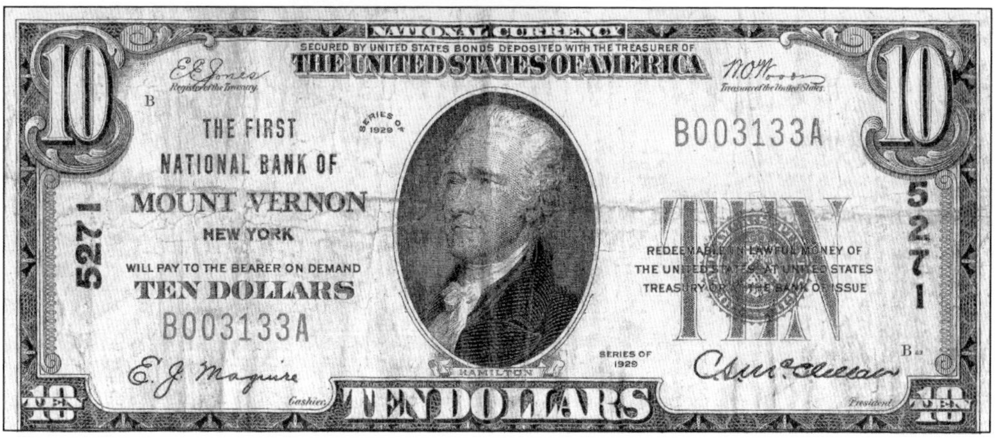

BIBLIOGRAPHY

Creamer, Robert, ed. *The Story of a Town, 1664–1964*. Eastchester, NY: Town of Eastchester, June 24, 1964.

Davis, Ernest D. *Mount Vernon, New York, A City at the Crossroads, The Past Meets the Future, 1853–2003*.

———. *Mount Vernon, New York, The City That Believes*. Mount Vernon, NY: Mount Vernon City Hall, 2003.

Franko, Alfred. *Place of Mount Vernon's Village Green and St. Paul's Church in American History*. Mount Vernon, NY: Self-published, 1985.

Gordon, Dorothy Gay. *The Social and Cultural Development of Mount Vernon, New York*. Mount Vernon, NY: Mount Vernon Public Library, 1951.

Holmes, William. *Chronicle of the Public School System, 1851–1940*. Mount Vernon, NY: Mount Vernon Board of Education, 1940.

Huffeland, Otto. *Early Mount Vernon*. Mount Vernon, NY: Mount Vernon Public Library, 1940.

Joffe, Roland D., ed. *Mount Vernon, 1892–1992, The Centennial Journal*. Mount Vernon, NY: City of Mount Vernon, 1992.

Mount Vernon Centennial, Centurama, Commemorating Mount Vernon's One Hundredth Anniversary. Mount Vernon, NY: Mount Vernon Chamber of Commerce, 1953.

Spruill, Larry. *A Time to Remember, A Portrait of African-American Life in Mount Vernon*. Mount Vernon, NY: Afro-American Workshop Publishers, 1987.

———. *On the Avenue, A Pictorial History of Small Business in Mount Vernon*. Mount Vernon, NY: AC-BAW Center for the Arts Publishers, 1983.

———. *Making Progress, The Mount Vernon School Board, 1894–1994*. Mount Vernon, NY: Mount Vernon Board of Education, 1994.

———. *When the Train Came*. Mount Vernon, NY: St. Paul's Church and National Parks Service, 1998.

Spruill, Larry, ed. *Mount Vernon, New York, City of Happy Homes, 1853–2003*. Mount Vernon, NY: Mount Vernon Chamber of Commerce, 2003.

Wintjen, John G. *The Village of Mount Vernon New York from 1851 to 1891*. Mount Vernon, NY: Mount Vernon Public Library, 1940.